Lecture Notes in Artificial Inte

Subseries of Lecture Notes in Computer Sc
Edited by J. G. Carbonell and J. Siekmann

Lecture Notes in Computer Science
Edited by G. Goos, J. Hartmanis and J. van Leeuwen

Springer

Berlin
Heidelberg
New York
Barcelona
Hong Kong
London
Milan
Paris
Singapore
Tokyo

Markus Hannebauer   Jan Wendler
Enrico Pagello (Eds.)

Balancing Reactivity and Social Deliberation in Multi-Agent Systems

From RoboCup to Real-World Applications

Springer

Series Editors

Jaime G. Carbonell, Carnegie Mellon University, Pittsburgh, PA, USA
Jörg Siekmann, University of Saarland, Saarbrücken, Germany

Volume Editors

Markus Hannebauer
GMD - German National Research Center for Information Technology
Research Institute for Computer Architecture
and Software Technology (FIRST)
Kekuléstr. 7, 12489 Berlin, Germany
E-mail: markus.hannebauer@gmd.de

Jan Wendler
Humboldt-Universität Berlin
Institut für Informatik
Unter den Linden 6, 10099 Berlin, Germany
E-mail: wendler@informatik.hu-berlin.de

Enrico Pagello
Universitá degli Studi di Padova
Dipartimento di Elettronica e Informatica
Via Gradenigo 6/a, 35131 Padova, Italy
E-mail: epv@dei.unipd.it

Cataloging-in-Publication Data applied for

Die Deutsche Bibliothek - CIP-Einheitsaufnahme

Balancing reactivity and social deliberation in multi-agent systems : from
RoboCup to real world applications / Markus Hannebauer ... (ed.). - Berlin ;
Heidelberg ; New York ; Barcelona ; Hong Kong ; London ; Milan ; Paris ;
Singapore ; Tokyo : Springer, 2001
(Lecture notes in computer science ; Vol. 2103 : Lecture notes in
artificial intelligence)
ISBN 3-540-42327-3

CR Subject Classification (1998): I.2.11, I.2, C.2.4

ISBN 3-540-42327-3 Springer-Verlag Berlin Heidelberg New York

Springer-Verlag Berlin Heidelberg New York
a member of BertelsmannSpringer Science+Business Media GmbH

http://www.springer.de

© Springer-Verlag Berlin Heidelberg 2001
Printed in Germany

Typesetting: Camera-ready by author, data conversion by PTP Berlin, Stefan Sossna
Printed on acid-free paper   SPIN 10839508   06/3142   5 4 3 2 1 0

Preface

The present volume of Springer's "Lecture Notes in Artificial Intelligence" focuses on the challenge of balancing between the two extremes of pure reactivity and in-depth social deliberation in the context of multi-agent systems. Finding a balance between these two extremes will lead to an overall behavior of the individual agents and of the multi-agent system that meets the demands of the environment but also the demand for high-quality problem solving results. This book collects selected and revised papers from "Balancing Reactivity and Social Deliberation in Multi-Agent Systems" – a workshop held at the 14th European Conference on Artificial Intelligence (ECAI 2000) – and additional papers from renowned researchers in the field. All the papers contained in this book have undergone at least one complete phase of reviewing and correction with typically three reviews, the large majority of them have been through two phases. In the first phase, papers were reviewed by members of the advisory committee, in the second phase, papers were peer-reviewed among the authors with additional comments from members of the advisory committee.

Although several contributions to this book stem from members of the RoboCup community and as such also deal with related topics, this is not a book on RoboCup. The target of "Balancing Reactivity and Social Deliberation in MAS" is to make a first step towards the main target of RoboCup: to transfer insights gained from a real or artificial gaming environment and to develop generic multi-agent systems techniques, such that they can be applied to other application domains. All the contributing authors have managed to meet this demand as you will see when taking a closer look at their contributions.

The workshop at ECAI 2000 has turned out to be only a starting point for this kind of research. The same holds for the present book. Nevertheless, the problem is evident, in particular in robotics and collaborative problem solving with resource bounds. Some contributions of this volume start at different points on the spectrum between the two observed extremes and try to make their way towards the other extreme stopping at the right point. Others propose integrated frameworks that can cover the full range of reactive and socially deliberative behavior. Though all of the contributions show success in dealing with our main problem they also underline the need for further research. With our collection of contributions we hope to have laid a sound foundation for this future work.

Berlin, May 2001   Markus Hannebauer

Advisory Committee

Table of Contents

I   Introduction

Balancing Reactivity and Social Deliberation in Multi-Agent Systems –
A Short Guide to the Contributions 3
  Markus Hannebauer, Jan Wendler, Enrico Pagello

Reactivity and Deliberation: A Survey on Multi-Robot Systems 9
  Luca Iocchi, Daniele Nardi, Massimiliano Salerno

II   Architectures and Frameworks

Bridging Deliberation and Reactivity in Cooperative Multi-Robot Systems
through Map Focus 35
  Stefano Carpin, Carlo Ferrari, Enrico Pagello, Pierluigi Patuelli

Balancing between Reactivity and Deliberation in the ICAGENT
Framework 53
  Vangelis Kourakos Mavromichalis, George A. Vouros

On Augmenting Reactivity with Deliberation in a Controlled Manner 76
  Jacek Malec

HAC: A Unified View of Reactive and Deliberative Activity 92
  Marc S. Atkin, David L. Westbrook, Paul R. Cohen

III   Enhanced Reactivity

Team Cooperation Using Dual Dynamics 111
  Ansgar Bredenfeld, Hans-Ulrich Kobialka

A Hierarchy of Reactive Behaviors Handles Complexity 125
  Sven Behnke, Raúl Rojas

Reinforcement Learning for Cooperating and Communicating Reactive
Agents in Electrical Power Grids 137
  Martin Riedmiller, Andrew Moore, Jeff Schneider

Being Reactive by Exchanging Roles: An Empirical Study 150
  Olivier Sigaud, Pierre Gérard

IV   Controlled Social Deliberation

Situation Based Strategic Positioning for Coordinating a Team
of Homogeneous Agents.. 175
    Luís Paulo Reis, Nuno Lau, Eugénio Costa Oliveira

Deliberation Levels in Theoretic-Decision Approaches for Task Allocation
in Resource-Bounded Agents 198
    Maroua Bouzid, Hossam Hanna and Abdel-Illah Mouaddib

Cognition, Sociability, and Constraints............................. 217
    Gerhard Weiß

Author Index 237

Part I

Introduction

Balancing Reactivity and Social Deliberation in Multi-Agent Systems – A Short Guide to the Contributions

Markus Hannebauer[1], Jan Wendler[2], and Enrico Pagello[3,4]

[1] GMD – German National Research Center for Information Technology,
Research Institute for Computer Architecture and Software Technology (FIRST)
Planning and Optimization Laboratory, Kekuléstr. 7, D-12489, Germany
markus.hannebauer@gmd.de
[2] Humboldt University Berlin, Department of Computer Science,
AI Laboratory, Unter den Linden 6, D-10099 Berlin, Germany
wendler@informatik.hu-berlin.de
[3] University of Padua, Department of Electronics and Informatics,
Intelligent Autonomous Systems Laboratory,
Via Gradenigo 6/a, I-35131 Padova, Italy
epv@dei.unipd.it
[4] LADSEB-CNR, Padova, Italy

Abstract. The focus of "Balancing Reactivity and Social Deliberation in Multi-agent Systems" is the right balance between the two extremes of pure reactivity and in-depth social deliberation in the context of collaborative work in multi-agent systems. This article briefly motivates this problem and provides a short guide to the contributions contained in this volume.

1 Covered Topics

Today's envisioned applications of intelligent systems in general and multi-agent systems in particular confront researchers and developers with the difficulty of finding the right balance between reactive and socially deliberative behavior. Reactive systems are capable of adapting very quickly to unforeseen changes in the environment and are hence said to be more robust and efficient. On the other hand, they usually lack the necessary overview to produce behavior that can compete with the results of in-depth reasoning techniques. In contrary to that, socially deliberative systems allow for exploiting environmental information and coordination mechanisms to build up through-thought individual and even team-oriented strategies. Though their problem solving results are usually much better than that of reactive systems, deliberative systems are much more susceptible to dynamic environments and often lack the potential for real-time computation.

This book focuses on theoretical, technical and practical work on balancing between these two extremes in the context of collaborative work in multi-agent systems. The call for contributions for this book directed the attention to the following topics of interest.

M. Hannebauer et al. (Eds.): Reactivity and Deliberation in MAS, LNAI 2103, pp. 3–8, 2001.
© Springer-Verlag Berlin Heidelberg 2001

- Extension of reactive systems by cooperation
- Teaching deliberative systems reactivity and real-time
- Efficient coordination, cooperation and organization approaches
- Anytime approaches and algorithms
- Design and evaluation of hybrid multi-level agent architectures
- Short-term, medium-term and long-term intentionality
- Enriching group behavior by environmental, opponent and social models
- Individual and social adaptivity

As application areas we had encouraged practical contributions to be directed at the following.

Multi-agent problem solving Real-world problems often require distributed solving strategies, because of natural distribution, social competence and efficiency matters. Multi-agent approaches to such problems are said to be more robust than monolithic systems, but usually entail worse solutions. How can this be overcome by better balancing between reactive and deliberative behavior?

RoboCup RoboCup has proven to be a great and challenging benchmarking scenario both to Robotics and Artificial Intelligence. In RoboCup reactivity and real-time are a must, but social deliberation gets more and more important to match the world's leading teams.

2   The Contributions

2.1   General Observations

From the beginning on, the difficulty of defining the notions of "reactivity" and "social deliberation" in a commonly acceptable way was evident. Though all authors had a more or less precise personal understanding of these categories it showed up in a lengthy discussion that a common understanding was quite far away. A first step towards creating a sound taxonomy for this kind of area is made by Iocchi, Nardi and Salerno in their introductory chapter on reactivity and deliberation in multi-robot systems (page 9). The taxonomy is mainly based on the system's cooperative capabilities. It consists of four levels: cooperation, knowledge, coordination and organization which characterize the major features of multi-robot systems. The concepts of reactivity and social deliberation are then assigned to the nodes of the taxonomy. Finally several deployment fields for multi-robot systems are described, examined, and characterized according to the proposed taxonomy. Apart from this introduction, all other authors of this book clarify their understanding of reactivity and social deliberation in the very beginning of their contributions.

As a second important point, even though most of the contributions do not mainly focus on applications, in almost all of them the authors show the relevance of the described techniques or theories by applying them to application areas from multi-agent problem solving. These areas are represented by *testbeds*, such as coordinated foraging (Carpin, Ferrari, Pagello, and Patuelli, page 35), tile-world chessboards (Mavromichalis and Vouros, page 53), "Capture the Flag" (Atkin, Westbrook, and Cohen, page 92), "Robot Sheepdogs" (Sigaud and Gérard, page 150) and RoboCup soccer (Bredenfeld and Kobialka, page 111; Behnke and Rojas, page 125; Reis, Lau, and Oliveira, page 175), as well as by *real-world case studies*, such as driver support systems (Malec, page 76), electrical power grid control (Riedmiller, Moore, and Schneider, page 137) and task allocation for cooperative rovers (Bouzid, Hanna and Mouaddib, page 198).

We have compiled the contributions in three parts according to the special focus they put on reactivity, social deliberation and the transition between them. These parts and the contributions belonging to them are briefly described in the next subsections.

2.2   Architectures and Frameworks

The first part deals with architectures and frameworks that comprise reactive components as well as deliberative components in a unique system. In the work of Carpin et al. and Malec reactive and deliberative components are clearly distinguishable, whereas Mavromichalis and Vouros or Atkin et al. do not represent reactivity and deliberation by distinct parts of their frameworks but by hierarchical planning concepts that allow for a fluent transition between reactive and deliberative behavior.

Carpin, Ferrari, Pagello and Patuelli (page 35) analyze the problem of balancing reactivity and social deliberation in the case of cooperative multi-robot systems. They outline the issues which need to be coped with to solve this problem and introduce a balancing method based on the "map focus" concept. This concept couples the reactive and the deliberative module of their architecture. The basic idea of the "map focuser" is to compute a simplified and localized version of the deliberative module state that can be used by the reactive module. The architecture proposal is supported by a case study of a simulated coordinated multi-robot system that performs a foraging task.

The contribution of Mavromichalis and Vouros (page 53) discusses a framework called ICAGENT that allows an agent designer to specify behaviors that combine reactivity with deliberation. Some internal mental states of the agent are explicit in this framework to allow the agent to decide when to react and when to deliberate. The transition between reactive and deliberative behavior is realized by the amount of external and internal information that is incorporated into a hierarchical planning process. The article addresses balancing only for single agent systems, but the authors state that it can be generalized to multi-agent systems. The framework is evaluated with a tile-world example as testbed.

In his contribution Malec (page 76) discusses the controlled augmentation of predictable reactivity with limited deliberation to preserve hard real-time requirements. The author illustrates his thoughts in terms of the "Generic Layered Architecture", which in its current status can be used for creating reactive agents that act in dynamic environments. The behavior of the agents is subject to worst-case guarantees in the sense of temporal predictibility. The problem of guaranteeing similar worst-case bounds for deliberation processes is presented and the factors that influence the problem are discussed. The paper also surveys existing approaches to the problem and a number of other layered agent architectures.

Whereas many other well-known architectures conceptually distinguish between reactive and deliberative behavior, Atkin, Westbrook and Cohen (page 92) introduce an agent architecture with a uniform representation of both. To achieve this, the behaviors/actions of the agents are arranged into a hierarchy. All the behaviors are represented in the same manner and have the same interface to a generic planner. Additionally, this agent architecture, called "Hierarchical Agent Control Architecture", does not distinguish between single-agent and multi-agent behaviors. The architecture and the planner have been applied to the competitive, real time scenario "Capture the Flag".

2.3   Enhanced Reactivity

This part collects contributions that concentrate on techniques to enhance existing reactive approaches in particular from robotics by social behaviors. All these contributions argue that socially deliberative behavior observed by an external observer can emerge from the interaction of complex reactive behaviors. But they also show that the extended reactive systems do not only "show" deliberative behavior but also dominate their purely reactive ancestors in efficiency and problem solving capability. This is proven by various testbed simulations and case studies.

Bredenfeld and Kobialka (page 111) present a team coordination approach, which is an extension of the behavior-based Dual Dynamics scheme. They specify team behaviors to realize team coordination in multi-agent systems by introducing special blackboard-like "team variables" that are exported and read by the local reactive decision makers. They also show that the set of design, simulation and monitoring tools developed for the Dual Dynamics approach is also suitable for allowing a smooth integration of team behavior with non-team behavior. The approach has been successfully applied to the coordination of soccer playing robots.

The work of Behnke and Rojas (page 125) builds upon the Dual Dynamics scheme. It introduces a temporal hierarchy of behaviors, fast and simple at the bottom of the hierarchy and getting slower and more complex to the top. Each layer in this hierarchy consists of a sensor module, an activation module and an actuator module. All of these modules are subject to the temporal hierarchy, i.e. not only the activation module (the decision maker) but also the sensors and actuators are classified according to their temporal characteristics. The generic approach is substantiated by a precise description of its application to robots in the small size league of RoboCup.

Riedmiller, Moore and Schneider (page 137) extend purely reactive agents by the ability to learn cooperative patterns via reinforcement. Driven by a global optimization goal the agents are forced to establish communication mechanisms.

The authors investigate two different settings of distributed power grid control to assess their approach. The learning agents fail more seldomly in solving the stated problems and produce globally better problem solutions.

Following a nice discussion of the notion of reactivity in the behaviors research community and in the Markov decision process research community, Sigaud and Gérard (page 150) enhance reactive controllers, which are based on the Classifier System formalism, by social roles. Though the performance of the system with handcrafted roles dominates the performance of a set of purely reactive agent without social roles, the latter approach turns out to be more robust to the size of the problem. To cope with this, the authors propose "social reactivity" enabling the reactive agents to dynamically change the social roles initially assigned to them. This approach turns out to be both more efficient and more robust than the system without roles.

2.4   Controlled Social Deliberation

The last part of the book is devoted to contributions that stem from the opposite direction of the spectrum compared to the contributions in the preceding part. Contributions in this part start from deliberative methods and propose techniques to constrain the resources needed by the deliberative reasoning process. Hence, they are trying to "teach deliberative systems reactivity".

Reis, Lau and Oliveira (page 175) facilitate a classification of the environment observed by an agent into active and strategic situations to balance between reactivity and social deliberation. In active situations that demand a very responsive behavior the agent uses high level and low level skills to directly manipulate the environment. As soon as the situation is classified as strategic more thorough reasoning techniques are used including social ones such as "situation based strategic positioning" and "dynamic role and position exchange". These concepts are evaluated by their impact on RoboCup soccer matches.

Bouzid, Hanna and Mouaddib (page 198) compare two quite different architectures for task allocation in collaborative problem solving and investigate their responsiveness properties. The first architecture consists of a completely deliberative central task allocator and reactive worker agents. The second architecture comprises deliberative worker agents making local task allocation decisions that are coordinated by a central instance. Decisions in both architectures are made based on Markov decision processes. Evaluation criteria include the overall quality of the task allocation process as well as the communication overhead in the second architecture.

The book closes with a contribution of a speculative yet visionary character. Weiss (page 217) argues that existing agent architectures often tend to inherently limit an agent's flexibility because they imply a discrete cognitive and social behavior space. He proposes a constraint-centered architectural framework that restricts the deliberative and social behavior by constraint handling and such forms a continuous behavior space. This behavior space is characterized by the two dimensions cognition (reactive vs. deliberative) and sociability (isolated vs. interactive). Four special conditions are highlighted under which constraint handling seems suitable to guide an agent with controlled social deliberation capabilities. The work additionally provides an extensive review of the current literature.

Reactivity and Deliberation:
A Survey on Multi-Robot Systems

Luca Iocchi, Daniele Nardi, and Massimiliano Salerno

Dipartimento di Informatica e Sistemistica, Università "La Sapienza"
Via Salaria 113 00198, Roma, Italy.
{iocchi,nardi,salerno}@dis.uniroma1.it

Abstract. Multi Robot Systems are, nowadays, an important research area within Robotics and Artificial Intelligence. Although Multi Robot Systems can be regarded as a particular case of Multi Agent Systems, it seems appropriate to study the Multi Robot Systems from a specific viewpoint, because of the issues which arise from the embodiment of agents operating in real environments. In this paper, we present an analysis of Multi Robot Systems by looking at their cooperative aspects. In particular, we propose a taxonomy of Multi Robot Systems and a characterization of reactive and social deliberative behaviors of the Multi Robot System as a whole. Finally, we address some Multi Robot Systems, which we consider representative of the various nodes in our taxonomy.

1   Introduction

Multi Robot Systems (MRS) have been proposed in the last decade in a variety of settings and applied in several tasks. Special attention has been given to MRS developed to operate in a dynamic environment, where uncertainty and unforeseen changes can happen due to robots and other agents that are external to the MRS itself.

In this paper, we regard MRS as a particular form of Multi Agent System (MAS), by specifically addressing reactivity and social deliberation. The work on MRS is pursued based on rather different goals. A significant body of work on MRS has been originated from motivations that are essentially of engineering nature. A MRS can improve the effectiveness of a robotic system either from the viewpoint of the performance in accomplishing certain tasks, or in the robustness and reliability of the system, which can be increased by modularizing it. Let us first address the improvement of performance. In [14] it is emphasized that there are tasks that require multi robots to be accomplished. This situation can arise not only when the robots can accomplish different functions, but also when they have the same capabilities. Moreover, even when a single robot can achieve the given task the possibility of deploying a team of robots can improve the performance of the overall system. With regard to robustness, following [40], we emphasize that, MRS can be designed and implemented in such a way to guarantee two important features: adaptivity and fault tolerance. Adaptivity refers to the ability of the MRS to modify its own behavior over time, depending

M. Hannebauer et al. (Eds.): Reactivity and Deliberation in MAS, LNAI 2103, pp. 9–32, 2001.
© Springer-Verlag Berlin Heidelberg 2001

on changes due to the dynamic environment, changes in the system mission, changes in the system composition or capabilities, so that the performance of the entire system can either be improved or at least not degraded. Fault tolerance is the ability of the MRS to deal with individual robot failures or communication failures, between two or more robotic agents, that may occur at any time during the mission. MRS which present both the above features can be said robust, where robustness is, therefore, the ability of the MRS to be both adaptive and fault tolerant.

Another significant development of MRS stems from the studies on biological systems or complex models arising in cognitive science and economics (see for example [9]). In this framework the development of simulation models has led also to implementations of real robot systems, built to provide additional evidence to the behaviors studied in the simulations. Many of these systems deal with a large number of robotic agents and the MRS is thus viewed as a swarm [9,40], or a colony [2] or, more generally, as a robot collective [14]. While in this work we are more interested in the system engineering aspects of the MRS, we consider to some extent also a few biologically inspired approaches.

A significant boost to the work on MRS has recently been given also by the Robotics competitions and RoboCup [27], in particular. In fact, the design of MRS is regarded as one of the major scientific challenges to be developed in the RoboCup environment [3]. In particular, according to the league organization of RoboCup, the real robot leagues as well as the simulated league provide different settings, where different hypotheses underly the design of the MRS. The most distinguishing feature, as compared with previous work on MRS, is that the RoboCup environment is highly dynamic and includes an opponent team; thus the RoboCup setting provides significantly new challenges in the design of MRS.

While the above mentioned motivations may seem very far apart, the technical solutions that are being developed have several common features. However, the discipline is still relatively young and a common framework for the work on MRS is difficult to identify. A MRS cannot be simply regarded as a generalization of the single robot case and the proposed approaches need to be more precisely characterized in terms of assumptions about the environment and in terms of the internal system organization.

Interesting contributions towards a classification of the work on MRS are the surveys by Cao et al. [9] and by Dudek et al. [14]. In [9] several axes for characterizing a MRS are discussed, while in [14] a classification of MRS that is more focussed with the communication and computation aspects of MRS is presented. In addition, MRS can be regarded as MAS and thus many aspects of the system organization of MRS can be analyzed by referring to the literature about MAS.

The aim of the present work is to address the most recent developments of MRS by classifying the proposed approaches in terms of a number of features concerning the system organization and specifically focusing on reactivity and social deliberation.

The paper is organized as follows. In the next section we propose a classification structure that is suitable for characterizing the major features of MRS. In Sect. 3 we specifically focus on the issue of reactivity versus social deliberation. In Sect. 4 we present some of the approaches that we consider as representative of various nodes in the taxonomy, characterizing them according to the task accomplished by the MRS. Section 5 concludes the paper by providing some reflections on the problems to be addressed by future research.

2   Multi-Robot System Taxonomy

In this section we present a taxonomy of the Multi Robot Systems (MRS) centered on their cooperative capabilities. The taxonomy allows for a precise classification of different typologies of MRS, with a special interest to those design choices concerning cooperation within the MRS. Following the approach in [9], we propose several classification dimensions. The *classification dimensions* used in the taxonomy are defined via a top down approach by refining the level of the system structure characterization. Four different levels are individuated in the taxonomy and presented in detail: a *Cooperation Level*, a *Knowledge Level*, a *Coordination Level* and an *Organization Level*. Subsequently, we recall two additional dimensions which can characterize the systems, independently of their classification in the taxonomy: communication and system composition. The issue of reactivity versus deliberation is addressed in the following section. In addition, an analysis of some of the most relevant works on the MRS according to our taxonomy will be presented in Sect. 4.

The taxonomy proposed for classification of MRS is shown in Fig. 1. The first level of the taxonomy is concerned with the ability of the system to cooperate

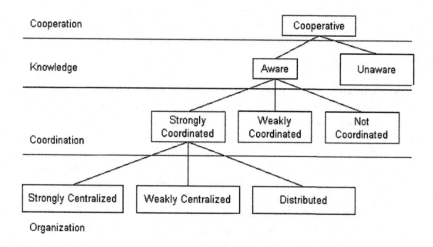

Fig. 1. MRS Taxonomy

in order to accomplish a specific task. At the *Cooperation Level* we distinguish cooperative systems from not cooperative ones.

> ***Cooperation***: situation in which several robots operate together to perform some global task that either cannot be achieved by a single robot, or whose execution can be improved by using more than one robot, thus obtaining higher performances (see [39]).

In this work we are interested only in those MRS which present many robotic agents (we also call them a *team*) having, as a whole, a common global goal to achieve. As a consequence, systems consisting of robotic agents that operate in the same environment, but that are not related to each other by a common objective (called *not cooperative* MRS) are not taken into account in this article. Therefore, in the following, the term MRS will refer to a team of cooperative robots.

Among the cooperative systems a first important characterization can be introduced depending on how much knowledge each robot has about the presence of other robots in its own team. This dimension represents the second level of the proposed taxonomy, that is called *Knowledge Level*.

> ***Awareness***: the property of a robot in the MRS to have knowledge of the existence of the other members of the system [47].

Conversely, unaware robots perform their tasks as if they were the only robots present within the system. Cooperation among unaware robotic agents is the weakest form of cooperation. For example in a box-pushing task many robots can contribute to the achievement of the common goal while behaving as single entities, i.e. without taking into account the presence and the actions of the other robots, as in [28].

In the category of aware systems we can identify the modes through which cooperation among robots can be achieved. We therefore introduce a third level in our taxonomy: the *Coordination Level*, that is concerned with the mechanisms used for robot cooperation.

> ***Coordination***: cooperation in which the actions performed by each robotic agent take into account the actions executed by the other robotic agents in such a way that the whole ends up being a coherent and high-performance operation (see [15]).

Coordination is not a prerogative of the cooperative MRS, in fact there exist robotic systems in which coordination between the members is required, but the robots have different goals which often are not related to each other. For example, the industrial robots often share tools and coordination is needed to avoid interferences, which take place when a single indivisible resource is requested by multiple robots. These kind of systems are not considered in the present article, which is concerned with cooperative MRS.

It is obvious that systems of unaware robots cannot be coordinated in the above sense because their members do not have knowledge of the existence of the others.

There are different ways a robot can take into account the actions of the other members of the team; we can further classify the coordinated MRS by introducing a distinction between two different kinds of coordination based on the use of a *coordination protocol*, that is defined as a set of rules that the robots must follow in order to interact each other in the environment.

Strong (Weak) coordination: a form of coordination that relies (does not rely) on a coordination protocol.

Strongly coordinated systems are based on a system of signals by which a robot exerts its influence on the behavior of another. In other words, strong coordination is based on the application of predefined or learned rules concerning the way two or more robots have to interact.

Coordination is not always a necessary property for the cooperative MRS, in fact while it introduces more flexibility within the system organization by allowing for a better use of the available resources, there are tasks which can be accomplished effectively by not coordinated MRS, as in [6] where a formation maintaining task is addressed. The advantage of a not coordinated MRS relies in its less complex design which involves a lower risk of fault, but as a consequence there could be a large waste of resources either because the robots execute contrasting tasks, or because interferences arise. A coordinated MRS, on the contrary, can avoid, or at least reduce, the previous kind of problems, but a more complex design is needed. The weakly coordinated MRS, as in [16], are not dependent on a protocol and consequently more robust to communication failures, but they lack of many of the organizational capabilities which a coordination protocol offers. The more the environment is dynamic and the goal is complex, the more a strongly coordinated MRS is effective in achieving its goal.

The fourth level of our taxonomy is concerned with the way the decision system is realized within the MRS. The *Organization Level* permits a distinction between centralized approaches and distributed ones [9].

Centralization: the organization of a system having a robotic agent (a leader) that is in charge of organizing the work of the other robots; the leader is involved in the decisional process for the whole team, while the other members act according to the directions of the leader.

Distribution: the organization of a system composed by robotic agents which are completely autonomous in the decisional process with respect to each other; in this class of systems a leader does not exist.

A centralized system can have a hierarchical structure, in which the robots operating under control of a leader, can be themselves leaders of other sub team of robots within the multi robot system.

A further classification of centralized systems can be introduced depending on the way the leader role is played.

Strong centralization: centralization in which decisions are taken by
a leader that remains the same during the entire mission duration.

It is possible that more than one member in the MRS is allowed to acquire the
role of leader, all of them can potentially plan the activity of the other members,
but, when the MRS is strongly centralized, at the beginning of the mission the
leader role is univocally assigned to only one of the robots, and kept by it till
the completion of the mission itself.

Weak centralization: centralization in which more then one robot is
allowed to become a leader during the mission.

The role of leader is assigned dynamically during the accomplishment of the
mission either depending on environmental changes, or forced by the failure of
the current robot leader.

Centralization, both weak and strong, allows for a simpler task assignment
between the team member because only one of them, the leader, is in charge
of it. Centralized MRS, as the one proposed in [49], have the disadvantage that
they strongly rely on communication. Thus, when a communication failure take
place, it results in a failure of the entire system. Moreover, a strongly centralized
system can fail in accomplishing its task when its leader goes out of order; a
weakly centralized system tries to recover from a leader failure by selecting a
new leader, as in [39]. An advantage of the strongly centralized MRS is that
a well suited robotic agent can be realized to be the leader, for example by
having the appropriate computing capabilities to analyze the environmental data
used to take decision. On the contrary, the distributed MRS, as in [42], offer
a greater robustness to the above mentioned problems by letting each team
member decide autonomously, but a greater complexity is required to realize
coordination between them.

As already mentioned, along with the classification introduced by the taxonomy, two more dimensions can be identified which are orthogonal to the
previous ones: communication and system composition.

Cooperation among robots is often obtained by a communication mechanism
that allows the robots to exchange messages among each other. For a detailed
analysis of the various technical problems related to communication see [15]. Here
we limit ourselves to present few basic aspects about communication, so that its
connection with our taxonomy can be illustrated. In fact, strongly coordinated
systems must necessarily communicate (in order to execute the coordination protocol), weakly coordinated and not coordinated systems can be developed with
or without communication, while unaware systems do not use communication
(because any robot does not know of the existence of the others).

We can distinguish two different types of communication depending on the
way the robots exchange information. All the communicating systems can use
either direct or indirect communication.

Direct communication: communication that makes use of some hardware on board dedicated device to signal something that the other team
members can understand.

Indirect communication: communication that makes use of stigmergy[1], both active and passive, for the communication among the team members.

Communication is a very important issue in MRS because many property of the system itself rely on it. Direct communication is the easier and most powerful way to exchange information between the members of a MRS, but due to noises or to hardware failures it often becomes a critical point. To avoid this problem, techniques like stigmergy have been developed and applied, as in [28], so that the members of the system can deal with communication failures. This more robust communication system implies a more complicated MRS design because each member of the team has to interpret the surrounding environment and, moreover, less information can be exchanged between the members themselves.

Finally, a design choice that must be taken into account for developing a MRS is the type of robots composing the system. We can distinguish two different system compositions: heterogeneous, homogeneous (see for example [46]).

Homogeneity: property of a team of robots whose members are exactly the same both in the hardware and in the control software.

Heterogeneity: property of a team of robots whose members have a difference either in the hardware devices or in the software control procedures.

If the robots of a deterministic homogeneous system are subject to the same inputs they have the same behavior, by producing the same outputs. They operate in a different way only when they act under different conditions in the environment in which they operate, or if the system is not deterministic. On the contrary, heterogeneous robots usually have different control mechanisms, different representations of the information, or different behaviors due to the experiences collected during the system existence via learning techniques.

The homogeneity or the heterogeneity of the members can influence the way in which robustness is achieved. In a homogeneous system every agent can execute the same actions as the other team members with the same results, so that a failure of a member can be easily compensated by another robot in the system, in such a way that fault tolerance is guaranteed. On the contrary adaptivity is weakly ensured because there is no differentiation among the robots. Therefore, homogeneous systems are typically used in the so called swarm-type approach, where a large number of autonomous robots are utilized to realize a distributed system. This method allows the system to achieve the desired goals when the repetitive execution of a set of actions is needed and time is not a critical resource.

---

[1] Stigmergy is a term coined by the biologist P.Grassé which means to incite work by the effect of previous work [28], in the robotics field there exist two type of stigmergy: active and passive. The first kind occurs when a robot alter the environment so as to affect the sensory input of another robot, the second one occurs when a robot action alter the environment so that the effects of another robot's action change.

The accomplishment of the task usually relies on some mathematical convergence results, and the relevant question with these systems is the realization of the correct laws to ensure the achievement of the desired goal.

On the other hand, for assuring adaptivity without giving up fault tolerance, heterogenous MRS are preferred. Heterogeneous robots allow the MRS to adapt more easily to the different situations which could emerge in a dynamic environment, since they offer a better chance to deal with new and unpredicted needs. The system does not rely on the fact that the robots are all the same, thus making it easier to modify the system composition so as to support a team configuration change by gathering new members within the MRS itself and/or changing some of the existing ones. Moreover, in a heterogeneous system it is still possible for more than one robot to execute the same task, even though with different modalities (because of different hardware and/or software). In this way, when a failure occurs, another member of the MRS can perform the required work to keep achieving the task, thus ensuring fault tolerance. Obviously, working with heterogeneous systems implies a higher effort in realizing the software needed to control the MRS.

3   Social Deliberation vs. Reactivity

Deliberation and reactivity are important features of a robotic system: both in the case of a single robot and in a robotic team. In this section we first recall the architectural issues that have been addressed for a single robot in order to develop a reactive and/or a deliberative behavior. Then, we characterize which behavior is expected from a reactive or a deliberative MRS. Finally, we discuss reactivity and social deliberation with respect to the taxonomy introduced in the previous section.

3.1   Deliberation and Reactivity for a Single Robot

The problem of realizing a reactive and/or a deliberative behavior in a single robot has been addressed by introducing different architectures for the robotic agent, specifically developed to suite the desired behavior. Three main approaches have been largely considered in the literature [33]: the behavior-based, the sense-model-plan-act and the hybrid one.

Behavior-Based Architecture. The subsumption architecture presented in [8] has been the first example of this kind of approach. A behavior-based controller consists of a collection of behaviors that activate and/or maintain goals [33]. Each behavior is implemented substantially as software or hardware control laws receiving inputs from the robot sensors and/or from other behaviors in the system, and sending outputs to the robot actuators and/or to other behaviors. Thus, the resulting architecture consists in a network of interacting behaviors, whose activation depends on a set of rules (behavior arbitration), such as prefixed priority among behaviors or a voting mechanism. Reactivity is ensured in these systems because of their quick real time responses due to the embedment of a collection of preprogrammed, concurrent condition-action rules. Finally, a behavior-based system is realized in a bottom up fashion and a distributed internal representation of the robot state can be used for building more and more abstract behaviors by laying them one on top of the other.

Sense-Model-Plan-Act Architecture. This approach is based on the explicit representation of the robot internal state and on the realization of four steps which give the architecture the name of sense-model-plan-act architecture [38]. The first step is called sensing and consists in collecting sensor data of the environment where the robot is situated; the data collected are then used to build a model of the environment which will be different depending on the way the system is implemented and on the aspect that are relevant to decide which action to execute. The model is usually constituted by a set of symbols composed by predicates and values which can be manipulated by a logical system, for example propositional or first-order logic. A planner module is in charge of analyzing the information contained in the environment model, by deciding a sequence of actions to be executed to achieve the desired goal, and verifying through logical inference if the sequence itself is compatible with the knowledge base of the system. Once a suitable sequence, called plan, has been found, the high level commands must be converted in low level commands to be sent to the actuators so that the robot can actually execute the plan. The deliberative system is realized in a top down fashion. This architecture is suited to deal with complex situations, but the need of higher computational resources (due to the modelling phase and the planning one), causes severe limitations in the response time (and thus in the reactivity) of the system.

Hybrid Architecture. To use the advantages of both the behavior-based architecture and the deliberative one, several hybrid architectures have been proposed (see for example [17,18]). This approach is realized by integrating in the same architecture: 1) behaviors that control the low level functions and that are in charge of the reactivity of the system, 2) a decisional module (a planner) in charge of the high level decision making. The hybrid architecture is often composed by two different layers: the planner and the reactive system. Sometimes an intermediate module is used for reconciling the possibly different representations used by the two layers and solving any conflict between the outputs.

The pure sense-model-plan-act architecture, which is used to realize a high level deliberative behavior, is not currently used because of its intrinsic limits, while the behavior-based and the hybrid architectures are quite common, especially when the robot is situated in a highly dynamic environment, where a quick reaction to a new input is very important, being the environment itself uncertain and unpredictable.

3.2 Social Deliberation and Reactivity in MRS

A precise characterization of MRS with respect to reactivity and social deliberation is difficult to identify in the literature on MRS, although these characteristics can be found in several MRS and are addressed for example in [10].
In addition, in the case of MAS reactivity and social deliberation are addressed
either through the study of a specific agent architecture (see for example [34,
30]), or by considering two different kinds of cooperation called reactive and
intentional, as described in [15].

We propose to address these notions based on the ability of the team of robots
to act in response to the dynamics of the environment. We thus characterize
social deliberation and reactivity for MRS as follows.

> **MRS social deliberation**: a system behavior that allows the team to
> cope with the environmental changes by providing a strategy that can be
> adopted to reorganize the team members' tasks, so as to use all the re-
> sources available to the system itself to effectively achieve the global goal.

> **MRS reactivity**: a system behavior in which every single robot in the
> team copes with the environmental changes by providing a specific solu-
> tion to reorganize its own task in order to fulfill the accomplishment of
> its originally assigned goal.

The main difference between social deliberation and reactivity in the proposed definition relies on the different modalities applied by the MRS to recover
from an unpredicted situation: in a social deliberative MRS a long term plan
involving the usage of all the available resources to accomplish a global goal is
provided; in a reactive MRS a plan to cope with the problem at hand is provided
by the robotic agent directly involved with it. In a social deliberative system a
global representation of the environment that is shared by all the team members
may exist, but it is not required. In fact, a system can be deliberative without
a global reconstruction of the environment, by imposing some constraints on
the overall system behavior. While a reactive system architecture allows for the
implementation of MRS that are able to quickly react to environmental changes,
without affecting the entire MRS organization.

To clarify this distinction we can consider a case where the MRS composed,
for instance by three robots, has the goal to open a room door and to move
the robots into the room. Let us suppose that all the robots can accomplish the
same tasks, even if in different ways. One of the robots has the specific task to
open the door and then enter the room, while the others have the task to go
directly to the door and, when open, enter the room. If the first robot encounters
an obstacle two different things can happen depending on the type of system
organization.

In a reactive system the robot that encountered the obstruction tries to avoid
it, so that it can continue the execution of its original task without affecting
the behavior of the other team members. If it fails to bypass the obstacle, the
other robots would remain in front of the closed door, until one of them tries to

exit from the impasse by opening the door by itself, but without a global task redistribution.

In a social deliberative system the same situation would be faced by deciding to reorganize the entire mission for example by exchanging the task allocation among the robots, in any case by elaborating a new strategy involving several members of the team.

3.3   Reactivity and Social Deliberation in the Proposed Taxonomy

As previously argued, when looking at reactivity versus deliberation, there is the need to distinguish between the case in which these concepts are referred to a MRS and that in which they are referred to a single robot. In fact, the former can be either social deliberative or reactive independently of the kind of architecture used to realize the single robots. In the previous example the way the robot reorganizes its own task to open the door is irrelevant with respect to its behavior as a member of the system. The single robot architecture could be either behavior-based, or hybrid, without affecting the reactive or social deliberative behavior of the entire system. On the contrary, in order to properly characterize the system, it is necessary to consider other features different from the single robot architecture.

As shown in Fig. 2, in order to have social deliberation in a MRS it is necessary to consider whether a system is coordinated or not, in particular, whether it is strongly coordinated or not. As evidenced by the taxonomy all the systems that are not strongly coordinated are reactive, while the strongly coordinated ones can be either reactive or social deliberative. This happens because of the need to have a coordination protocol for reorganizing the MRS task allocation. Among the strongly coordinated MRS only the distributed ones can be reactive,

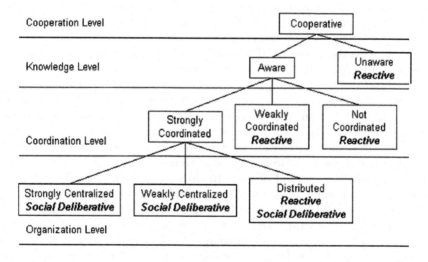

Fig. 2. MRS Taxonomy

because centralization implies that the task allocation among the different team members is executed by the robotic agent which takes the role of the leader, thus enforcing the behavior of the overall system, by providing a strategy.

As a consequence, among the orthogonal dimensions of communication and system composition, only communication is a required feature for social deliberative systems which rely on strong coordination, while composition of the team is not a constraining characteristic.

4   MRS Application Domain

In this section we are going to discuss several works related to MRS. We collect them according to the task used to test the techniques proposed, so that a comparison among them is more natural. It is worth emphasizing that our goal is not to provide a complete survey of existing approaches. Rather, we aim at characterizing more precisely some aspects of the taxonomy presented in Section 2, by providing concrete examples of implemented MRS.

We consider five different kinds of tasks for MRS: foraging, multi target observation, box pushing, exploration and soccer. These domains are representative of a large number of issues which arise from the study of cooperative MRS.

4.1   Foraging

Foraging is a testbed often used for MRS because of its analogies with tasks like rescue and search operations, toxic waste cleaning, mine cleaning [4,24,32,40, 12]. The task requires the MRS's robotic agents to pick up objects scattered in the environment; along with the foraging task also the multi foraging has been defined [4], which is a variation of the first one where different kinds of objects must be collected. Different techniques to cope with problems like interferences (especially when a homogeneous MRS is used), communication and knowledge sharing are involved in this task.

In [4] an unaware, reactive MRS, composed by behavior based robotic agents, is proposed to deal with a multi foraging task, in which two typology of objects must be collected and also delivered to different locations depending on their own type. Three strategies are presented and the results obtained with the different settings are compared by considering the relation between performance and a metric, called social entropy, introduced by the author. The social entropy measures the amount of the robotic agent diversity within the MRS. In the first setting, a homogeneous MRS is realized; each robot is capable of collecting and delivering both the types of objects. In the second setting, the MRS is heterogenous and the robotic agents can only pick up either one type of object or the other. In the third case, the MRS is again heterogenous, but this time the specialization is concerned with the task the robots can execute: by using a territorial division, some robots are in charge of collecting the objects around the environment and to drop them on the edge of an area which include the retrieving location. Inside the area, the remaining robotic agents collect the dropped objects and deliver them to the predefined areas. Experimental results show that a homogeneous MRS performs better than a heterogeneous one as long as the complexity of the task does not require a diversification of the capabilities of the MRS members.

In [24] a reactive, strongly coordinated, distributed MRS is presented. The heterogeneous robotic agents, realized in a behavior based architecture, have the common goal to clean an office like environment. One of the robotic agent is the vacuum and the other is the sweeper. The work studies the possibility to realize a grounded symbolic knowledge and communication. Three levels of representation are proposed, one on top of the other: the iconic representation, the indexical representation and the symbolic representation. Each of the levels is learned by the robots. The cooperation is realized with the superposition of four different modules, each of which is related to a representation level. The first module makes use of no representation and no communication, so that each robot acts for itself, by just executing correctly its own task. The input sensor data are the icons for the environmental objects (the sensors are the same so that the robots have the same icon). The second module lets the robots have knowledge of each other. An indexical representation is realized by the robotic agents by associating an icon to a robot. The sweeper becomes the index for the dust, so that the vacuum relates the sweeper position to the dust pile position, by watching where the sweeper stops. The third module introduces a direct communication among the agent so that the indexical representation can be shared. In the final module the symbolic representation is introduced, so that a more complete information can be exchanged by the robots. It lets the robotic agents be able to accomplish the task even if they are not in a direct view.

In [32] a reactive, distributed, strongly coordinated MRS is proposed to accomplish a foraging task. The system is composed by behavior-based homogeneous robots. The objective of the work is to obtain social behaviors via learning techniques, which allows for reducing the interferences between the robotic agents. The main problem is to find the appropriate reward, so that greedy robots act in a social way even if the effect of the acquired behavior are not of immediate benefit for the single robotic agent. Three different types of reinforcement are proposed to let the MRS present the social rule of yielding. The first is based on the perception that each robot has about the way its own task is being accomplished. The second kind of reinforcement, called observational reinforcement, encourages the robotic agent to repeat the behaviors observed for the other robots. The third type of reinforcement is obtained directly from the other robotic agents, based on their experiences. This kind of reinforcement does not require the robotic agent to model the internal state of the other robots, because, if the social rules are consistent, the punishment or the reward received would have been the same if the robotic agent were directly involved in the situation which generated them.

In [40] a reactive, distributed, strongly coordinated MRS, composed by heterogeneous behavior-based robotic agents, is tested with a foraging task. The focus of the work presented is the ALLIANCE architecture. All the robotic agents have sets of behaviors, each of which lets the robot itself to execute a corresponding task for which it is allowed. These behavior sets inhibit more basic and reactive behaviors, and are controlled by modules called motivational behaviors, which can cross inhibit each other. ALLIANCE's motivational behaviors are activated on the basis of a threshold mechanism; two parameters regulate their activation modalities, by characterizing the speed growth to the thresholds of the control functions. The first parameter is representative of the impatience of a robotic agent to take care of a task that is already assigned to an other agent within the system, so as to cope with the fault tolerance aspect. The second parameter is representative of the acquiescence of a robotic agent to give up the task which it is executing, so that it can accomplish another task for which it is more suitable and leaving the current one to a more adequate robot. Inputs to the control functions are the information that the robotic agents exchange, and the data coming from the each robot's sensors.

Other MRS which address the foraging task that are based on the swarm approach are described in [12,31,1]. All these works presented reactive MRS.

According to the characterization of social deliberation and reactivity proposed in the previous section, all the MRS presented in the above works are classified as reactive. In fact, in presence of an unforeseen event, each team member elaborates an individual solution, based on its own capabilities, to cope with the new situation. Therefore a single robot never modifies the global strategy to achieve the team's goal. In [4] the MRS is reactive because of its unawareness, the team cannot reorganize itself since each member ignores the existence of the others, hence only individual solutions can be addressed. The other works, on the contrary, present strongly coordinated MRS, but in each of them the social deliberative aspect is not realized, letting the robots face the unpredicted situations by providing individual specific tactics.

As highlighted by above discussion, foraging tasks have been usually addressed by reactive MRS, extending previous work on behavior-based architectures for a single robot. To the best of our knowledge deliberative approaches have not been proposed for this task. This may be explained by the fact that the major issue in foraging is to avoid spatial interferences among team members, which may be effectively addressed without the need to realized a social deliberative MRS.

4.2   Multi Target Observation

The multi target observation (also known as CMOMMT: Cooperative Multi Robot Observation of Multiple Moving Targets) is a very recent MRS testbed, first introduced by Parker in [41]. The task consists in maximizing the time during which each of the moving target is being observed by, at least, one of the robotic agents within the MRS. There are many connections with security, surveillance and recognition problems [41,50,23], where targets moving around in a bounded area must be observed. Problems like those connected with communication, sensor fusion, cooperation and coordination are involved in the multi target observation.

In [41], a reactive, distributed, strongly coordinated MRS, composed by homogeneous, behavior-based robotic agents (even if the system is allowed to cope with heterogeneous robots), is proposed to deal with the CMOMMT. The system is realized through the behavior based ALLIANCE architecture, combined with techniques based on potential fields and a target seeking system. In [50] the multi target observation task is achieved by using a social deliberative, distributed, strongly coordinated MRS. The robotic agents are behavior based and homogeneous, but the technique proposed is perfectly applicable to a heterogeneous system as well. The proposed architecture, called Broadcast of Local Eligibility (BLE), is an extension of the subsumption architecture, to enable for coordination between the robotic agents. Each behavior of each robot has a function which locally evaluates the robot's eligibility to accomplish a given task; the values are then exchanged between the robotic agents "peer behaviors". The robot whose behavior performed the highest value, inhibits the corresponding behaviors on the other system's members, thus claiming the task. This process, called cross-inhibition, can be executed only among peer behaviors. Internally to each agent the subsumption architecture selects the current behavior to be activated, by making use of a behavior arbitration possibly tuned so that priority is given to the task each robot is specialized for. Both the internal subsumption and the cross subsumption are sufficient to permit a heterogeneous MRS assigning the optimal task to each robotic agent within it.

The two above described works pinpoint a very interesting aspect: the difference between a reactive MRS and a reactive single robot architecture. They both present strongly coordinated MRS whose members are behavior based robotic agents, but while the ALLIANCE architecture implements a reactive system, with the BLE architecture a social deliberative MRS is realized. ALLIANCE ensures the robustness of the system by letting each member decide when to employ itself in accomplishing a task, without any need to reorganize the other members activity. A robot can take over the task assigned to another team member even if that member is still attempting to accomplish it. In the BLE architecture this is not possible, because when a robot starts accomplishing a task it inhibits the peer behaviors of the other members. Thus, when something happens which imposes a selection of a different action to be executed by a member of the MRS, all the other members will be involved in this reorganization and the new action will be executed by the robots which better fit the requirements, thus obtaining a new strategy.

Another work related to Multi-Robot target observation is presented in [23], where the authors describe a preliminary system that is focussed on tracking only one moving target (Paparazzi problem).

The multi target observation task is similar to the foraging one, with the addition of dynamic targets that must be continuously tracked. The more complex environment becomes an interesting testbed where deliberative systems could be effectively used.

4.3 Box Pushing

The box pushing task has analogies with problems like, for example, stockage or truck loading and unloading [28,42,39]. Moreover, for a MRS, different issues, like task allocation, robustness or communication, are related to it; thus the box pushing task is a very common MRS testbed to verify all those techniques which cope with such issues.

In [28] a reactive, unaware MRS is realized. The system proposed is a classical example of swarm approach; the robotic agents are homogeneous and rely on a behavior based architecture. The authors implemented a set of behaviors inspired by the way some ant species organize themselves to accomplish a pushing task. The system's members do not have direct communication capabilities, and they select their actions driven by their own reactivity. Three different primitive behaviors are implemented: a behavior which provides a pose (position and orientation) modification attracted by the input stimuli, a behavior which acts exactly the opposite of the previous one and, finally, a behavior which activates a set of preprogrammed actions used to escape from a deadlock. The robots, by using behaviors relying on the previous ones, manifest a real cooperative effort in the box pushing task.

In [42] the box pushing task is used as a testbed for a reactive, distributed, strongly coordinated MRS. The system is composed by heterogeneous robotic agents realized with the behavior based architecture L-ALLIANCE, developed by the author. L-ALLIANCE extends ALLIANCE capabilities by introducing learning techniques to adjust the parameters which regulate the ALLIANCE working modes. These parameters, called impatience and acquiescence motivations, control the capability of a robot to handle situations when other robots (outside itself) fail in performing a given task, and the capability of a robot to handle situations in which it fails in accomplishing a task respectively. The way the entire MRS operates depends on the values assigned to the above mentioned parameters. Because in a long term mission the robotic agents can degrade their operational capabilities, an external robotic agent should be in charge of setting the motivation values depending on the actual state of the MRS. This is needed to avoid, by relying on a learning technique, to adapt the parameters to the current system configuration.

In [39] the task of box pushing is proposed to test a strongly coordinated, weakly centralized, social deliberative MRS, whose heterogeneous robotic agents are realized in a hybrid architecture. The cooperative aspect of the MRS is here faced by dividing it in four different sequential phases: decomposition, allocation, local planning and execution. In the first phase a leader robot decomposes the global task into subtasks executable by a single robot or a group of them. Once the subtasks are individuated, they are scheduled and the robot's capabilities that are necessary to accomplish them are pinpointed. In the second phase the leader selects, by making use of a negotiation protocol, the available robots which fit the required capabilities. In the third phase the leader assigns them their own tasks, and each subordinated robot decomposes it into an action sequence which it can execute. If conflicts due to some kind of interference among the MRS's members arise, they must be solved in this phase. In the fourth phase the actions planned are executed by taking care of the possible unpredictable faults that could arise. If a leader presents some malfunction it can be replaced by another member of the team.

The work on box pushing is based on both reactive and social deliberative MRS. The reactive systems are implemented relying on various kind of techniques, in fact in [28] the system is unaware and the cooperation is obtained by letting each team member achieve its individual goal, without realizing any explicit coordination, thus the system reactivity is inherited by the single agent reactivity. In [42] the MRS is reactive, but it is also strongly coordinated, so as to reduce the situations in which the robotic agents could interfere with each other. Anyway each robot takes decision about how to cope with unpredicted events autonomously, by considering its knowledge about the environment and the team global state. In [39] each team member can notify an unforseen situation to its leader, so as to reorganize the roles of the robots and the task assigned to each of them. This MRS is then a social deliberative system, able to eventually create a new strategy to deal with the environment modification or to provide robustness.

Applications in the box pushing domain have been realized by using both reactive and deliberative approaches. Indeed, as compared with the foraging and multi target observation problems, in box pushing one may take advantage of explicit cooperation in the accomplishment of the task to the extent in which box maneuvering requires coordination.

4.4   Exploration and Flocking

Under the label of exploration and flocking different tasks can be grouped: these tasks differ on the way they are realized, but have the common feature to require MRS's members to move around in the environment. Behaviors like flocking, formation maintenance or map building [6,39,22,20,45] are, thus, part of the same task class. In the exploration task there is the need to distribute the robots as sparsely as possible so that the information they can collect does not overlap, while in the flocking task the goal is that the robotic agents move around together, such as in a flock. The formation task can be seen as a way to realize either the exploration one or the flocking one, in fact, depending on which kind of formation is chosen, the robotic agents can be as far as possible from each other, or as close as possible to each other.

In [6] a reactive, aware, not coordinated, homogeneous MRS, composed by not communicating behavior based robotic agents, is proposed to cope with the formation maintaining task, by using the potential function technique. The authors, inspired by the way the molecules snap into place as they form crystals, set each robotic agent with "attachment sites" to which the other system's members are drawn. The attachment site is not a physical device, but a position in the space surrounding a robotic agent. In this work the robotic agents are not forced to occupy a prefixed position within the formation, but they have different attachment sites disposition and, depending on which one is selected, they search for the first available position in the formation. The choice of one position respect to another depends on the robot's overall behavior generated by the superposition of the potential functions, called by the authors social potentials.

In [22] an exploration task in a office like environment is used to test a distributed, reactive MRS, designed to study the problem of grounding representations and communications of the robotic agents in real perceptions. The approach is strongly coordinated since, even though the robots are not coordinated for navigation, a protocol for exchanging representations of perceptual data is used. The author presents a technique to build a primitive language composed by a set of symbols obtained by classifying the robotic agent perception with a self-organizing classifier. The MRS's members cooperate in building a common knowledge about the environment by broadcasting their high-level representation of the perception data over the entire MRS. The process of building the set of symbols is divided into four subprocesses: perception, broadcast, singularity filtering and classification. In the first process each robot explores its portion of the environment producing perceptions, then, in the second phase, it broadcasts them to the other team members. The third phase consists in filtering the collected perceptions by retaining only those which are sufficiently singular with respect to the whole set. In the classification phase the robotic agents classify the set of perceptions so as to obtain the same resulting class.

The architecture presented in [39] is also used for a formation maintaining task. The resulting MRS is an example of strongly coordinated, weakly centralized, social deliberative MRS, composed by heterogeneous robotic agents realized in a hybrid architecture. In this work two robots travel in a office like environment in a convoy formation. Cooperation is obtained by dividing the task in four different sequential phases: decomposition, allocation, local planning and execution. A leader robot decomposes the global task into subtasks executable by a single robot or a group of them and directs them to the execution of these subtasks.

Other effective social deliberative MRS applications in the exploration domain have been realized by using strongly coordinated and centralized approaches [20,45], or distributed ones [44].

The works concerned with exploration and flocking task realize both reactive and social deliberative systems. In [6] the MRS is not coordinated and thus it is classified as reactive since its robotic agents execute their task by filling the gaps available in the formation, without communicating with each other. The work in [22] tests the possibility to realize a grounded language within the team, so it is not important to implement a MRS that presents a social deliberative behavior. Each team member can react to environmental changes by taking individual decisions without any necessity to reorganize the entire system strategy, while strong coordination is an essential property to realize the common grounded knowledge base. If the main task had been the exploration finalized to map building instead of a grounded language realization, a social deliberative system would have been more effective by letting the MRS better employ its resources. Finally in [39], as previously said, the system is social deliberative.

MRS for exploration or map building can be based on both reactive and social deliberative approaches. For this kind of tasks, with the increasing of the complexity of the environment social deliberative approaches could become more effective in ensuring a stronger level of cooperation.

4.5   Soccer

Robotic soccer is one of the tasks that has been considered in the last years as an interesting testbed for research in multi-agent and multi-robot cooperation [3, 13,27]. Indeed the soccer games played by robotic teams provide an interesting setting in which cooperation among robots is fundamental for an effective accomplishment of the task in a a highly dynamic and uncertain environment.

Depending on the different RoboCup leagues, different issues in multi-agent cooperation have been studied. The *Simulation league* is concerned with simulated agents, that are implemented by separate programs and can communicate among each other. Because of the lack of global information about the environment for the single agent, this setting provides an interesting environment for experiments in coordinating a multi-agent system [21,35]. The other RoboCup leagues are instead composed by actual robotic teams and the dynamic and uncertain environment in which they operate makes coordination of the multi-robot system a more challenging problem.

In the *Small-Size league* robots are small and very fast, they are usually controlled by a remote host that can take advantage of a global vision system (a camera positioned above the field). The availability of global information about the environment and the use of a remote host for robots' control allows for the implementation of centralized strategies [49]. Most of these systems are strongly centralized and deliberative, since the remote host can be considered as an agent acting as the leader of the team. However, reactive approaches can also be found in the behavior based hierarchical control architecture proposed in [43].

On the contrary, in the *Middle-Size league*, all the robot's sensors must be on board; therefore robots are more autonomous and have to deal with high uncertainty in reconstructing global information about the environment. The approach in [16] represents an example of reactive, weakly coordinated system, in which two robots are able to exchange the ball by using direct communication of their roles and a field-vector based collision avoidance that takes into account in a proper way the role of the robots. Other behavior based reactive MRS are presented in [7,10] On the other hand, successful deliberative centralized approaches in the Middle-Size league are used when it is possible to reliably reconstruct global information about the environment. For example the CS Freiburg team [19] makes use of very precise measurements given by laser scanners to reconstruct a global representation of the field and a social deliberative weakly centralized approach is obtained by dynamic selection of the robot that acts as the leader. However, possible communication failures, that are very common in this environment, as well as the general difficulty of reconstructing a global reliable view of the environment, require full autonomy on each robot and distributed approaches are to be preferred. Distributed heterogeneous robots cooperating by using explicit communication is described in [51]. The Azzurra Robot Team also presents a distributed heterogeneous robotic soccer team [11] based on a simple and flexible coordination protocol. From a technical perspective the proposed approach makes use of a *formation/role* mechanism and of dynamic assignment of roles by explicit communication of information about the status of the environment. A simple form of negotiation is used in order to realize a deliberative, distributed MRS that does not require a global representation of the environment. In fact each robot has the knowledge necessary to play any role, and robots switch roles on the fly, when a distributed agreement on the actions to be performed is achieved. A distributed architecture has the advantage that, in case of communication failures, the system degrades its performance, but it still keeps on the execution of the task. Finally, in the *Sony Legged league* three Sony AIBOs robots are used to form a team. Therefore the robots are the same in hardware and heterogeneity can be only given by different software control. At this time, mostly because of the lack of network devices on the robots, there are very simple forms of cooperation: in SPQR team [36] the robots are unaware of each other, but cooperation is still obtained by a static assignment of the roles (i.e. GoalKeeper, Defender and Forward). Other teams (for example [29,48]) have developed a different software only for the goalkeeper, while the other two robots are the same. For an effective game the robots should not obstruct each other when approaching the ball. Using different roles can help to accomplish this task; when the robots have exactly the same behavior it is not possible to guarantee that robots do not interfere.

The RoboCup teams have chosen reactive or deliberative approaches for their MRS, mainly depending on the capabilities of the robots involved in the competitions. In fact, the global vision system allowed in the *Small-Size league* has led to centralized and deliberative approaches; in the *Middle-Size league*, in which robots are fully autonomous, the deliberative approach has been mostly used, but also reactive MRS are present; finally, in the *Sony Legged league* we have only reactive MRS, due to the difficulties of communication among robots.

In general, the need of dynamically adapting different strategies during the game, has been considered an important aspect of social deliberation. For example, in order to realize in a robotic team the capabilities of passing the ball, a strong cooperation is required and social deliberative approaches based on centralized techniques [37] as well as on learning [46] have been proved to be successful.

5   Conclusions

In this paper we have presented a classification of MRS with the goal of highlighting reactivity and social deliberation. It is worth emphasizing that, although a MRS can be regarded as a kind of multi-agent system, the need to cope with the acquisition of knowledge from the environment, makes it more challenging to build actual experimentation settings for MRS. In addition, the forms of cooperation used in MRS need to take into account the uncertainty, the limitations, and the mistakes arising from the processing of sensor information.

We have first introduced a set of dimensions for the classification of MRS and provided a taxonomy of the type of cooperations that can be found in MRS. In addition, we have discussed two dimensions that can be considered orthogonal to the taxonomy in the sense that they do not interact with the features used to build the taxonomy. Then, we have focussed our attention on the issue of reactivity and social deliberation, by distinguishing the single robot from the MRS setting, and by proposing a characterization of MRS in terms of reactivity and social deliberation. In addition, we have seen that reactive approaches are viable in the settings where no coordination takes place, for example when the robots are unaware of the presence of other robots, as well as in distributed, strongly coordinated system organizations. On the other hand, social deliberation is based on coordination and it is implicit in the centralized approaches, while being suited also to distributed ones.

Finally, we have presented some of the MRS described in the literature by arranging them according to the task accomplished. As it turns out, reactive and social deliberative approaches are pursued in order to solve any of the problems examined, possibly with the exception of the foraging task. The outcomes of this analysis show that reactive approaches tend to be used when there are several robots and the task can be independently achieved by a single robot. However, when the task requires some degree of coordination social deliberation can be effectively applied. The models that are used for coordination in MRS are often not complex: the critical aspect is rather on their actual application, given all the difficulties arising in copying with dynamic environments.

We believe that, given the growing interest in practical application of MRS, we will have a significant increase of the work in this field. A major issue to be addressed by future work is the definition of suitable evaluation methodologies, in order to assess the adequacy and effectiveness of various forms of cooperation in MRS (see for example [5]). A major role in this respect can be played by the competitions [26,25], which provide a common set up that is a basic requirement for comparing different approaches.

Acknowledgments. This research has been carried out within the project "Robot Calciatori" funded by Italian Consiglio Nazionale delle Ricerche and the projects RAMSETE and MISTRAL funded by Italian Ministero dell'Università e della Rricerca Scientifica e Tecnologica. The authors also wish to thank the reviewers for their detailed comments which helped to improve the quality of this article.

References

1. R. C. Arkin. Cooperation without communication: Multiagent schema-based robot navigation. *Journal of Robotic Systems*, 9(3), 1992.
2. R. C. Arkin and G. A. Bekey. *Robot Colonies*. Kluwer Academic Publishers, 1997.

3. M. Asada. The RoboCup physical agent challenge: Goals and protocols for Phase-I. In H. Kitano, editor, *RoboCup-97: Robot Soccer World Cup I*, 1998.
4. T. Balch. The impact of diversity on performance in multi-robot foraging. In *Proc. of Agents '99*, 1999.
5. T. Balch. Hierarchic social entropy: an information theoretic measure of robot team diversity. *Autonomous Robots*, 8(3), 2000.
6. T. Balch and M. Hybinette. Social potentials for scalable multirobot formations. In *Proc. of IEEE International Conference on Robotics and Automation (ICRA-2000)*, 2000.
7. A. Bredenfeld and H. U. Kobialka. Team cooperation using dual dynamics. In M. Hannebauer, J. Wendler, and E. Pagello, editors, *Balancing Reactivity and Social Deliberation in Multi-agent Systems (this volume)*, pages 111–124. Springer, 2001.
8. Rodney A. Brooks. A robust layered control system for a mobile robot. *IEEE Journal of Robotics and Automation*, RA-2(1), 1986.
9. Y. Uny Cao, A. Fukunaga, and A. Kahng. Cooperative mobile robotics: Antecedents and directions. *Autonomous Robots*, 4:1–23, 1997.
10. S. Carpin, C. Ferrari, E. Pagello, and P. Patuelli. Bridging deliberation and reactivity in cooperative multi-robot systems through map focus. In M. Hannebauer, J. Wendler, and E. Pagello, editors, *Balancing Reactivity and Social Deliberation in Multi-agent Systems (this volume)*, pages 35–52. Springer, 2001.
11. C. Castelpietra, L. Iocchi, D. Nardi, M. Piaggio, A. Scalzo, and A. Sgorbissa. Coordination among heterogenous robotic soccer players. In *Proc. of International Conference on Intelligent Robots and Systems (IROS'2000)*, 2000.
12. F. Chantemargue and B. Hirsbrunner. A collective robotics application based on emergence and self-organization. In *Proc. of Fifth International Conference for Young Computer Scientists (ICYCS'99)*, 1999.
13. S. Coradeschi, L. Karlsson, P. Stone, T. Balch, G. Kraetzschmar, and M. Asada. Overview of RoboCup-99. *AI Magazine*, 1999.
14. D. Dudek, M. Jenkin, E. Milios, and D. Wilkes. A taxonomy for multi-agent robotics. *Autonomous Robots*, 3(4):375–397, 1996.
15. J. Ferber. *Multi-Agent Systems*. Addison-Wesley, 1999.
16. M. Ferraresso, C. Ferrari, E. Pagello, R. Polesel, R. Rosati, A. Speranzon, and W. Zanette. Collaborative emergent actions between real soccer robots. In *RoboCup-2000: Robot Soccer World Cup IV*, 2000.
17. Erann Gat. Integrating planning and reacting in a heterogeneous asynchronous architecture for controlling real-world mobile robots. In *Proceedings of the Tenth National Conference on Artificial Intelligence (AAAI'92)*, 1992.
18. M. Georgeff and A. Lansky. Reactive reasoning and planning. In *Proceedings of the Sixth National Conference on Artificial Intelligence (AAAI'87)*, 1987.
19. J.-S. Gutmann, T. Weigel, and B. Nebel. Fast, accurate, and robust self-localization in the robocup environment. In *RoboCup-99: Robot Soccer World Cup III*, 1999.
20. D. Guzzoni, A. Cheyer, L. Julia, and K. Konolige. Many robots make short work. *AI Magazine*, 1997.
21. M. Hannebauer, J. Wendler, P. Gugenberger, and H. Burkhard. Emergent cooperation in a virtual soccer environment. In *Proc. of DARS-98*, 1998.
22. L. Hugues. Grounded representations for a robots team. In *Proc. of the 2000 IEEE/RSJ International Conference on Intelligent Robots and Systems*, 2000.
23. M. Jenkin and G. Dudek. The paparazzi problem. In *Proc. of International Conference on Intelligent Robots and Systems (IROS'2000)*, 2000.

24. David Jung and Alexander Zelinsky. Grounded symbolic communication between heterogeneous cooperating robots. *Autonomous Robots*, 8(3):269–292, 2000.
25. H. Kitano. Robocup rescue: A grand challenge for multi-agent systems. In *Proc. of ICMAS 2000*, 2000.
26. H. Kitano, M. Asada, Y. Kuniyoshi, I. Noda, E. Osawa, and H. Matsubara. Robocup: A challenge problem for ai and robotics. In *Lecture Note in Artificial Intelligence*, volume 1395, pages 1–19. Springer Verlag, 1998.
27. H. Kitano, E. Pagello, and M. Veloso, editors. *RoboCup-99: Robot Soccer World Cup III*. Springer-Verlag, 1999.
28. C. Ronald Kube and E. Bonabeau. Cooperative transport by ants and robots. *Robotics and Autonomous Systems*, 30(1):85–101, 2000.
29. M. Lawther and J. Dalgliesh. Unsw united. In *RoboCup-99: Robot Soccer World Cup III*, 1999.
30. J. Malek. On augmenting reactivity with deliberation in a controlled manner. In M. Hannebauer, J. Wendler, and E. Pagello, editors, *Balancing Reactivity and Social Deliberation in Multi-agent Systems (this volume)*, pages 76–91. Springer, 2001.
31. M. Mataric. *Interaction and Intelligent Behavior*. PhD thesis, MIT, 1994.
32. Maja J. Mataric. Learning social behavior. *Robotics and Autonomous Systems*, 20:191–204, 1997.
33. Maja J. Mataric. Behavior-based robotics. In Robert A. Wilson and Frank C. Keil, editors, *MIT Encyclopedia of Cognitive Sciences*, pages 74–77. MIT Press, 1999.
34. V. K. Mavromichalis and G. Vouros. Balancing between reactivity and deliberation in the ICAGENT framework. In M. Hannebauer, J. Wendler, and E. Pagello, editors, *Balancing Reactivity and Social Deliberation in Multi-agent Systems (this volume)*, pages 53–75. Springer, 2001.
35. F. Montesello, A. D'Angelo, C. Ferrari, and E. Pagello. Implicit coordination in a multi-agent system using a behavior-based approach. In *Proc. of DARS-98*, 1998.
36. D. Nardi, C. Castelpietra, A. Guidotti, M. Salerno, and C. Sanitati. S.P.Q.R. In *RoboCup-2000: Robot Soccer World Cup IV*. Springer-Verlag, 2000.
37. B. Nebel, J. S. Gutmann, and W. Hatzack. CS Freiburg '99. In *RoboCup-99: Robot Soccer World Cup III*, 1999.
38. N. J. Nilsson. Shakey the robot. Technical Report 323, SRI Artificial Intelligence Center, 1984.
39. Fabrice R. Noreils. Toward a robot architecture integrating cooperation between mobile robots: Application to indoor environment. *International Journal of Robotics Research*, 12(1):79–98, 1993.
40. Lynne E. Parker. ALLIANCE: An architecture for fault tolerant multirobot cooperation. *IEEE Transactions on Robotics and Automation*, 14(2):220–240, 1998.
41. Lynne E. Parker. Cooperative robotics for multi-target observation. *Intelligent Automation and Soft Computing*, 5(19), 1999.
42. Lynne E. Parker. Lifelong adaption in heterogeneous multi-robot teams: Response to continual variation in individual robot performance. *Autonomous Robots*, 8(3):239–267, 2000.
43. S. Behnke and R. Rojas. A hierarchy of reactive behaviors handles complexity. In M. Hannebauer, J. Wendler, and E. Pagello, editors, *Balancing Reactivity and Social Deliberation in Multi-agent Systems (this volume)*, pages 125–136. Springer, 2001.
44. A. Saffiotti, N.B. Zumel, and E.H. Ruspini. Multi-robot team coordination using desirabilities. In *Proc of the 6th Intl Conf on Inteligent Autonomous Systems (IAS)*, pages 107–114, Venice, Italy, 2000.

45. R. Simmons, D. Apfelbaum, D. Fox, R. P. Goldman, K. Z. Haigh, D. J. Musliner, M. Pelican, and S. Thrun. Coordinated deployment of multiple, heterogeneous robots. In *Proc. of International Conference on Intelligent Robots and Systems (IROS'2000)*, 2000.

46. P. Stone. *Layered Learning in Multiagent Systems*. MIT Press, 2000.

47. C. F. Touzet. Robot awareness in cooperative mobile robot learning. *Autonomous Robots*, 2, 2000.

48. M. Veloso, S. Lenser, E. Winner, and J. Bruce. Cm-trio-99. In *RoboCup-99: Robot Soccer World Cup III*, 1999.

49. M. Veloso and P. Stone. Individual and collaborative behaviors in a team of homogeneous robotic soccer agents. In *Proceedings of the Third International Conference on Multi-Agent Systems*, 1998.

50. B. B. Werger and M. J. Mataric. Broadcast of local eligibility for multi-target observation. In *Proc. of DARS*, 2000.

51. K. Yokota, K. Ozaki, N. Watanabe, A. Matsumoto, D. Koyama, T. Ishikawa, K. Kawabata, H. Kaetsu, and H. Asama. Uttori united: Cooperative team play based on communication. In *RoboCup-98: Robot Soccer World Cup II*, 1998.

Part II

Architectures and Frameworks

Bridging Deliberation and Reactivity in Cooperative Multi-Robot Systems through Map Focus

Stefano Carpin[1], Carlo Ferrari[1], Enrico Pagello[1,2], and Pierluigi Patuelli[1]

[1] Department of Electronic and Informatics
The University of Padua, Italy
[2] LADSEB – National Research Council
Padua, Italy
epv@dei.unipd.it
http://www.dei.unipd.it/ricerca/airg

Abstract. This paper is on balancing reactivity and deliberation in cooperative multi-robot systems. We outline which are the challenging issues that has to be addressed to get an effective solution. Then, a balancing method, based on introducing a concept of "Map Focus", is proposed. The framework is also enhanced with "Cooperative Behaviors", useful for robotic cooperation for accomplishing tasks in dynamic environments. We provide the details of the implementation and of the experimental results.

1 Deliberation, Reactivity, and Cooperation in Multi-Robot Systems

1.1 Multi-Robot Systems and Cooperative Robotics

Starting from the nineties there has been a great effort towards the development of multi-robot systems, which led to the introduction of a great variety of hardware and software configurations and architectures. In this work the term **multi-robot system** indicates *a team of two or more autonomous robots performing in the same shared environment*[1]. We focus our attention on Distributed Autonomous Robotic Systems (DARS), i.e. multi-robot systems where the control is not centralized, but rather distributed over the members of the team.

The starting point which led to the development of multi-robot systems, is that in many situations a team of robots may perform better (i.e. more robustly, or in less time) in dynamic environments or may be less expensive than a single robot. It is also clear that for some tasks a single robot is not able to reach the goal, like a multi-robot in the case of surveillance of a building or of a wide area, or for the transportation of big and/or heavy objects ([1]). However, at

---

[1] Note that accordingly to this definition two robotic arms operating in the same work cell, as well as a team of mobile platforms, constitute a multi-robot system. The key issues concerns the autonomy and the shared environment.

M. Hannebauer et al. (Eds.): Reactivity and Deliberation in MAS, LNAI 2103, pp. 35–52, 2001.
© Springer-Verlag Berlin Heidelberg 2001

the moment there is no criterion which indicates when switching from a single robot to a multi-robot is advantageous, nor widely accepted metrics to compare different solutions to the same problem (see [6] and [24] for some examples of metrics for measuring multi-robot performance).

Such systems may be organized in very different ways because of the many degrees of freedom which influence the overall architecture design (extensive descriptions can be found on [14], [16] and [20]). Even if multi-robot research directly follows from traditional autonomous robotics, multi-robot systems exhibit some unique features. Thus new approaches, analysis and design tools and challenging goals emerge ([28]). For example, in the design of a multi-robot system, one has to face the choice of implementing an identical team (in which every robot is equal in the hardware and in the software), an homogeneous team (in which the hardware is the same, but the control laws may differ) or a heterogenous one (in which the hardware, and then the control, is not the same for all the components).

Another important issue concerns the nature of **cooperation**, i.e. *the collective working towards a common goal (or set of goals)*. Cooperation may be gained through a "swarm effect", in which every robotic agent is driven by a simple set of rules without an explicit model, or even knowledge, of other members of the team (see for example [18]). This approach, derived from biological observations and from cybernetics ([11]), proved to be effective, but it is still not clear how to design individual control laws which drive to a satisfactory collective performance; the works of Steels ([32]), Pfeifer ([29]), Beni and Wang ([8]) are directed toward the development of suitable models to address this problem.

Cooperation can also be obtained through "intentional cooperation", also called coordination, in which every element of the team is aware of the presence of the others, and of the fact that they are working towards the same goal(s). In this situation is important to handle communication and to manage a model of the team and of its behavior. This approach strictly relates to DAI (Distributed Artificial Intelligence), and in fact it is often based on concepts like "negotiation", and "cooperative problem solving". A number of interesting architectures, like [4], [9], [10] and [27], were developed to address this point (for a general discussion on coordination techniques see [34]).

1.2   Deliberation and Reactivity in Multi-Robot Systems

Artificial intelligence concepts have been used in the past to control robots; in literature there are some well known systems that have been widely used for that purpose, like STRIPS ([17]) or NOAH ([31]). STRIPS, for example, used first-order logic to develop a navigational plan for a robot performing in an indoor environment. Such systems were based on an explicit model of the world, where the state was modeled as a collection of first order predicates, and the reaching of the goal was implied by the proving of a theorem on that assumptions. With this approach the system then performs obeying the *sense-think-act* paradigm, where the acting phase modifies the knowledge base and thinking means proving a theorem over it.

In this context **deliberative systems** *are intended to be systems with an explicit model of the world and with a planner working on it, in term of logical inferences*[2].

It is well known that the reactive approach ([12]) was introduced to address the issue of performing in highly dynamic environments, where the operating conditions are rapidly changing, and deliberative systems are then not able to perform correctly, because of the too fast changing of the world with respect to the time spent to update and "reason" on the model. The strict coupling of perception to action proved to be very effective and led to the development of intelligent systems totally based on the reactive approach. An intelligent behavior by a situated agent can then be achieved without an explicit model of the environment ([13]).

In this context **reactive systems** *are intended to be systems which do not own an explicit complex model of the environment, but that are instead organized with shortcuts between sensors and actuators* (with or without a layered or parallel architecture).

It is worth noting that this is quite different from the AI point of view of "reactive reasoning" ([19]).
Soon after the introduction of the reactive paradigm, and starting also from biological observations, hybrid architectures were introduced ([2], [3]), with the goal of putting together real-time responsiveness and deep reasoning capabilities.

In the case of multi-robot systems the situation is much more complicated. Multi-robot systems add significant dynamics to the world they live in, so real-time performance is a must, in order to let the system survive in its operating environment. The information flow coming from sensors needs to be carefully handled; in fact not only there are more events to track, but it is also necessary to distinguish between external stimuli, coming from the environment, and system's stimuli, coming from other members of the team (*proprioception*). This overloaded flow of information should lead to a pure reactive approach, in order to deal with the proper dynamic constrains, but this is not the appropriate case. In fact each member of the team risks to behave in a *"skizophrenic"* manner, with a continuous and useless switching between different behaviors caused by the overflow of perceptual stimuli. So some kind of deliberation should be embedded in the system, but with the caveat that traditional single-robot hybrid approaches are not straightly applicable, because of the different time scale and of the different nature of the problems which arise.

---

[2] The system is not limited to use first-order logic but some kind of logic; there is a huge literature of systems based on temporal-logic, non-monotonic logic and so on.

2   Coupling Reactivity and Deliberation through Map Focus

In this section we investigate the problem of coupling reactivity and deliberation in the case of *cooperative distributed autonomous robotic systems*. We briefly summarize the basic hypothesis:

- we deal with a *distributed* system; this mean that the system is composed of two or more units, each one with its own control system
- the system is composed of *autonomous* units, so every robot is possibly equipped with sensors and actuators, and is never operated from an external entity
- the team *cooperate* to accomplish a common goal; success or failure will concern the whole system

Additionally, we suppose that the team is composed by a small number of robots (say less than 10).

In this context we outline three points which need to be addressed to propose an effective solution:

- *Awareness.* Each robot is member of a team of robotic agents and is aware of this membership. This means that each robot owns individual and group goals and has to be able to make a choice when they conflict. In fact it is not the case that when a conflict of interests occurs it is always a group goal which needs to be honored. This assumption is reasonable, since we assumed to work with a small group of robots. Awareness of this social citizenship implies some sort of communication, implicit or explicit ([26]).
- *Locality.* As already pointed out, a multi-robot system is a physical entity situated in an operating environment and with bounded capabilities. This means that, if we do not restrict the system to trivial tasks and environments, it will not be able to elaborate the whole amount of information, neither by reactivity nor by deliberation. So, in the case that the system is not able to process everything it should, a choice has to be done, and only a subset of the amount of data is processed. The natural choice is to consider only local information, since it is more reliable (less noisy) and almost always more critic to deal with.
- *Active Sensing.* Sensing is expensive, and generally speaking, the more a sensing activity is rich of information, the more expensive it is. It is then necessary to drive the sensing process in such a way that only the information needed to usefully act locally and socially is gathered. Furthermore, it is worth noting that since a multi-robot system performs a distributed sensing of its operating environment, sensing activity should be scheduled from a social point of view, as illustrated later. This is very effective in the case of explicit communication between the agents where sensed data can be shared between robots.

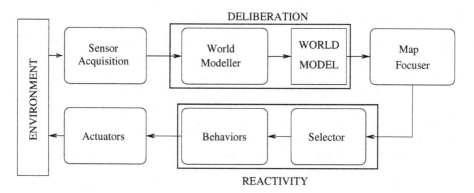

Fig. 1. High-level architecture

Starting from the former considerations, we develop our proposal for the balancing between reactivity and deliberation. While other authors do not explicitly distinguish between these two extremes ([5], [35]), we chose to clearly separate the two subsystems which are devoted to reactivity and deliberation. The system is composed of two levels which operates in parallel and communicate through a buffer of logic trigger conditions (see fig. 1). This means that the reactive and deliberative blocks are not coupled, but rather operate asinchronously, in a producer/consumer-like fashion. Also it has to be noticed that the buffer (inditcated in the figure as "Map Focuser") is not a passive entity but an active component which filters out details which are not needed in the current situation (this justifies the name, since it keeps the focus on the part of the map which is considered relevant).

The displayed architecture, which will be now discussed, is instantiated in each member of the robot team; however it is necessary to point out that this is a functional scheme, which may be implemented in different ways in each robot, so we are not restricting our attention towards identical systems.

The components of the architecture are now discussed.

2.1 World Modeler

The "World Modeler" reads the sensorial inputs and uses them to build a complete description of the world. This is a pure deliberative subsystem and there is freedom to organize, build, and update the world-model in a preferred way. It may be a geometric based model, a logic based model or whatever. At this level sensed data may be processed scheduling a suitable amount of time; for example a reading from a range scanner which indicates that there is an obstacle very near should be quickly processed and added to the model, while less time-critic sources of information could be allocated more time. Moreover, in this case it is possible to read the map contents to get a better interpretation of the sensed information. The modeling may be obtained with more modelers working concurrently, each one processing inputs coming from different sensors.

2.2   Map Focuser

The "Map Focuser" is the core of the system. It works on the model produced by the World Modeler block and outputs a simplified version of it. This simplified version is a localized version, and its composition is also influenced by the state of the reactive subsystem described later. The output map needs not to be organized in the same way of the whole world model, even if this would simplify the focus process. This subsystem addresses the point of "locality" previously pointed out, in the sense that at this level details not relevant are cutted of the scene. The relevance of a detail is determined on the basis of a metric based on the distance, the goals and the current situation of the reactive subsystem.

2.3   Selector

The "Selector" operates on the simplified map and outputs high-level logical conditions which will be used to drive the reactive subsystem. This is nothing new, and could also be incorporated in the behavior stage, as usual in reactive system, but we design it as a separate block to allow the building of more sophisticated conditions. For example some conditions can be activated also on the basis of explicit messages coming from other robots.

2.4   Behaviors

"Behaviors" are selected and executed on the basis of the high level conditions produced by the selector; this level may be implemented as the user prefers, and in Sect. 3 we demonstrate how to use this level to add cooperative behaviors using "shared activation conditions".

2.5   Focus is the Key to the Balancing

The aim of this contribution is towards the balancing between reaction and deliberation in cooperative multi-robot systems: how is it obtained?

The key concept of the system is the focus of the map. With a strong focus on the world model, in the reduced map a lot of details are cut off. This means that few selected high level conditions are available to the selector. Thus it is possible to face the problem of the "*skizophrenic*" switching between different behaviors and to obtain a more deliberative system.

On the other hand, if no focus is performed on the map, no filtering is obtained, so the whole amount of sensorial data is available for building the high level conditions for the behaviors selector; in this way it is possible to handle external stimuli useful for real-time responsiveness of the system (see Fig. 2). The whole spectrum of possibilities lies between these two extremes.

And how do we address social issues?

Once again the key is the focus; since the world model is build by a deliberative subsystem, this may include also the modeling of the intentions of other robots, based on the sensed data and on the eventual communications. We now introduce

Weak Focalization   Strong Focalization

Low   Map Details   High

Reactive Behavior   Deliberative Behavior

Fig. 2. Balancing through focusing the map

the concepts of Low Level Behavior (LLB), High Level Behavior (HLB) and Cooperative Behavior (CB) and illustrate how to scale them with the size of the team.

2.6   Social Behaviors

The reactive subsystem is two-layered. The first layer is a finite state automaton (FSA), whose inputs are the high level constraints output by the selector working on the reduced map. From a given input the FSA triggers High Level Behaviors (HLBs) or Coordination Behaviors (CBs) in a winner-take-all manner. The distinction between a HLB and a CB is that a CB is shared between two agents, i.e. the activation and execution of such a behavior involves two or more robots. Such "coordinated behavior activation" is fully distributed and can be modeled with the Petri net formalism, as usual in the field of distributed algorithms.

Figure 3 shows how two distinct robots coordinate themselves; the behavior "Homing with puck" is triggered and executed by two robots. The same figure also shows that there is a third level, the level of Low Level Behaviors (LLBs), which are the building blocks used to realize HLBs and CBs. With regard to

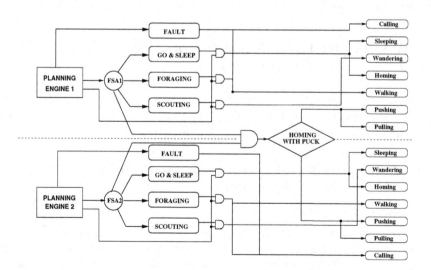

Fig. 3. CBs, HLBs, and LLBs (taken from the case study presented in Sect. 3)

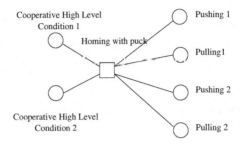

Fig. 4. Petri Net model for the coordinated behavior "Homing with Puck" shown in Fig. 3

Petri net modelling, and according to standard notation (see for example [30]), "Homing with puck" is a transition, and the input high level conditions to the *AND* gate are two places which holds a mark if and only if the conditions are active (see Fig. 4 for the corresponding graphical translation).

An interesting feature of this approach is that it is vertically scalable. This means that if we move up and consider two multi-robot systems which need to perform some coordination, they will need at least a CB at the fleet level, whose enabling conditions are shared between the two multi-robot systems involved. In this situation the CBs at the single-robot level became HLBs at the multi-robot level and the robot level HLBs become LLBs of the multi-robot, while robot level LLBs still remain global LLBs.

This process, which is a sort of clustering of behaviors, may be further scaled up, if we consider fleets of multi-robot systems which needs to coordinate, but also scaled down. In fact it may also be used to coordinate local behaviors, i.e. behaviors executed by one robot which need some degree of coordination.

3   A Case Study: A Multi-Robot System for Coordinated Foraging

Up to now we have talked only about the general idea of focusing the map to get the balancing between reactivity and deliberation; in this section we describe the experimental set up we developed to validate our proposal.

3.1   Cooperative Foraging: The Task, the Environment, and the Multi-Robot System

The given task is the following:

a team of N robot, with $N \geq 2$, performs in a room where M items are scattered on the floor. The team goal is to bring the items back to a home area with the constrain that two robots are needed to carry an item.   The task has been studied in simulation, using our VLAB simulator ([15]), a software designed

Fig. 5. An example of simulation

to study heterogeneous multi-robot systems (see Fig. 5 for an example of the rendering obtained with the VLAB simulation environment). Since the goal is to study the effectiveness of the proposed framework, in the devised context of the balancing between reaction and deliberation, in the simulation stage the constrain that two robots are necessary to bring an item back to the home area has been considered as a logic constrain. This means that no problem about the cooperative transportation of the item has been faced, so when a robot catch an item, all it has to do is to wait that another robot will help him, but this help is limited to following him while he is bringing the item in the home area. This suffices in order to study the cooperation aspect of the problem.

The Operating Environment. The room is square shaped with a side of 10 meters and the home area is a 2×2 meters square and is located in a corner of the room. The floor is covered with a wood-like texture; items are red, walls are green and the home area is yellow (both the floor and the walls). Figure 6 shows the details. In our simulations we posed $M = 10$.

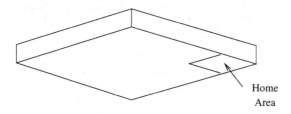

Fig. 6. Foraging environment

The Robots. In simulation we implemented an homogeneous multi-robot system. Each robot is a mobile platform which may turn in place and move forwards or backwards in its heading direction.
Each robot is equipped with the following sensors and actuators:

- a gripper device to pick up items; the gripper is also equipped with a sensor which allows to know if something has been caught
- a communication device which allows broadcast and unicast communications
- a GPS-like device, which tells each robot its position (relative to a room based coordinate system)
- 12 range scanners disposed on the perimeter which measures the distance of the other robots (but not of the walls)
- a camera and a frame grabber

The VLAB simulator allows the user to add noise components to the sensorial inputs; in the experiments presented a noise component of the 10% was added to the range scanner inputs, while the frame grabber and the communication device was considered to be error free. Someone could argue that the sensing capabilities of the robots are a bit "oversized". This is true, but these assumptions have been made because our goal is to study the mechanisms for balancing the two extremes, and we are not interested in sensor fusion.

3.2   Implementation Details

We now look closer at how we implemented the proposed framework. Figure 7 shows the details that will be discussed.

As previously stated, the three main blocks (World Modeler, Map Focuser and Selector) run concurrently. This has been achieved implementing them as different threads, which already showed to be a good choice for the programming of intelligent multi-agent systems ([21]).

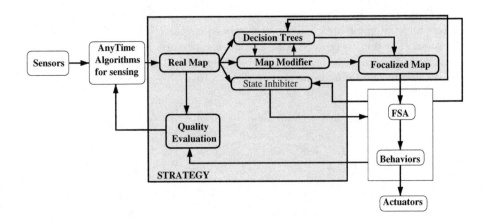

Fig. 7. Implementation of our proposal

Designing the Map. The complete map is built as a set of "generalized geometric objects". A generalized geometric object is an object which is located in the generalized space GS, where GS is defined as[3]

$$GS = \mathbb{R}^3 \bigcup \{EveryWhere\} \tag{1}$$

Everywhere is a symbol added to the Euclidean space $\mathbb{R}^3$ and its function is explained later.

The map is organized as a set, so there is not an order between the objects. The space GS is introduced because the map keeps not only the model of physical objects (like robots or items) which has a physical location in the Euclidean space, but also the models of the intentions of the agents and of the information they are exchanging. Such entities are not located in the precise point of the space, but rather affect the whole environment. For example if a robot asks for some information, this fact will be modeled as an object of type "Communication" whose location is *EveryWhere*, so every other robot should consider it as relevant. The map is owned and managed by the World Modeler module which is now discussed. This means that inserting and deleting on and from the set is possible only to that module. Other modules may only read the contents of the set, but may not modify it. In Fig. 7 it is also mentioned that the sensing process may be scheduled obeying to an Anytime policy to get an even better real time performance. This approach is actually been investigated and will not be discussed; however this is not a problem, since the approach does not rely on this assumption.

Implementing the World Modeler. The World Modeler is implemented as a set of threads which run concurrently. Every thread is responsible for the handling of a sensor, so that we have one thread for the GPS, one for the camera and so on. Once a data is read, it is processed and "interpreted", also according to the current elements which are in the map; then the map is updated accordingly, with the suitable insertions and deletions (this process resembles the post-conditions operations in STRIPS).

Implementing the Map Focuser. Thanks to the choices made for the map, the Map Focuser is extremely simple: it is a thread that continuously scans the set of objects which constitutes the map and outputs a subset of it. An element belongs to the output subset if is considered local to the robot.

Algorithm 1, which shows how the focus is obtained is based on some routines:

- *SerialCopy* gives a serialized copy of the map, so that it is possible to sequentially scan it (remember that the map is generated as a unordered set of objects)

---

[3] Since we do not deal with flying objects, GS could also be defined as $\mathbb{R}^2 \bigcup \{EveryWhere\}$. However the given definition does not raise any computational complication, so we think to objects as entities in $\mathbb{R}^3$.

Algorithm 1. Algorithm for building the focused map

INPUT Map: the global map
OUTPUT FocusedMap: the focused version of the global map
loop
   MapCopy ← SerialCopy(Map)
   for j=0 to | MapCopy | **do**
     Obj ← MapCopy[j]
     local ← IsLocal(Obj,CurrentState)
     if In(FocusedMap,Obj) *AND* local **then**
       Update(FocusedMap,Obj)
     else if In(FocusedMap,Obj) *AND NOT* local **then**
       Delete(FocusedMap,Obj)
     else if local **then**
       Insert(FocusedMap,Obj)
     end if
   end for
end loop

- *IsLocal* is a boolean function which determines if the object has to be inserted in the focused map; this selection is based on the generalized position of the object and on the state of the system
- *In* is a boolean function which tells if the object is present in the focused map
- *Insert, Delete,* and *Update* performs the corresponding operations on the focused map

It is worth noting that the routine which performs the focus on the map is extremely simple and can be implemented in a very efficient way, so that newly introduced geometric objects are processed in a short time. Figure 8 shows an example of the performed filtering on the map.

Selector and Decision Trees. The Selector is simply a routine which scans the reduced map and accordingly gives a value to a set of boolean conditions. In this stage it is possible to add a selection mechanism aimed to get better social behavior, accordingly to the sensing and to the communication. In our case study we exploited the possibility to use some simple *game theory* related concepts in order to get a prediction about the actions of other team members. Game theory, and Dynamic Game Theory in particular, has already been used in robotics (see for example [22] and [23]), and its use appears to be very effective in the field of multi-robot systems (for a formal definition and discussion of dynamic non-cooperative games see [7]).

The selector implements an algorithm based on the *game tree* concept. The game tree is the tree of all the possible decisions which could be made by all the possible decision takers, i.e. the robots. Since the system is distributed, we lack a central handler and the tree is built by each robot accordingly to the sensed

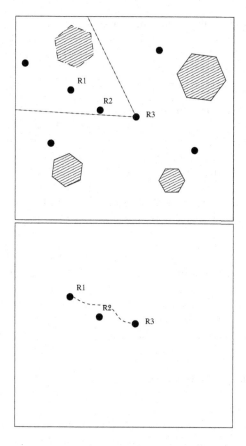

Fig. 8. An example of map focus

data and the explicit communication. Let us consider the j-th robot which keeps a model of all n robots, say $r_1, r_2 \ldots, r_n$; let $s_1, s_2, \ldots, s_n$ be the set of actions[4] that each robot may execute. Each tree is build as follows:

− the root of the tree is a dummy node
− the i-th level of the tree is assigned to r_i
− each node at the level k represents one of the possible choices of the robot r_k related to the choices made by $r_1, \ldots, r_{k-1}$. Every action is given a weight

So each path from the root of the tree to a leaf is a complete specification of actions performed by each robot. This tree needs to be carefully built and handled, and it is often necessary to avoid to use all the available information, since the tree may considerably grow in size. In fact if we consider N robots and

---

[4] In this context action is used as a synonymous of low level behavior.

L possible actions ($L \geq 1$), we obtain a tree with

$$\sum_{j=0}^{L} N^j = \frac{N^{L+1} - 1}{N - 1} \tag{2}$$

nodes, with N^L leafs. Once the tree has been built, it may be used to select the more appropriate action, and this choice is also based on a guess on the choices made by other decisors. This prediction is possible since every robot performs obeying the same rule. To select the candidate action, every robot assigns a weight to each node and then it chooses its action on the path from the root to the leaf with the lowest weight. The weight of the root is the weight of the action it represents, and the weight of every other node is the sum of the weight of its parent and of the action it represents.

Behaviors. Behavior selection is based on the condition set handled by Selector and on the robot internal state; it is implemented by a Finite State Automaton (FSA) and it obeys a *winner take all* policy. Since conditions are build on the basis of the reduced map and explicit communication affects both the general and the reduced map, it is possible to schedule the Cooperative Behaviors (CBs) shared between different robots. The set of available LLBs implemented is the following:

- *Wander*: randomly move in the environment
- *GoToItem*: move toward a recognized item
- *CatchItem*: grasp an item
- *Call*: send a message requiring help to bring an item in the home area
- *WaitForAMate*: if a previous request has been positively answered, wait for the incoming mate
- *GoToHome*: moves toward the home area grasping an item
- *WaitForHomeFree*: if other robots are in the home area, wait outside
- *EnterHomeArea*: enter in the home area
- *AnswerYes*: positively answer to a help request
- *AnswerNo*: negatively answer to ha help request
- *GoToMate*: reach a robot
- *Support*: move towards the home area supporting a robot which holds an item (remember that two robots area needed to bring an item to the home area)

Based on the shown LLBs, two HLBs has been implemented:

- *GET-ITEM*: moves in the environment, find an item and get it
- *NEGOTIATE*: ask for help and wait or answer and eventually move to the mate

The only CB is *BRING-ITEM-TO-HOME*, which is performed in a different way by the leading robot and by the supporting robot.

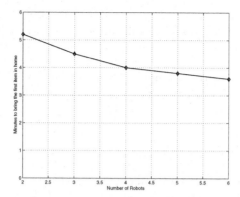

Fig. 9. Team performance

Experimental Results. In a numerous set of simulations we have tested the effectiveness of our proposal. It is easy to predict that the main difficulty is to find the suitable degree of focus, i.e. to determine a criterion to say when an object has to be considered local or not, and in fact this is the case. However in a few simulations this can be easily set up. In our experiments an object was considered local if its position was *EveryWhere* or internal to a circle whose center was the robot and with a radius of $2m$. As stated in Sect. 4 in would also be possible to learn from experience the right threshold.

Figure 9 shows how with the increasing of the number of robots in the team, the time necessary to bring the first item in the home area decreases. It is possible to observe that even if the population grows so that it becomes harder to navigate in the environment to seek items or to support mates, combining reactivity and strategy via decision trees results in an increased of performance.

4   Discussion of the Related Work

In this section we briefly compare our proposal[5] with previous published works in the field of cooperative robotics.

One of the most similar architecture is ALLIANCE ([27]), which proposes a behavioral framework for heterogenous multi-robot cooperation. Through *motivational behavior*, ALLIANCE superbly addresses the problem of achieving fault tolerance in heterogeneous systems, with much more robustness than in our approach. However we also feel that ALLIANCE's fault tolerance, which allows to perform even in case of communication lack, comes at the expenses of the deliberative capabilities of the system. One interesting point is that ALLIANCE has been implemented for a team engaged in collective foraging, but once again the lack of a well defined metric of performance prevents an analytical comparison between the two solutions.

---

[5] It is worth noting that we consider the general framework proposed in Sect. 2 and not the case study presented.

Other approaches to the problem of cooperative behavior in multi-robot systems are very often based on learning techniques (see [25] for an example of a cooperative system for foraging). In these systems the hypothesis are quite different, so at the moment a comparison is not possible. However for our architecture it is possible to introduce the learning of the suitable degree of focusing activity while performing the task (for a general discussion about learning in multi-agent context and the related problems, see [33]).

5   Conclusions

We introduced a general discussion about the problem of balancing reaction and deliberation in multi-robot systems, and we analyzed the most challenging problems one has to deal with. Then, we proposed an architecture with deliberative and reactive subsystems. This architecture is based on the idea of focusing on the map which models the environment and of exploiting shared activation conditions to trigger "Cooperative Behaviors" between the robots. The proposed framework has been implemented in simulation. The details and the results of the performed simulations has been illustrated.

Acknowledgements. This research has been partially supported by the Ministry for Education and Research (MURST Certamen project), by the Italian National Council of Research (CNR special project), and by the Italian Energy Agency (ENEA Parallel Computing Project). The authors would like to thank Federico Montesello for his cooperation to this research.

References

1. T. Arai and J. Ota. Let-us work together – task planning of multiple mobile robots. In *Proceedings of the IEEE/RSJ International Conference on Intelligent Robots and Systems*, pages 298–303, 1995.
2. R. Arkin. Path planning for a vision-based autonomous robot. In *Proceedings of the SPIE Conference on Mobile Robots*, pages 240–249, 1986.
3. R. Arkin. Integrating behavioural, perceptual, and world knowledge in reactive navigation. *Robotics and Autonomous Systems*, 6:105–122, 1990.
4. H. Asama, K. Ozaki, A. Matsumoto, Y. Ishida, and I. Endo. Development od task assignment system using communication for multiple autonomous robots. *Journal of Robotics and Mechatronics*, 4:122–127, 1992.
5. M.S. Atkin, D.L. Westbrook, and P.R. Cohen. HAC: A unified view of reactive and deliberative activity. In M. Hannebauer, J. Wendler, and E. Pagello, editors, *Balancing Reactivity and Social Deliberation in Multi-agent Systems (this volume)*, pages 92–107. Springer, 2001.
6. T. Balch and R.C. Arkin. Communication in reactive multiagent robotic systems. *Autonomous Robots*, 1(1):27–52, 1994.
7. T. Basar and G.J. Olsder. *Dynamic Noncooperative Game Theory*. SIAM, 1999.
8. G. Beni and J. Wang. On cyclic cellular robotic systems. In *Japan-USA Symposium on Flexible Automation*, pages 1077–1083, 1990.

9. S.C. Botelho and R. Alami. Cooperative plan enhancement in multi-robot context. In E. Pagello et al., editor, *Intelligent Autonomous Systems 6*. IOS Press, 2000.

10. S.C. Botelho and R. Alami. A multi-robot cooperative achievement system. In *Proceedings of the IEEE International Conference on Robotics and Automation*, pages 2716–2721, 2000.

11. V. Braitenberg. *Veichles: Experiments in Synthetic Psychology*. MIT Press, 1984.

12. R.A. Brooks. A robust layered control systems for mobile robot. *IEEE Journal of Robotics and Automation*, RA-2(1):14–23, 1986.

13. R.A. Brooks. Intelligence without reason. In *Proceedings of the International Joint Conference on Artificial Intelligence*, pages 569–595, 1991.

14. U. Cao, A.S. Fukunaga, and A.B. Kahng. Cooperative mobile robots: Antecedents and directions. *Autonomous Robots*, 4(1):7–27, 1997.

15. S. Carpin, C. Ferrari, and E. Pagello. A framework for distributed simulation of multirobot systems: the vlab experience. In L.E. Parker, G. Bekey, and J. Barhen, editors, *Distributed Autonomous Robotic Systems 4*, pages 45–54. Springer, 2000.

16. G. Dudek, M.R.M. Jenkin, E. Milios, and D. Wilkes. A taxonomy for multi-agent robotics. *Autonomous Robots*, 3(4):375–397, 1996.

17. R. Fikes and N. Nilsson. Strips: A new approach to the application of theorem proving to problem solving. *Artificial Intelligence*, 2:189–208, 1971.

18. T. Fukuda, S. Nakagawa, Y. Kawauchi, and M. Buss. Self organaizing robots based on cell structures – cebot. In *Proceedings of the IEEE International Workshop on Intelligent Robots and Systems*, pages 145–150, 1988.

19. M. Georgeff and A. L. Lansky. Reactive reasoning and planning. In *Proceedings of the Sixth National Conference on Artificial Intelligence*, pages 677–682, 1987.

20. L. Iocchi, D. Nardi, and M. Salerno. Reactivity and deliberation: a survey on multi-robot systems. In M. Hannebauer, J. Wendler, and E. Pagello, editors, *Balancing Reactivity and Social Deliberation in Multi-agent Systems (this volume)*, pages 9–32. Springer, 2001.

21. K. Kostiadis and H. Hu. A multi-threaded approach to simulated soccer agents for the robocup competitions. In M. Veloso, E. Pagello, and H. Kitano, editors, *Robocup-99: Robot Soccer Word Cup III*, pages 366–377. Springer, 2000.

22. S.M. LaValle. Robot motion planning: A game-theoretic approach. *Algorithmica*, 26:430–465, 2000.

23. S.M. LaValle and S.A. Hutchinson. Optimal motion planning for multiple robots having independent goals. *IEEE Transactions on Robotics and Automation*, 14(6), 1998.

24. M.J. Mataric. Minimizing complexity in controlling a mobile robot population. In *Proceedings of the IEEE International Conference on Robotics and Autonomation*, pages 830–835, 1992.

25. M.J. Mataric. Reinforcement learning in the multi-robot domain. *Autonomous Robots*, 4(1), 1997.

26. E. Pagello, A. D'Angelo, F. Montesello, F. Garelli, and C. Ferrari. Cooperative behaviors in multi-robot systems through implicit communication. *Robotics and Autonomous Systems*, 29(1):65–77, 1999.

27. L. Parker. *Heterogeneous Multi-Robot Cooperation*. PhD thesis, Massachusetts Institute of Technology, January 1994.

28. L.E. Parker. Current state of the art in distributed autonomous mobile robots. In L.E. Parker, G. Bekey, and J.Barhen, editors, *Distributed Autonomous Robotic Systems 4*, pages 3–12. Springer, 2000.

29. R. Pfeifer. Building fungus eaters: Design principles of autonomous agents. In *Simulation of Adaptive Behavior*, pages 3–12, 1996.

30. W. Reisig. *Elements of Distributed Algorithms*. Springer, 1998.
31. E. Sacerdoti. *A structure for plans and behavior*. American Elsevier, 1977.
32. L. Steels. Exploiting analogical representation. In P. Maes, editor, *Designing Autonomous Agents*, pages 71–88. MIT Press, 1990.
33. P. Stone and M. Veloso. Multiagent systems: A survey from a machine learning perspective. *Autonomous Robots*, 8(3):345–383, 2000.
34. E. Todt, G. Raush, and R. Suàrez. Analysis and classification of multiple robot coordination methods. In *Proceedings of the IEEE International Conference on Robotics and Automation*, pages 3158–3163, 2000.
35. G. Weiss. Cognition, sociability, and constrains. In M. Hannebauer, J. Wendler, and E. Pagello, editors, *Balancing Reactivity and Social Deliberation in Multi-agent Systems (this volume)*, pages 217–235. Springer, 2001.

Balancing between Reactivity and Deliberation in the ICAGENT Framework

Vangelis Kourakos Mavromichalis and George A. Vouros

Dept. of Information and Communication Systems
University of the Aegean
Karlovassi, Samos, Greece
{emav,georgev}@aegean.gr

Abstract. The aim of this paper is to present a framework for developing intelligent agents that act in dynamic and unpredictable environments in a robust and efficient way. To achieve this objective, agents must be able to balance between reactive and deliberative planning. This paper emphasizes on the seamless integration of these planning techniques and on the smooth transition between reactive and deliberative planning in terms of agents' mental attitudes and agents reasoning capabilities. The framework is thoroughly explained and the behaviour of an agent that acts in the tile-world chessboard is examined.

1 Introduction

Agents, to achieve their goals successfully in dynamic and unpredictable environments, must be able to generate plans in a timely way, monitor changes in their environment, change and adapt their plans accordingly.

It is well known that reactivity is necessary when agents face unpredictable events/obstacles. Reactive behaviour is considered to be a kind of reflective behaviour: Agents react in the same way when they face the same situation [6].

However, this is a very restrictive type of behaviour even for reactive agents: Agents recognize a situation and *execute the* precompiled procedure that is *hard-linked* to the recognized situation. Doing so, agents commit to the achievement of a specific action and start executing a procedure without considering (a) whether they should postpone execution until a time point, (b) other preferences and commitments they may have, (c) other options towards performing that action.

In order agents to intermix and balance between reactivity and deliberation, they must be able to "move" across the continuum from reactive to deliberative planning depicted in Fig. 1. To balance between these planning techniques it is important to make fine-grained distinctions between the features that allow an agent to deal with the considerations mentioned above, and provide reasoning services for reconciling between options, preferences and commitments that the agent holds.

Reactive planning, as it is mentioned in [6], concerns with the difficulties of direct interaction with a changing world. Planning reactively, an agent builds and/or adjusts its plans in response to changes in the environment. However, in order agents to

M. Hannebauer et al. (Eds.): Reactivity and Deliberation in MAS, LNAI 2103, pp. 53-75, 2001.

exhibit robust behaviour, must be able to deliberatively evaluate their options, consider all their desires and commitments, prioritise alternatives, form plans, and reason about the consequences of their actions [6,3]. Planning deliberatively, an agent may deal with goals that need careful, although in general not detailed, planning. Although classical planning techniques can be utilized for deliberative planning, we need to integrate these techniques with methods for managing agents' mental attitudes, and describe these techniques in terms of agents reasoning capabilities.

Fig. 1. The continuum from reactive to deliberative planning

Putting this in another way, we may distinguish between deliberation and reaction in terms of:

1. Features that are recognized and exploited by an agent in order to decide "the amount of planning needed for achieving its goals".
2. The representation of these features
3. The reasoning services needed for exploiting these features.

For instance, to achieve a purely reactive behaviour, agents may utilize features that are characteristics of the environment itself. In this case, features are represented by procedures' conditions and agents execute a procedure whose conditional part describes the perceived situation. On the other hand, to deliberate, an agent must exploit features related not only with the environment itself, but also with its mental state (beliefs, intentions, desires and goals), the overall context of action (actions already planned and/or performed, constraints related to these actions), options and commitments it has, and with the mental states of its collaborators or antagonists. The representation of these features must enable agents to plan and adapt their behaviour effectively.

Furthermore, for agents to plan and act effectively in dynamic and unpredictable environments, they must decide in which situations they must react or deliberate, balancing and intermixing reaction and deliberation.

Let us for instance assume that while driving to work, an agent intents to withdraw money from the bank, make some shopping and pass from a specific point. Let us further assume that this agent plans her/his route deliberatively: The agent examines and reconciles alternative plans and decides which alternative to pursue. We must notice that this does not mean that the agent has a detailed plan for achieving her/his intentions. The agent may have a partial plan that is further extended towards fine-grained (*basic-level*) actions. While the agent extends and refines the plan, she/he must decide which segments of the plan to form reactively and which ones deliberatively. Reconciling between alternative plans, the agent chooses a route deliberatively and starts following it. Following certain parts of the route in a purely reactive way, means that the agent does not consider other options she/he may have: The agent follows the planned route and reacts to changes in the environment. For instance, obstacles that the agent can avoid reactively, it does avoid them. In such cases the agent does not need to consider other alternatives, reform its commitments or abandon any of them. However, obstacles that prohibit him/her to follow the planned route, such as heavy traffic due to an accident, may force him/her to re-schedule the route, change its preferences and even abandon some commitments. To choose which commitment to abandon, the agent must deliberate. Choices depend on the relative strength of agent preferences and commitments, on its commitments for the future, as well as on contextual constraints.

The aim of this paper is to report on progress towards our efforts to establish a generic framework for developing agents that reason about their plans and balance between deliberation and reaction. Key issues towards this aim are the following:

- Provide clear definitions of deliberative and reactive planning in terms of agents' reasoning tasks and management of agents' mental state. This requires considering agents' mental attitudes and reasoning tasks in an integrated way. Agents are considered to move across the continuum presented in Fig. 1 by choosing the features to exploit during deliberation. This enables them to plan more deliberatively or more reactively.
- Provide an *explicit and an as detailed as possible representation of agents' mental state,* so as to support effective plan management, effective reactive, robust deliberative and collaborative behaviour.
- Provide the necessary reasoning tasks for agents to plan towards achieving their commitments, to monitor changes happening in their environment, to manage their preferences and commitments, to assess alternatives, to cooperate with other agents and to change/extend their plans accordingly. This requires agents to be equipped with *advanced plan management reasoning tasks* [12].

While commitments towards performing actions are expressed by means of *intentions*, preferences are represented by *desires*. The desire to perform an action A represents the state in which the agent has a preference for A, but has not decided whether it shall perform A. Successful reconciliation of this desire with intentions that the agent already holds, drives the agent to form a *goal* towards A. The goal represents the state in which the agent knows a partial plan for performing A, and it believes that this is consistent with other intentions it holds. The *intention* to perform A, represents the state in which the agent has either a complete plan to perform A, or it has a partial plan towards A and a complete plan for completing the partial plan for A. The representation of these mental attitudes are described in section 4.1.

To distinguish between pure deliberative and pure reactive planning, this paper conjectures that deliberation requires agents to assess alternatives and *reconcile* their *desires* with their *intentions*, taking into account the overall context of action. Planning reactively, agents recognize a situation and commit to the achievement of a specific action by forming intentions towards it. In this case, agents do not consider other desires and/or intentions that may hold, and therefore, do not reconcile their desires with other intentions.

Reconciliation forces agents to assess their options and form a consistent set of intentions. This means that the distinction between deliberation and reaction is not based on whether an agent plans or invokes a hard-wired procedure, but on how plan operators (*recipes*) are utilized during planning.

To achieve the objectives and tackle the above-mentioned key issues, the proposed agent development framework is based on the collaborative planning framework of [7], which is further extended with advanced plan management tasks [12].

It must be mentioned that although the proposed framework is based on a collaborative planning framework, it does not deal with social deliberation since it does not handle shared plans at the moment. The paper focuses on the principles and reasoning tasks that distinguish between reaction and deliberation and provides the basis for dealing with social deliberation.

The paper is structured as follows: Section 2 presents work related to plan formation and plan management and presents major agent frameworks that support reactive and deliberative behaviour. Section 3 presents the tile-world example, which provides a dynamic and unpredictable environment in which an agent must balance and intermix reaction and deliberation. Section 4 explains thoroughly the ICAGENT framework: The knowledge base and all modules that enable an agent to plan and act. Section 5 presents the behaviour of an agent that acts in the tile-world environment and has been implemented using the ICAGENT framework. The section explains how the agent intermixes and balances between reactive and deliberative planning and depicts its behaviour. Finally, conclusions and further work are sketched in section 6.

2 Related Work

As Pollack and Horty [12] indicated, in order agents to achieve their goals in uncertain, unpredictable and dynamic environments, they must be able to form plans and manage them in an effective way. Plan management aims to tackle problems related to the agents being omniscient, acting in deterministic and instantaneous ways, having goals that are fixed and to their environment being static.

As it proposed in [12], to manage plans effectively, agents should be equipped with the following reasoning tasks:

1. *Plan generation*: Agents must be able to perform classical planning.
2. *Environment monitoring*: Agents must be able to monitor their environment and focus their attention to specific environmental changes.
3. *Alternative assessment*: Given contextual constraints and their capabilities, agents must be able to assess the costs and the benefits of the options that are presented to them.
4. *Commitment management*: Agents must be able to reason about the relative strength of their commitments and to decide which to give up.
5. *Plan elaboration*: Agents must be able to interleave planning and execution in order to elaborate their partial plans. In dynamic and unpredictable environments agents may have not all the needed knowledge to complete their plans at planning time.
6. *Meta-level control*: Agents, for some activities, may need to do a lot of careful planning, while for others may decide to have a less-than-optimal solution.
7. *Cooperation with other agents*: Agents acting in a multi-agent environment may need to cooperate (or at least interact) with other agents in order to realize their tasks.

Balancing between deliberation and reaction and intermixing these planning techniques is a plan management problem, because agents have to:

1. Decide whether they shall commit to fulfil a desire or they shall reason about the relative strength of their desires and intentions,
2. Decide whether they shall assess their options towards fulfilling a desire or, acting purely reactively, will fetch a good solution and start pursuing it, and consequently,
3. Determine how to generate and elaborate their plans.

Major agent frameworks that intermix deliberative with reactive planning are dMARS [10], and InteRRaP [11].

dMARS provides a framework for developing agents capable to perform in dynamic and unpredictable environments. dMARS does not support distinguishing in a comprehensive way plans (or plan portions) that are generated in a reactive or in a deliberative way. The abilities of the framework to support balancing between deliberation and reaction are further constrained, since agents' mental attitudes are not represented and handled in an explicit way.

InteRRaP uses a hybrid-layered architecture, which combines reactive and deliberative planning and incorporates the ability to interact with other agents. This architecture distinguishes reactive and deliberative planning using two different control and knowledge layers: The behaviour-based layer, incorporating reactive and procedural knowledge for routine tasks and the local planning layer that provides the facilities for means-ends reasoning for the achievement of complex level action producing a goal-directed behavior. InteRRaP distinguishes between deliberation and reaction by goal classification (reaction, local planning, cooperative) and by distinguishing the above-mentioned layers. It does not consider reconciling desires and intentions, which would involve dealing with incompatibilities between plans. Furthermore, InteRRaP does not arbitrarily intermix between deliberative and reactive behavior: The local planning layer can invoke procedures from the behavior-based layer, without procedures to be able to either invoke reactors from the behavior-based layer or establish a goal state to the local planning layer.

HAC [1] is a framework for building agents that act in dynamic environments. HAC, among others, deals with the problems of reacting to changing environments in a timely manner, integrating reactive and cognitive processes to achieve abstract goals and interleaving planning with execution. However, it does not clearly distinguish between deliberation and reaction in terms of agents' reasoning tasks and management of their mental states. It assumes that in a hierarchical plan, high-level actions are of a deliberative character, while lower-level actions are more of a reactive character. Consequently, it assumes that reaction and deliberation do not need extra mechanisms to implement them.

Another approach is the one used for developing AT-Humboldt [2]. Intentions in this approach correspond to long-term plans (that can be partial) for achieving a chosen goal. Then, the execution of each intention is split into short-term plans that are precompiled plan skeletons. In this approach, each new sensor information results in a complete deliberation process, which result in new plans created. Therefore, according to this approach, although agents react to the changes in the environment, they do not balance between reaction and deliberation effectively. The major problem arises from the fact that new commitments are formed independently from previous ones.

J.Blythe and W.S.Reilly in [3] present a hybrid reactive-deliberative system. The reactive component, Hap, of the system starts with a predefined set of goals and hand-coded plans for achieving them. In case this component has no stored plan for handling a situation, it calls the deliberative planner Prodigy. This system neither balances between reaction and deliberation, nor it intermixes these planning modes. Furthermore, the conditions under which Prodigy is called are contained in pre-defined Hap productions.

Concluding the above, existing systems either do not distinguish in a clear way between reactive and deliberative planning, or when they distinguish between them, they do not intermix these two "modes" of planning. Taking into account the continuum depicted in Fig. 1, existing systems cannot move in an arbitrary way across this continuum, choosing the amount and type of planning needed in a situation. As already mentioned, in order agents to react in a responsive and timely way to changes happening in their environment, they must balance between deliberative and reactive planning, and must be able to arbitrarily intermix these planning modes. To achieve this objective, an agent developing framework needs to provide an explicit and an as detailed as possible representation of agents mental state, and provide the reasoning tasks needed for forming and managing plans.

Furthermore, although not a goal of this paper, to support social deliberation, the framework should provide collaborative planning facilities, in order agents to ascribe attitudes to each other, share goals, plan towards these goals and integrate their individual plans towards their shared goal. Towards these directions, we propose using the framework for collaborative planning proposed by B.Grosz and S.Kraus in [7]. This framework can form the basis for constructing agents that have advanced plan generation and elaboration abilities, and provides the basis for designing agents that have advanced plan management facilities.

3   The Tile-World Example

The tile-world example proposed by M. Pollack and M. Ringuette [13] provides the dynamic and unpredictable environment that abstracts many real world tasks in which an agent needs to balance between deliberation and reaction, such as the "driving to work" example presented in Sect. 1. However, for the purposes of this paper a variant of this example is utilized.

The tile-world is a chessboard like environment with empty squares, obstacles, holes and an agent that carries a number of tiles with him. The agent is a unit square. The goal of the agent is to put all its tiles into the holes making the least possible moves. Obstacles are blocks that the agent has to move in order to reach the holes. Holes and blocks change their position randomly on the board. Each hole can be filled by only one tile. It is not possible to have a block over a hole or to have two blocks one over the other. The agent is able to move in all directions, except diagonally and backward, by one square per move. The agent is also able to move an obstacle to a neighbour empty square, except to the square that is behind the agent.

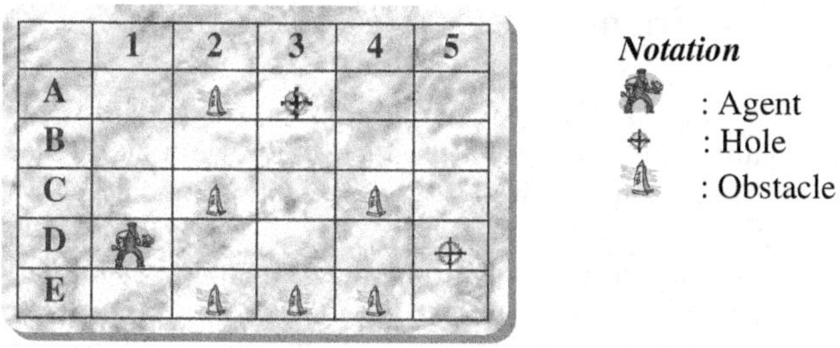

Fig. 2. A configuration of the tile-world chessboard

This environment is dynamic, because it continuously changes and it is non-deterministic, because at each time point the next state of the environment can not be determined by its current state and the actions performed by the agent.

Figure 2 shows a configuration of a 5x5 chessboard with 6 obstacles and 2 holes. The agent must fill the two holes with tiles, performing the least possible moves. We assume that the agent is fully aware of the changes in the environment and therefore, at any time point it knows the complete chessboard configuration.

Given the configuration depicted in Fig. 2, the agent initially recognizes the two holes, forms two desires to fill them and, purely reactively, finds the shortest path to each of them. Doing so, the agent has a path to each hole: one for A3 and one for D5. The agent deliberatively commits to fill the hole with the shortest route, i.e. D5, following the path (D2,D3,D4,D5), and starts to move to D5 reactively. In this case it does not check for conflicts that may arise with other intentions it may hold. The agent elaborates its plan based on the perceived environment configuration and its capabilities. Let us now suppose that when the agent reaches the square D3, two blocks appear at D4 and C3. Recognizing this situation, the agent tries to react by moving the obstacle to a neighbour square. It soon realizes that this cannot be done and that it is impossible to continue its route to D5. In this case, the agent reconsiders its desires, its intentions and their relative strengths. This results in committing to fill the hole A3. However, the agent does not abandon its desire to fill D5. It postpones filling D5 and keeps its desire "in the background of its mind".

Therefore, the agent balances between reactive and deliberative planning taking into account the configuration of the environment, its mental state and the overall context of its interaction with the environment (i.e., its commitments and constraints associated with the corresponding actions). For instance, when the agent recognizes that it cannot move an obstacle to a neighbour position, it starts deliberation by assessing the relative strengths of its desires and intentions. On the other hand, when there are not obstacles, or when the agent is able to avoid an obstacle, it follows its route in a reactive way. Furthermore, the agent intermixes reaction and deliberation in an arbitrary way. For example, it reactively finds two paths to the perceived holes, it deliberatively decides which route to follow, and follows one of the routes reactively. It skips obstacles reactively, but it deliberates by reconsidering its desires and intentions when an obstacle cannot be avoided.

4   The ICAGENT Framework

As Fig. 4 shows, the ICAGENT overall architecture comprises two units: the Deliberation Control Unit (DCU) and the Plan Elaboration and Realization Control Unit (PERCU). These units, as well as the perception module consult and update agent's knowledge base.

Based on this architecture, an agent monitors its environment via the perception module and updates its beliefs about the environment. The term *environment* denotes the physical environment as well as the mental attitudes of other agents acting in the physical environment.

Although the perception module can be quite sophisticated, involving planning and multi-modal perception, this paper assumes that the agent, somehow, is aware of everything occurring in its environment.

The agent recognizes situations and forms desires to perform actions. While the agent may have many and possibly conflicting desires, depending on the situation at a specific time point, it must decide which action to pursue and whether it shall elaborate its plan towards that action reactively or deliberatively. Depending on whether the agent reacts or deliberates, it commits to the corresponding action, or it reconciles its desires with its intentions, reasoning about the relative strength of conflicting actions, about the strength of its commitments and its desires, and about the overall context of action. Therefore, it is the reconciliation module that consults agent's knowledge on the environment, agent's mental state, and the overall context of action, and enables the agent to deliberate rather than react. However, the "amount of planning" that the agent performs, i.e., "how much it deliberates", depends on the "amount" of careful planning that it performs. This will be explained in detail in Sect. 4.2.2 (reconciliation module) and will be depicted with an exemplary case in Sect. 5.

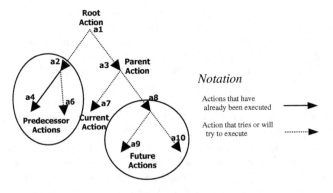

Fig. 3. A hierarchical plan

Each action is either a basic level action or a complex one. A basic level action is an action that can be executed directly in the environment. A "complex action" is an action that needs further planning and refinement.

Each action is realized by one or more alternative recipes. Each recipe comprises conditions for being selected, applicability conditions and, as far as complex actions are concerned, a sequence of sub-actions that the agent must pursue for completing the plan. During plan formation, the agent selects relevant recipes, tests for their applicability and adds them in the overall plan. In this way, the agent constructs a hierarchical plan such as the one presented in Fig. 3. This plan, augmented with constraints that must hold during plan formation and execution (e.g. preconditions of recipes) is referred as the *context of action*.

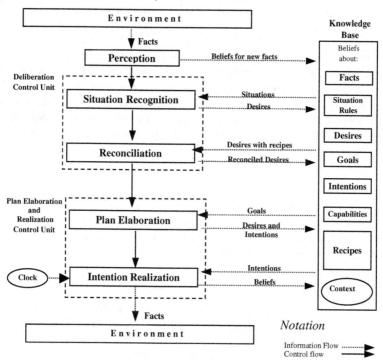

Fig. 4. Overall ICAGENT Architecture

Referring to the actions in the context of action, we shall refer to an action A that is currently added in the context, as the *current action* (e.g. action a7 in Fig. 3). The action in the parent node of A is the *parent action* of it, and the top-level action in this context shall be referred as the *root action*. Each action to a path from the root to action A is an *ancestor action* (or a *high-level* action) of A and each action located to a left-hand sub-tree of an ancestor action of A is a *predecessor action* of A. Furthermore, each action that is located to the right-hand sub-tree of an ancestor of A is a *future action* for A.

Elaborating a plan, the agent reaches basic-level actions (i.e., actions that may be performed directly in the environment) and decides whether these actions shall be performed at the current time point, interleaving planning with execution, or their execution shall be postponed until it has completed the corresponding part of the plan. Subsections that follow, explain in detail the structure and content of the resources depicted in Fig. 4, as well as the function of the individual modules.

4.1 Knowledge Base

The agent's Knowledge Base comprises beliefs about its environment. As already explained, the environment of an agent comprises its physical environment and the mental states of the agents acting in it, including itself. Similarly to the approach in [14], beliefs are recorded as facts and have the following form:

$$fact(T,bel(Agent,C,fact(FT,Prop)))$$

where, `Agent` is an agent id, `C` is a certainty factor about the occurrence of the `fact(FT,Prop)`, `FT` is the time point where the `fact(FT,Prop)` occurred, `T` is the time point where the agent learned about the occurrence of `fact(FT,Prop)` and `Prop` is a logical proposition. This logical proposition can be any combination of the agents' mental attitudes, or of the corresponding mental attitudes for other agents, using and, or and not logical connectives. The mental attitudes of agents are as follows:

Desires

$$desire\_to(Agent, Action).$$

where `Agent` is an agent id and `Action` is a complex or a basic level action. As already explained in section 1, a desire is an abstract notion that specifies a preference to achieve a particular mental or external world state, or to take over an action. The agent may hold an inconsistent set of desires.

Goals

$$goal\_to(Agent, Action).$$

where `Agent` and `Action` are as it is specified above. Following Cohen-Levesque [5], goals are desires that have passed the reconciliation process. Therefore, a goal represents the state in which the agent knows a partial plan for performing `Action`, and it believes that this is consistent with other intentions it holds.

Intentions to act

$$intent\_to(Agent, Action).$$

Intentions represent the commitment of an agent to perform the `Action`. The mental attitude `intent_to` corresponds to the Int.To mental attitude proposed in [7] according to which the agent has either a complete plan to perform `Action` or it has a partial plan towards `Action` and a process to elaborate that plan in order to complete it. Intentions are consistent with the goals of the agent as well as among themselves: This is true only for the intentions that correspond to actions that the agent plans purely deliberatively.

Capabilities

$$cap(Agent, Action).$$

A capability statement represents agent's ability to perform the basic level action `Action`.

Situation rules

$$situation(SituId, MntlCond, Mode, Action).$$

The agent utilizes situation rules to recognize situations occurring in the environment for which it must take the initiative to act. This results in new desires for the corresponding actions. Situation rules comprise four arguments:

♦ SituId. This is an Id that identifies the situation.

♦ MntlCond. This is a logical proposition that combines beliefs using and, or and not logical connectives. This proposition must be true in order the agent to form the desire to perform Action.

♦ Mode has the form

```
mode(BMntlCond,Behaviour)
```

where, BMntlCond has the form of the MntlCond constituent, and Behaviour is a variable that is instantiated to a, possibly empty, list of check directives that involve features that must be checked during reconciliation. Further details about the check function will be given in section 4.2.2. BMntlCond is tested when the agent has found a recipe for performing Action. BMntlCond drive the agent to decide whether it will deliberate, by proceeding to the reconciliation module, or it will react, by proceeding to the plan elaboration module. BmntlCond instantiates the Behaviour variable. This is further explained in subsection 4.2.2.

♦ *Action* has the form

```
Action_Name(Time, List of Action arguments).
```

Time is the time point that the Action will be performed. Time, as well as all arguments may be either constants or variables. These are instantiated either by checking the MntlCond part of the rule or by elaborating a recipe for that action.

```
situ( /*SituId*/     empty_hole,
      /*MntlCond*/   bel( square(X,Y,hole(H)) ) AND
                     bel(empty(hole(H)) ),
      /*Mode*/       mode( bel(Behaviour=[]), Behaviour ),
      /*Action*/     achieve( now, not(empty(hole(H))) ) ) ).
```

Fig. 5. Example of a situation rule

Returning to our tile-world example, Fig. 5 provides a situation rule, according to which, in case the agent believes that there is an empty hole in the square (X,Y), it will form a desire to fill this hole with a tile. The mode constituent of this rule specifies that the agent shall proceed planning in a purely reactive way: The Behaviour argument is an empty list of directives for the reconciliation module.

Recipes

```
rec( Action, RecId, MntlCond, Mode, Interleave,
     CapConstr, CConstr, ActionsList, Effects).
```

Recipes represent the knowledge of an agent to perform actions.
Figure 6 gives three examples of recipes for performing actions in the tile-world environment. Constituents of these recipes shall be used as examples in discussing recipes' constituents.

A recipe comprises the following constituents:

♦ `Action`, which is of the form

   `Action_Name(Time, List of Action arguments)`.

`Time` is the time point that the `Action` will be performed. `Time`, as well as all arguments may be either constants or variables. Arguments are instantiated by checking the `MntlCond` constituent, or during recipe selection.

For instance, the `Action` part of the recipe `clear_next_square` is

   `clear_next_square( _T, hole(H) )`,

where `T` is the Time variable and `hole(H)` denotes an empty hole to be filled.

♦ `RecId` is an Id for the recipe.

For instance, the `RecId` part of the recipe `clear_next_square` is `clear_next_square`.

♦ `MntlCond` is a logical proposition that combines beliefs using and, or and not logical connectives. When this proposition is true, the recipe is determined to be *relevant* for the `Action`.

The mental condition of the recipe `clear_next_square` depicted in Fig. 6, is quite a complex one and is the disjunction of three parts. It must be noticed that depending on the beliefs of the agent, mental conditions may determine the effects of the recipe and instantiate variables (e.g. `Path = [sq(Nx,Ny) | NewPath]` and `NewCost is Cost-1`). For instance, the first part of this disjunction tests whether there is not an obstacle in the square that is next on the route to the hole H. If this is true, then the action `clear_next_square` is determined to have no effect.

```
bel( path(square(X,Y,hole(H)),Path,Cost)) AND
bel( next_move(Path, Nx,Ny) )             AND
( not bel( square(Nx,Ny, obstacle(O)) )   AND
bel( Effects=[] )
```

♦ Mode has the form

   `mode(BMntlCond,Behaviour)`

where, `BMntlCond` has the form of mental conditions and `Behaviour` is a variable that is instantiated to a, possibly empty, list of check directives that involve features that must be checked during reconciliation. Further details about the check function will be given in section 4.2.2. `BMntlCond` is tested in order for the `Behaviour` variable to be instantiated. If `Behaviour` has no value and is not instantiated by `BMntlCond`, then the recipe inherits the `Behaviour` of its parent action (in the context of action). In case the action has no parent action, then the recipe inherits the `Behaviour` of the corresponding situation recognition rule.

In case `BMntlCond` is a variable, then the recipe inherits the `BMntlCond` of the situation recognition rule or of its parent action.

For instance, the mode part of the recipe `clear_next_square` is a disjunction of three conjunctions. The first conjunction expresses the belief that if there is not any obstacle to the path, then the agent must proceed reactively, and therefore, it is determined that no reconciliation is needed (the Behaviour list is empty).

```
( not bel( square(Nx,Ny, obstacle(O)) )    AND
  bel( Behaviour=[] )
```

However, the second conjunction expresses the belief that if there is an obstacle that cannot be avoided, then the agent must proceed deliberatively by reconciling the recipe clear_next_square. The corresponding check directives and the features that shall be taken into account during reconciliation are explained thoroughly in sub-section 4.2.2.

```
bel( square(Nx,Ny, obstacle(O) ) )                    AND
bel( not empty_neighbour_square(Nx,Ny, Nx1,Ny1)) AND
bel( Behaviour=[check(precondition,mstate),
               check(effects, effects_parent) ])
```

♦ Interleave is a true/false variable. If true, then the agent interleaves planning with execution. Otherwise, the agent constructs the full plan for the corresponding action (either reactively or deliberatively) and executes the resulting plan afterwards. This argument is specified either by the agent developer or it is instantiated by checking the mental conditions of the recipe. Considering our examples in Fig. 6, the recipe clear_next_square is specified to be executed when it is integrated in the overall plan (i.e., Interleave=true).

♦ Capability Constraints represent constraints that should hold for the agent to have the ability to perform/reconcile the recipes of basic level actions. It comprises a logical proposition that combines agent beliefs using and, or and not logical connectives. Capability constraints are checked when the agent reconciles the recipe (deliberatively) and when it tries to execute it (either deliberatively or reactively). During reconciliation the agent checks these constraints against its mental state and tests whether they are in conflict with the effects of predecessor actions.

The capability constraints of the recipe clear_next_square specify that the agent must believe that, either the next square has an obstacle and there is an empty neighbour square (i.e. the obstacle can be moved), or there are no obstacles.

```
( bel( square(Nx,Ny, obstacle(O) )        AND
  bel(empty_neighbour_square(Nx,Ny,   Nx1,Ny1))
)
or
not bel( square(Nx,Ny, obstacle(O)
```

♦ Contextual Constraints represent constraints that should be maintained when the agent plans deliberatively towards Action. In other words, contextual constraints of actions must be preserved by the effects of their sub-actions. Contextual constraints is a logical proposition that combines agent beliefs using and, or and not logical connectives. They are checked against the effects of sub-actions during reconciliation and, for a basic level action, when the agent executes that action.

Recipe `fill_a_hole` specifies that this recipe applies when there is not any other path to a hole with less cost than the cost of the known path to H.

```
bel(path(H,Path,Cost))        AND
bel(path(H1,Path1,Cost1))     AND
bel(Cost<Cost1)
```

Capability and contextual constraints constitute the *preconditions* of the recipe and determine the *applicability* of a recipe.

♦ `Actions List`. It specifies the sequence of sub-actions that should be performed in order the agent to perform `Action`. If this list is empty, then the action is a basic level one.

The action list of the recipe `clear_next_square` is an empty one. This is in contrast to the action list of the recipe `fill_a_hole` which comprises three subactions that should be performed for the action `fill(T,hole(H))` to be executed.

♦ `Effects`. This is a list of facts that the agent shall believe, when the plan towards `Action` has been performed successfully.

As already explained, the `Effects` of the recipe `clear_next_square` is a variable list that is instantiated when the `MntlCond` part of the recipe is checked. Therefore, it depends on the beliefs of the agent. This is in contrast to the recipe `find_path`, whose effects specify that when the recipe has been executed successfully, the agent must believe that there is a path to the hole H with a specific cost (i.e., `path(H,Path,Cost)`).

4.2 Deliberation Control Unit

The modules in this unit enable an agent to monitor its environment, update its beliefs about the environment, recognize situations occurring in the environment and form desires to act. As it will be explained, the agent chooses recipes for actions and decides whether these recipes will be utilized reactively or deliberatively. Depending on whether the agent reacts or deliberates, it commits to the corresponding actions, or reconciles its desires and intentions, respectively. As already mentioned, when the agent deliberates, it reconciles its desires with its intentions, reasoning about the relative strength of conflicting actions, about the strength of its commitments in relation with its desires and about the overall context of action. Therefore, as already indicated, it is the reconciliation module that enables the agent to deliberate rather than react. However, the "amount of planning" that the agent performs, i.e., "how much it deliberates", depends on the "amount" of careful planning that it performs: This is determined by three factors:

1. The strategy that the agent follows in order to find a relevant recipe for each action.
2. The features exploited during reconciliation in order the agent to detect conflicts that are due to the selected recipes, and
3. The decisions and methods followed for resolving these conflicts.

```
rec(
/*Action*/     clear_next_square( _T, hole(H) ),
/*Recipe_Id*/ clear_next_square,
/*MntlCond*/
   bel( path(square(X,Y,hole(H)),Path,Cost)) AND
   bel( next_move(Path, Nx,Ny) )            AND
   ( not bel( square(Nx,Ny, obstacle(O)) )   AND
     bel( Effects=[] )
   )
   or
   ( bel( square(Nx,Ny, obstacle(O) ) )      AND
     bel( not empty_neighbour_square(Nx,Ny,
                                Nx1,Ny1) ) AND
     bel( Effects=[ path( square(X,Y,hole(H)),
                           Path, 10000) ] )
   )
   or
   ( bel( square(Nx,Ny, obstacle(O) ) )      AND
     bel( empty_neighbour_square(Nx,Ny,
                                Nx1,Ny1) )  AND
     bel( Path=[sq(Nx,Ny)|NewPath] )          AND
     bel( NewCost is Cost-1 )                 AND
     bel( Effects = [
            path( square(X,Y,hole(H)),
                  NewPath, NewCost),
            not square(Nx,Ny,obstacle(O)),
            square(Nx1,Ny1,obstacle(O)) ] ) ),

/*Mode*/
   mode(
   ( not bel( square(Nx,Ny, obstacle(O)) )   AND
(1)  bel( Behaviour=[] )
   )
   or
   ( bel( square(Nx,Ny, obstacle(O) ) )      AND
     bel( not empty_neighbour_square(Nx,Ny,
                                Nx1,Ny1)) AND
(2)  bel( Behaviour=[check(precond,mstate),
                     check(effects,effects_parent) ])
   )
   or
   ( bel( square(Nx,Ny, obstacle(O) ) )      AND
     bel( empty_neighbour_square(Nx,Ny,
                                Nx1,Ny1) )  AND
(3)  bel( Behaviour=[])
   ),
   Behaviour ),

/* Interleave */  true,

/* CapConstr */
   ( bel( square(Nx,Ny, obstacle(O) )        AND
     bel( empty_neighbour_square(Nx,Ny,
                                Nx1,Ny1)))
   or
   not bel( square(Nx,Ny, obstacle(O) ),

/* CConstr */       bel(true),

/* ActionList */   [],

/* Effects */      Effects

   ).
```

```
rec(
/*Action*/    fill( T, hole(H) ),

/*Recipe_Id*/ fill_a_hole,

/*MntlCond*/  bel(true),

/*Mode*/
   mode( Variable, Behaviour ),

/* Interleave */  true,

/*CapConstr*/  bel(true),

/*CConstr*/  ( bel(path(H,Path,Cost))
                 AND
               ( bel(path(H1,Path1,Cost1))
                 AND
                bel(Cost<Cost1)
               )
               or
               bel(unknown_path(H)) ,

/*ActionList*/ [
     find_path(now, hole(H) ),
     traverse_the_path_to(now,hole(H)),
     drop_tile_to(now, hole(H) ) ],

/*Effects*/     [ not empty(hole(H)) ]).
```

```
rec(
/*Action*/    find_path(T, hole(H) ),

/*Recipe_Id*/ find_path,

/*MntlCond*/  bel(true),

/*Mode*/
   mode( bel(Behaviour=[]),Behaviour ),

/* Interleave */  true,

/*CapConstr*/ bel(true),

/*CConstr*/  bel(true),

/*ActionList*/ [],

/*Effects*/    [ path(H,Path,Cost) ]).
```

Fig. 6. Examples of complex and basic level actions' recipes

4.2.1 Situation Recognition Module

This module exploits "situation rules" to recognize situations occurring in the environment. As already indicated, situation rules drive the agent to form desires towards actions and decide whether it shall react or deliberate to a corresponding situation. Consequently, each desire for an action results to a desire of the agent to find a recipe for the desired action.

The agent uses the action `find_recipe(Time,Action)` in order to select a recipe that is relevant for `Action`. `find_recipe` is a basic level action and is invoked in a purely reactive way. If the agent fails to find a recipe for `Action`, then it may insert a desire to find another recipe for `Action`, or it may plan towards finding a recipe for `Action`. The latter case, i.e. planning for the action `find_recipe` is not enabled in the current implementation of ICAGENT, because it may lead to infinite recursion (planning to find a recipe for the action `find_recipe`, and so on). However, the agent may search for alternative recipes for the action `find_recipe`. In case the agent fails to find a recipe for `Action`, and a method for selecting a recipe, then it will insert a belief expressing its failure.

If the desire for `Action` has been asserted from a parent action rather than from a situation rule, then in case the agent fails to find a recipe for `Action`, it will assert a new desire to find an alternative recipe for the parent action of `Action`.

Having a recipe for `Action`, the agent utilizes the BMntlCond of the situation rule and the BMntlCond of the selected recipe, to form a final decision concerning the way the recipe shall be utilized: Reactively or deliberatively.

In this point we must recall that (a) in case the BMntlcond argument of the mode constituent of a chosen recipe is a variable, then the recipe inherits the BMntlCond of the corresponding situation rule or of its parent action, (b) in case the Behaviour argument of the mode constituent is a variable, then the agent tries to instantiate it by checking the BMntlcond conditions of the recipe, (c) If the Behaviour argument is not instantiated after all, then the recipe inherits the Behaviour argument of the situation rule, or of the parent action.

If (Behaviour=[]), this means that the agent does not need to check any features for possible conflicts and therefore, it skips the reconciliation module and proceeds reactively. On the other hand, if the list includes features that the agent must check in order the recipe to be integrated in the overall plan context, then the agent shall proceed to the reconciliation module checking for possible conflicts with the commitments that it already holds.

4.2.2 Reconciliation Module

The reconciliation module enables the agent to find conflicts between (recipes resulting from) desires and intentions that the agent holds, as well as between desires and the overall context of action. Figure 7 shows the control flow and information flow between reconciliation's sub-modules and agent's knowledge base.

As already pointed, the Behaviour argument of the mode (Behaviour-Mode) constituent of recipes drives the reconciliation module to detect conflicts. Behaviour-Mode is a list of check directives of the form

```
check(Features_arg_1,Features_arg_2)
```

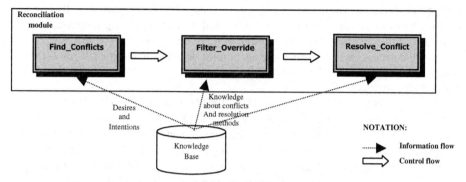

Fig. 7. The general architecture of Reconciliation Module

These directives specify the features that must be checked by the reconciliation module for the occurrence of possible conflicts. Therefore, the agent may determine to perform a subset of all possible checks, determining the "amount" of careful planning that is needed to perform in a specific situation. Figure 8 depicts all possible check directives that may be included in the Behaviour-Mode list (3rd column), the corresponding features that are involved in each check (2nd column) and the corresponding aspects that drive deliberation (1st column).

Deliberation Aspect	Reconciliation Features	Behaviour-Mode Element
Conflicts between the new desires and committed actions	preconditions of a new recipe (resulting from a new desire) and effects of its predecessors.	`check(preconditions, effects_predecessors)`
Conflicts between the new desires and high-level actions in the context of action	effects of a new recipe and preconditions of parent actions	`check(effects,preconditions_parent)`
Conflicts between the new desires and high-level actions in the context of action	effects of a new recipe and the effects of its parent actions	`check(effects,effects_parent)`
Conflicts between the mental state and new desires (i.e. applicability of the new recipe)	Mental state and the preconditions of the new recipe	`check(preconditions,mental_state)`
Conflicts between the mental state and high-level actions	Mental state and the preconditions of parent actions of the new recipe	`check(preconditions_parent, mental_state)`
Conflicts between the new desires and desires/intentions formed in the future	effects of a new recipe and the preconditions of future actions	`check(effects,preconditions_future)`

Fig. 8. Check directives and planning features

In order for the agent to detect possible conflicts between features occurring as arguments in a check directive, it uses conflict resolution rules of the form shown in Fig. 9a. Such a rule specifies that when the mental conditions (MntlCond) hold, then there is a conflict between propositions `Prop1` and `Prop2`, and therefore, there is a conflict between recipes with ids `Action1` and `Action2`. `Prop1` (respectively, `Prop2`) is either an effect or a precondition of `Action1` (respectively, `Action2`).

Having detected such a conflict, the agent must decide whether it shall resolve the conflict, or override it. In the former case, the agent must prioritise actions, deciding which recipe to reject.

To form such decisions, the agent must check the two mental conditions `Override_MntlCond` and `Action1_vs_Action2_MntlCond`, respectively. When `Override_MntlCond` is true, then the agent overrides the conflict. On the contrary, it proceeds checking `Action1_vs_Action2_MntlCond`. When `Action1_vs_Action2_MntlCond` is true, then it rejects `Action1`. If it is false, then it rejects `Action2`. For each action whose recipe is rejected, it forms a new desire towards that action.

For instance, the conflict rule depicted in Fig. 9b specifies that if the cost of a path to hole H is huge (>1000) and there is a path to a hole X with a manageable cost (<1000), then the agent must reject the recipe `Action1`.

```
fact( now,                                fact( now,
      MntlCond                                  (Cost1>=1000 AND
      =>                                         Cost2<1000)
      conflict( Prop1    %of Action1            =>
                Prop2,   %of Action2)           conflict(
                                                path(square(X,Y,hole(H)),Path,Cost1),
                Action1,                        path(square(X,Y,hole(X)),Path,Cost2)
                Action2,                        ),
                                                _Action1,
                Override_MntlCond,              _Action2,
                Action1_vs_Action2_MntlCond
      )).                                       fail,   %never override.
                                                fail    %always reject Action1
                                                )).
  (a)                                     (b)
```

Fig. 9. The general form of a conflict resolution rule

4.3 Plan Elaboration and Realization Control Unit

This unit comprises the following modules:

Plan Elaboration Module: This module converts goals of the agent to intentions and proceeds to elaborate the plan recipes as follows: In case the action realized by the recipe is a basic-level action, then it proceeds to the intention realization module. Otherwise, for each sub-action in the actions list of the recipe, the agent forms a desire to perform the sub-action and forms a desire to find a recipe for that sub-action. The agent proceeds in the way described in subsection 4.2.

Therefore, we may consider the plan elaboration and realization unit to be the behavior-based layer of the ICAGENT architecture. The agent elaborates its plan at this level, and may also decide if it shall perform its basic level actions, or it will postpone them until the whole plan has been constructed.

Intention Realization Module: This module realizes agent's intentions. When all the actions of a recipe have been performed, then the module updates the beliefs of the agent with the effects of that recipe. In case of a deliberative recipe, before executing it, the intention-realization module checks the preconditions (contextual and capability constraints) of this recipe, as well as of all its ancestor recipes. For reactive recipes, it checks the preconditions of the recipe. If these conditions are not satisfied, then the agent backtracks by turning the last intention into desire, until either it finds a recipe that can be executed in the current context, or until it has checked all alternatives. In the latter case, it forms a desire for the parent action in the context of action, and proceeds to find alternative recipes.

5 Example

Given the configuration of the tile-world chessboard in Fig. 10, the agent must fill holes D5 and A3. The agent at this time recognizes the configuration of the chessboard using situation recognition rules and forms two desires: One for filling hole D5 and one for filling hole A3.

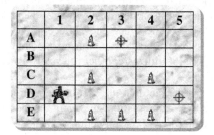

Notation

🦾 : Agent

⊕ : Hole

🏛 : Obstacle

Fig. 10. Initial configuration of the chessboard

Therefore, the agent has two options. To choose which option to pursue first, the agent finds recipes[1] for the desired actions and starts planning towards them deliberatively according to the Behaviour-Mode specified in the following situation recognition rule:

```
situ( /*SituId*/   empty_hole,
      /*MntlCond*/ bel( square(X,Y,hole(H)) ) and  bel( empty(hole(H)) ) and
                   bel( find_no_of_holes(Number_of_holes) ),
      /*Mode*/     mode( ( bel(Number_of_holes==1)   and
                           bel(Behaviour=[]) )
                         or
                         (bel(Number_of_holes>1)   and
                     bel(Behaviour=[check(preconditions,mental_state)]) ),
                     Bahaviour )
    ).
```

Figure 11 presents the plan formed by the agent towards completing the action 'fill(now,hole(d5))'. It must be mentioned that the agent, in parallel to the plan for d5, forms a similar plan for the action 'fill(now,hole(a3))'. Figure 12 shows the different states of the agent during the construction of the plan to fill hole d5.

As Fig. 11 shows, the agent proceeds towards filling holes d5 and a3, by finding a path to each hole reactively (action find_path).

Since the goal of the agent is to fill the holes in the chessboard making the least

---

[1] The agent forms desires to find recipes for each of the desired actions. Doing so, as already explained in Sect. 4.2.1, the agent elaborates the action 'find_recipe'.

possible moves, the agent chooses the hole that is nearest to it. In order to do so, contextual constraints of the recipe fill, depicted in Fig. 6, specify that this recipe is applicable only when the path found by the find_path sub-action of this recipe is the shortest path to any other hole. On the other hand, deliberation in traversing paths, guides the agent to check the constraints specified in the context of action (i.e. the preconditions of all ancestor actions in the context of action). Checking these conditions, the agent detects that the preconditions of the recipe fill hole a3 do not hold: The cost of the path to d5 is less than the cost of the path to a3. This means that the agent does not discard its desire to fill a3, but postpones planning towards it: The agent holds the desire to fill a3, as well as the intention to find a recipe towards filling a3. Furthermore, in every cycle, the agent reconciles its desires with its intentions, and decides whether to keep its intention to fill d5 or form a new intention to a3.

Let us now assume that when the agent reaches square d3 two new obstacles arise at squares c3 and d4. According to case (2) in the mode constituent of the recipe clear_next_square in Fig. 6, when there is an obstacle in a square on the route to a hole and this obstacle can not be moved to a neighbour square, then the agent must elaborate its plan deliberatively (checking the effects of clear_next_square with the effects of its ancestor actions). During reconciliation, in order the agent to detect possible conflicts, it utilizes conflict rules. At this time, the agent detects a conflict between the recipes clear_next_square and fill(now,hole(d5)). This is due to the fact that the cost of the path to hole d5 is very large and this hole is empty. After reconciliation, the agent decides to reject recipe fill(now,hole(d5)) and therefore, all its sub-actions.

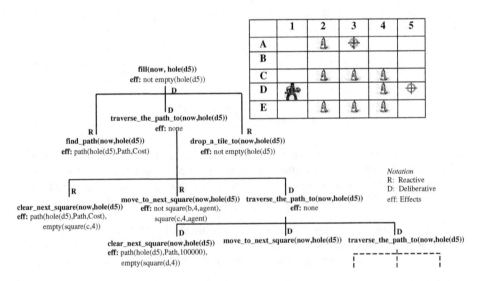

Fig. 11. The context formed towards the action "fill(now,hole(d5))"

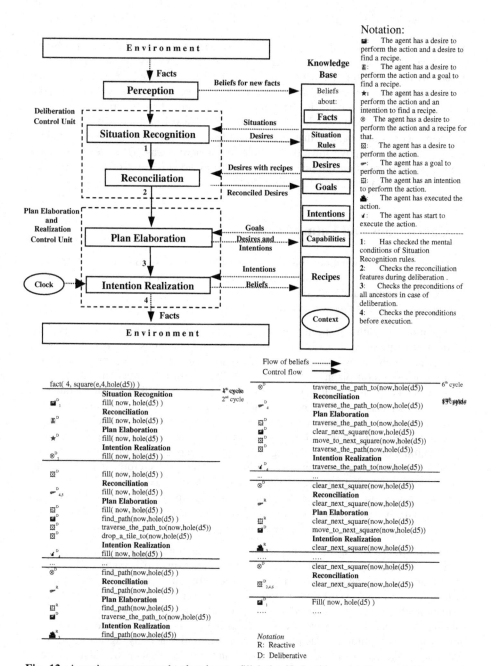

Fig. 12. Agent's states towards planning to fill hole d5. In this point the agent chooses to further pursue a plan to A3

Therefore, the agent, balancing between reaction and deliberation, it chooses to reconsider its intentions and desires and checks for possible conflicts in the overall context of action.

As Figs. 11 and 12 show, the agent intermixes deliberation and reaction in an arbirary way and may choose the same recipe to be used either reactively or deliberatively, depending on the conditions that determine the Behaviour-mode aspect of each recipe (BMntlCond). For instance, the recipe clear_next_square is invoked both reactively and deliberatively in the same plan. According to this recipe, as Fig. 6 describes, when the route to a hole has no obstacles (case 1 of the mode constituent), or when there is an obstacle that can be avoided (case 3 of the mode constituent), then the agent may move towards the hole in a reactive way. However, as already shown, when there is an obstacle that cannot be avoided (case 2 of the mode constituent), then the agent plans deliberatively.

6   Conclusions and Future Work

As stated in the introduction, this paper reports on progress towards establishing a generic framework for developing agents that reason about their plans and balance between deliberation and reaction.

Key issues towards this aim are the following:

- Equip agents with advanced plan management tasks [12]. This paper emphasized on generating plans towards achieving desires and intentions, on managing desires and intentions, assessing options and alternatives towards acting, and deciding the amount of careful planning that agents shall perform in a situation. These issues have been discussed with respect to balancing between reaction and deliberation.
- Provide a clear distinction between deliberation and reaction in terms of agents' reasoning tasks and management of agents' mental state. This paper conjectures that "careful" planning (deliberation) needs agents to reconcile desires and intentions. On the contrary, during reaction the agent focuses on the performance of a specific action without considering its options. Therefore, it is the reconciliation module that provides the agent with the ability to deliberate.
- Provide an explicit and an as detailed as possible representation of agents' mental state. This paper provides a comprehensive set of mental attitudes based on a well-defined framework for cooperative planning [7].

The framework as well as the agent presented has been implemented in Prolog.

Future work concerns extending the ICAGENT framework to support collaborative behaviour and balancing reaction and deliberation in a group of agents [7,8]. Collaboration comprises (a) recognition of the potential for collaborative activity, (b) formation of a group of intended actors, (c) recipe selection, and (d) allocation of subsidiary actions to group members or subgroups, and finally, (e) execution of actions. During recognition of the potential for collaborative activity, agents may reconcile among alternative recipes for an action and decide whether they shall proceed deliberatively or reactively, based on the recipes' mental conditions, recipes' preconditions and the overall context of action. Furthermore, during recipe selection, as well as task allocation, different agents may form different proposals for the same action A, proposing A to be elaborated either deliberatively or reactively. It is the responsibility of the group decision mechanism to decide whether the group shall proceed planning (individually or collaboratively) deliberatively or reactively towards A.

In these cases, the reconciliation mechanism must reconcile not only desires and intentions formed for individual plans, but also desires and intentions formed by a group of agents for achieving a shared goal [7]. As B.Grosz and S.Krause noted at [8], the community of agents may have different interests, so it is important agents to behave as rational, self-motivated individuals, which care for the good of the team.

The exact conditions and mechanisms, which allow agents to balance between reaction and deliberation as members of a group rather than as individuals, is an issue of further research.

References

1.   M. S. Atkin, D. L.Westbrook, and P. R Cohen. Capture the flag: Military simulation meets computer games. In *AAAI Spring Symposium on AI and Computer Games*. 1999.
2.   H. D. Burkhard, M. Hannebauer, and J. Wendler. AT Humboldt - Development, practice and theory. In *Proc. First International Workshop on RoboCup*. LNCS, Springer, 1997.
3.   J. Blythe and W. Scott Reilly. Integrating reactive and deliberative planning in a household robot. In *AAAI Fall Symposium on Instantiating Real-World Agents*. 1993.
4.   M. E. Bratman, D. J. Israel, and M. E. Pollack. Plans and resource-bounded practical reasoning. *Computational Intelligence* 4(3):349-355, 1988.
5.   P. Cohen and H. Levesque. Intention is choice with commitment. *Artificial Intelligence* 42: 213-261, 1990.
6.   R. Firby. An investigation into reactive planning in complex domains. In *Proceedings of the National Conference on Artificial Intelligence (AAAI-87)*. pages 202-206, Seattle, WA, 1987.
7.   B. J. Grosz and S. Kraus. Collaborative plans for complex group action. *Artificial Intelligence* 86:269-357, 1996.
8.   B. J. Grosz and S. Kraus. Intention reconciliation by collaborative agents. In *Proceedings of the Fourth International Conference on Multi-Agent Systems*, 2000.
9.   V. Hugel, P. Bonnin, and P. Blazevic. Using reactive and adaptive behaviors to play soccer. *AI Magazine*, Fall 2000.
10.   M. d'Inverno, D. Kinny, M. Luck, and M. Wooldridge. *A Formal Specification of dMARS*. Australian Artificial Intelligence Institute, Technical Note 72, 1997.
11.   J. P. Müller. *The Design of Intelligent Agents*. Volume 1177 of LNCS, Springer, 1996.
12   M. E. Pollack and J. F. Horty. There's more to life than making plans: Plan management in dynamic, multi-agent environments. *AI Magazine* 20(4), 1999.
13.   M. E. Pollack and M. Ringuette. Introducing the tileworld: Experimentally evaluating agent architectures. In *Proceedings of the Eighth National Conference on Artificial Intelligence (AAAI-90)*. pages 183-189. Menlo Park, Calif.: American Association for Artificial Intelligence, 1990.
14.   Y. Shoham. Agent0: An agent-oriented language and its interpreter. In *Proceedings of the National Conference on Artificial Intelligence (AAAI-91)*, 1991

On Augmenting Reactivity with Deliberation in a Controlled Manner

Jacek Malec

Department of Computer Science
Lund University
Box 118
221 00 LUND, Sweden
jacek@cs.lth.se

Abstract. We argue that a reactive agent obeying the requirement of predictability imposed by a hard-real-time application domain cannot be equipped with an arbitrarily powerful deliberation capability as this would jeopardize the predictability of the agent's behaviour. Therefore such augmentation should be performed in a principled, controlled manner. We illustrate our line of thought with the example of Generic Layered Architecture used for creating reactive agents acting in dynamic environments requiring real-time responsiveness.

1   Introduction

The interplay between reactivity and deliberation is one of the issues of paramount importance for intelligent agent[1] design. For many years AI research focused on deliberation as the basis for intelligent activity, neglecting the problems of situatedness and reactivity. Increasing complexity of the problems addressed by the researchers has led to the important insight that appropriate reactivity is probably as necessary and important to intelligent behaviour as are the deliberative capabilities. During the last fifteen years the reactive paradigm has gained much attention and popularity, especially in the area of autonomous robotics, and has led to important advancement in the field. However, probably the most important insight is that pure reactivity is much too weak to create any complex behaviours worth the adjective *intelligent*.

The coexistence of the two paradigms of building intelligent agents was not friction-free, but the debate between the proponents of either of the approaches has undobtedly led to better understanding of the problems within the paradigms and also to some solutions to those problems. In the last decade the two approaches began to merge, yielding a number of so called hybrid architectures offering both reactivity to cope with the dynamic environment of the agent and

---

[1] The term *agent* is understood rather broadly in this paper, encompassing both software agents (softbots living in a networked environment) and hardware agents acting in the real (physical) world, although the main association we would like the reader to have is that of an autonomous intelligent robot.

M. Hannebauer et al. (Eds.): Reactivity and Deliberation in MAS, LNAI 2103, pp. 76–91, 2001.

deliberation to deal with the cognitive tasks. Although the number of proposals is large and covers the whole spectrum between purely reactive and purely cognitive agents, there is no agreement as to how much of both should be used in each particular case.

The balance between reactivity and deliberation is a function of many factors. Among the most obvious ones we can count the designed agent's predominant tasks, or functions, constraining the number of possible implementation architectures, the architectural assumptions of the designer (revealing the designer's preferences), the availability of efficient algorithms for tasks imposed by the application domain (this is especially important for the deliberative part of the system), the necessity to switch between several types of representations used by different parts of the system, etc.

In particular it is important to notice that the space of possible choices is limited by the initial design decisions. Once the architecture is chosen and the representation languages defined the designer is faced with the constraints that have to be obeyed without exceptions. e.g. by choosing ATLANTIS [13] the designer accepts the way the control is imposed over the three layers of this architecture and the temporal dependencies between the layers become fixed. In most cases this is the intended result: the agent architecture is expected to help the programmer achieve maximal functionality in minimum time, relieving her from the tedious task of creating the agent from scratch.

Usually, an architecture assumes a fixed balance between reactivity and deliberation. For example, when using RAPS (Reactive Action Package System, [9]) one decides upon what functionality of an agent is to be implemented at the task (skill) level and what can be explicitly reasoned about at the highest RAP level. However, the price to pay may be some inflexibility of the designed agent. In complex domains one usually wants the possibility of adjusting this balance depending on the current circumstances - thus a reasonable requirement would be to expect the architecture to support such adjustments. In the extreme case one may wish to let the agent decide by itself in a principled manner about this balance, what would imply a meta-reasoning module in the system. Another important limitation imposed by an architecture is the set of representation languages available - architectures are usually centered around some ontological assumptions. The languages used induce a limit on what may be perceived and understood (or reasoned about) by an agent.

Therefore the choice of the languages underlying the used architecture is probably the most important design decision. Before a particular architecture is commited to one needs to carefully analyse its languages and their expressive power (and the associated computational complexity). The languages should allow rich interpretation domains but also efficient reasoning, be it on the reactive level or during deliberation. Moreover, the set of used languages must allow easy translation for effective representation switches.

Yet another dimension of analysis is that of the guaranteed *predictability*[2] of the agent's response. In many applications the agents have to satisfy the usual requirements put on hard-real-time systems. Traditionally AI wasn't concerned much about that issue although it has received some attention during past decades. However, all the applications where an agent might influence the safety of human beings require us to address the problem of predicatbility of the agent's behaviour.

The rest of the paper is organized as follows. In Sect. 2 we introduce an agent architecture called *Generic Layered Architecture* (GLA) and discuss its advantages and disadvantages, in particular for creating intelligent real-time agents. Section 3 introduces the postulate of controlled augmentation of the predictable reactivity with limited deliberation preserving the imposed hard-real-time requirements. Then in Sect. 4 we look at some other agent architectures, focusing mostly on the reactive side of the spectrum. Finally some conclusions are given.

2   Generic Layered Architecture

Our approach to intelligent system design and implementation builds on the three-layered software architecture developed during the last decade at the Linköping University [37] (recently renamed to GLA, the generic layered software architecture). The main distinctive property of this architecture is that it groups similar types of computations into *layers* (shown in Fig. 1), as opposed to the much more common approach where a functional decomposition into layers is typical.

Literally dozens of layered architectures have been recently proposed for autonomous system implementation (see e.g. [1,3,5,8,13] for just a few of them; good overviews can be found in [2,38,22]). Although there are differences both in the way of assigning various tasks to different layers and in the way the overall control of the system is executed, the general conclusion is that such layering is beneficial, if not necessary, in designing autonomous *intelligent* systems. We do not claim that the GLA architecture is novel in terms of extending the set of agent's capabilities, rather we expect that the functionalities implementable using GLA might be achieved by using other architectures as well. Our primary claim is that GLA has the following advantages in designing autonomous *real-time* agents:

1. Explicit separation of tasks requiring different conceptual and computational frameworks;
2. Providing a potential designer with a set of formal tools (languages, algorithms) simplifying and systematizing the design process itself;
3. Supporting the design process with a set of software tools enabling easy prototyping of complex real-time systems.

---

[2] The term *predictability* is used in this paper in the sense adopted by the real-time community[45]: A system is predictable if and only if all the timing constraints in the system are provably satisfied.

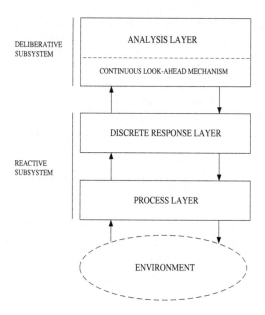

Fig. 1. The generic layered software architecture

The bottom layer, called the *process layer* (PL), is hosting implementations of numerical, periodic tasks, such as identification or control. Data handled by this layer is stored in dual-state vectors. Computations have the form of mappings from input vectors to output vectors and are performed periodically in synchronization with the sample rates of sensors.

The middle layer is called the *discrete response layer* (DRL), and performs tasks which are by nature asynchronous. For instance, it computes the responses to asynchronous events that are recognized by the PL. An example of such a task is the change of control mode (of the PL) due to the change of mode in the environment. The computational model assumed for the DRL is that of discrete event systems (DES). There exist several equivalent DES formalisms: automata, transition systems, rule-based systems, etc. All of them distinguish the notions of *state* and *transition* as central, although the details vary from model to model. We have used the rule-based approach for the purpose of specifying knowledge-based system prototypes. However, this does not preclude usage of other approaches [25,30]. The process and discrete response layers together form the reactive part of the GLA.

The top layer is called the *analysis layer* because it is defined to handle *symbolic* reasoning tasks such as prediction, planning and scheduling, which require reference to physical time. The output of this layer can be either control events that guide the DRL in its decisions, or parameter settings that are passed through the DRL and directly affect the operation of the PL. This layer has also been tested as a host for symbolic learning mechanisms which adapted the discrete response layer while maintaining its critical response requirements. An important sub-task of this layer, the *continuous look-ahead* (or limited prediction) mechanism has been distinguished in order to identify a predictable subset of the computations in this layer.

While the bottom two layers of GLA, forming the reactive part of the system, might be considered well-developed (both theoretically and in terms of the provided tools, see the description below) and stable, the analysis layer is the subject of on-going research and no design and verification tools have been provided yet.

2.1   Real-Time Software Tools

During our previous research we have thoroughly studied this architecture and its implications on software engineering issues [37]. One of the conclusions was that it facilitates prototyping of systems, especially because it allows development of generic software tools which can be used for implementation of each particular application system. Along this line we have developed software kernels, or *engines*, for development and implementation of the process layer and the discrete response layer. The set of tools includes:

– Process Layer eXecutive (PLX) [34]: a multi-threaded time-triggered real-time engine for implementation of process layer software. It has been implemented on a pSOS$^+$ based system and on a PC running VDX. A port to Real-Time Linux is currently developed.
– Process Layer Configuration Language (PLCL) [35] and its compiler: a language for specification of PL module interconnections and interfaces to both sensors and actuators on one side, and to the DRL software on the other side. The modules themselves are programmed in a subset of some conventional language, such as C or Java.
– Rule Layer eXecutive (RLX) [36]: an engine for implementation of rule-based discrete-event systems in the DRL. It has been implemented on Unix-based machines and on a PC with VDX; A port to Real-Time Linux is under preparation.
– Rule Language (RL) [24]: a rule-based language for declarative specification of discrete-event control.

2.2   The Process Layer Executive

The PLX supports the implementation and maintenance of the hard real-time parts of the application which perform the transformations of periodic data.

During processing, all data is stored in a *dual state vector*, which is a global data structure consisting of an input and an output vector. The values in the input vector represent either sensor readings or internal state, whereas the values in the output vector represent actuator outputs or new internal state.

A PL application defines a sequence of transformations that should be applied to the input vector in order to compute a new output vector. Since sensor values are read periodically, the transformations have to be applied with the same periodicity. When the transformations have been applied, actuator outputs are flushed to devices and the new internal state is installed in the input vector, thus establishing the new state of the process layer.

The PLX engine supervises a PL application, which includes managing the internal state, reading sensors and writing to actuators using user defined access functions, and supervise the execution of the periodical transformations of the dual state vector. The PLX supports decomposition of the vector into several sub-vectors, each of which has its own period, causing transformations to be executed at different rates.

The PLX engine and the PLCL compiler together form the basis for a worst case execution timing (WCET) analysis of a PL application [26,34].

2.3   The Rule Layer Executive

The rule layer executive supports the implementation of rule-based event processing. In the RLX the state of the world is represented by the time dependent values of a set of symbolic state variables called *slots*. A slot is updated only when its value changes, due to an external event or as a result of a change of another slot's value. Rules specify dependencies between slots, and typically have the following form: *if the value of a particular slot is changed in a certain way, then the value of another slot should also be changed as a result.* Internally, each such change may trigger additional rules, which lead to more updates. This forward chaining process may continue in several steps.

We take an object-oriented view of the rule base in the sense that we associate a set of rules with each slot. This view facilitates the flexibility and maintainability needed for complex systems.

The RLX tool has two major tasks. Firstly, it maintains the set of slots and rules which determines the behaviour of the discrete response layer. Secondly, it performs the forward chaining of rules. The forward chaining is typically initiated by an event recognized by the PL. The result of the forward chaining process may be the change of control algorithm used by some PL process or direct output to a device interfaced by the PL.

The language RL is essentially a syntactic variant of a simple temporal logic and is used for declarative specification of behaviour of the discrete response layer. A comprehensive set of tools for correctness and consistency checking, for timing analysis and for code generation have been developed during the recent years [23,25,27].

2.4   An Application Example

The GLA architecture has been used in recent years for specification and implementation of autonomous agents for several domains requiring hard-real-time guarantees. The original application that triggered our work on GLA was a driver support system [29]. Then we have applied GLA to robot control [31] and recently to RoboCup agent development, to flexible manufacturing cell control [28] and to simulated helicopter control in a traffic surveillance system [24] (an experiment within the WITAS project [7]).

In order to keep this presentation not overwhelmed by unnecessary details, we will briefly present here the first of the applications developed using GLA: the driver support system (DSS). The main function of the system was to provide the driver with accurate, reliable, necessary and sufficient, and timely safety-related support on the basis of unreliable and limited input information, while taking into account the driver's workload and attention capabilities.

The input devices used in our experiments were *autonomous intelligent cruise control* (AICC), *route guidance, road/tyre friction estimation system*, and *roadside information system*. However, as the number of intelligent devices available for mounting in a contemporary car becomes larger, there is an obvious need for modularity and incrementality. The reactive part of the GLA can provide at least the second of these properties.

As the support systems mentioned above generate a lot of data, the amount of information potentially available to the driver is very large, and sometimes contains even conflicting messages. In such situation there is an immanent danger of overloading the driver's perceptual and reactive capabilities. Clearly, there is a strong need for systematic handling of the output to the driver from different subsystems in the car, in order to guarantee that the driver gets the relevant information at the right time. This task is complicated by a number of circumstances, for instance:

- Output requests may come from many different sources (support systems) operating independently, or almost independently, without a coherent view of the information available in the whole system.
- Information is time-dependent, so it might prove useless, or even dangerous, if presented to the driver at the wrong time.
- The amount of information the driver can handle is not untimed nor static, but varies dynamically depending on, among other things, the traffic situation, the weather conditions and the kind of maneuvre the driver is performing.
- There may be several output channels available (for example display(s), voice output, and haptic actuators) whose appropriateness may change dynamically.
- Drivers may prefer some output channels to others, or may want to suppress some kinds of messages (e.g. speed excess messages).

The DSS has been specified using the rule language RL introduced in Sect. 2.3. The RL rules are the classical *event-condition-action* rules of the form

```
WHEN event IF condition THEN action
```

where all the events, condition and actions are modeled as value changes to discrete state variables called slots. Some of the actual DSS rules looked as follows:

```
WHEN aicc_distance_acc *= FIRM
  IF aicc_decision |= DISTANCE
  THEN aicc_warning := FIRM;

WHEN acceleration *= ACC
  IF direction_indicator |= LEFT AND car_in_front |= CAR_IN_FRONT
  THEN maneuver := OVERTAKING;

WHEN road_grip *= BAD
  IF skid   |= NO
  THEN road_conditions := BAD;

WHEN on_intersection *= ON_INT
  IF maneuver |= DRIVE_FREELY  OR maneuver |= FOLLOWING
  THEN workload := HIGH;

WHEN skill *= NOVICE
  IF workload |= VERY_HIGH OR light_conditions |= NIGHT OR
     maneuver |= OVERTAKING
  THEN channel := VOICE;

WHEN maneuver *= {FOLLOWING, TURNING}
  IF NOT light_conditions |= NIGHT AND NOT workload |= VERY_HIGH
  THEN channel := DISP_AND_VOICE;

WHEN preference *= NO_SPEED_MESSGS
  IF NOT aicc_state |= AUTO AND NOT aicc_state |= OFF
     AND aicc_decision |= SPEED_LIMIT
  THEN warning := OK;
```

The RL program for the DSS is rather large. It contains 275 rules and 80 slots, where some of the slots have more than 100 possible values. The total number of slot-value pairs is 1752. The program is stratifiable (see [24]) and therefore may be run using the stratified (i.e., simpler) RLX engine. Please note that the specification presented above is *executable*, that is, no further coding is necessary to obtain the implementation for this layer. An automated tool creates also stubs of the PLCL code, to be used in the Process Layer.

The consistency checker gave us guarantee that the DSS program is logically consistent. Then we have performed the timing analysis. Assuming that all the primitive operations take no more than $4\mu s$ (implementation-dependent constant), the one-step time bound for this engine was $T_{step} = 0.0108$s. As the maximal number of rules to be fired was 275, the upper bound for a response was $T = 0.88$s, what was deemed acceptable from the application point of view. Some experiments have been performed with computing tighter estimates for the DSS program, according to the proposal described in [27]. However, as the algorithms are NP-complete, the results were expectedly not encouraging - we

couldn't obtain any better estimate within 72 hours of computation time due
to the complexity of rule dependencies. However, more loosely coupled specifi-
cations would theoretically allow the possibility to tighten the estimates.

The Process Layer part of the DSS application was rather simple: it consisted
of a number of processes extracting the events from the raw data provided by
the input devices and another set of processes translating the discrete decisions
into appropriate signals to the output devices (display and voice synthesiser).
The timing analysis of this part of the system has provided guarantees that all
deadlines for the assumed period of the schedule (100ms) would be met.

The final comment about this application (as well as all others) is that it did
not require any advanced deliberation: all necessary decision making could be
specified as a set of fixed, effectively propositional, rules describing all modes of
the system and all possible transitions between the modes. As we did not posess
any possibility of extending our predictability framework onto the analysis layer,
we have avoided to face such applications that would require it to be present. In
particular, any dynamic cooperation of autonomous (robotic) agents, involving
situation analysis and possibly negotiation among agents, would fall into this
class and therefore has not been studied so far. The two-robot test case [28] has
been created using a simple, fixed communication protocol, and therefore could
be realised completely reactively.

3 Controlled Deliberation

It is no accident that the tools described in the previous section do not entail
the analysis layer. Our approach to the tool generation can be described as
bottom-up: we have assumed predictability as the main requirement and then
developed and extended the tools in such a way that the created agent can always
be subjected to predictability analysis. This way we can formally, declaratively
specify an agent's control system using the languages introduced earlier, then
subject the specification to correctness analysis, then (mostly) automatically
derive (most of) the code and finally analyse its worst-case timing properties.
However, the price we pay for this comfortable situation is very high: we can
only deal (so far) with purely reactive systems, as the work on development of
the tools suitable for creating non-trivial deliberative modules in the analysis
layer has lagged much behind the original schedule.

As we have decribed already five years ago in [32], the basic idea behind the
controlled deliberation in the analysis layer is to use one of a series of logical
formalisms with increasing expressive power and with well-defined computational
properties. The agent would dynamically choose the formalism suitable for the
environment and the reasoning task it is currently faced with and, possibly, the
temporal constraint currently active. The theory of *inhabited dynamical systems*
underlying such logical formalisms has been developed by Sandewall [44] where
he has introduced a family of logics of action of increasing complexity, suitable for
capturing evolution in worlds characterized by some of the assumed set of well-
defined criteria, such as temporal invariance of the domain, inertia, alternative

results of actions, delayed effects of actions, concurrency of actions, surprises, etc. However, an efficient implementation of such temporal reasoning systems did not appear yet and it seems very unlikely that it will in the near future. On the other hand, one of the most prominent results of this research has recently led to the development of an extremely efficient planning system — the TAL Planner — announced earlier this year [21].

One could imagine the use of TAL as the main tool for reasoning in the analysis layer. Unfortunately, TAL has some peculiarities that preclude its use as a general-purpose mechanism. It requires that for every task it is expected to reason about a specially crafted second-order "control" formula is provided. So far, this formula needs to be created by hand and there are no clues how one could automate the process.

Even if it were possible, the efficiency of TAL, however, is not sufficient to guarantee the success of the whole enterprise — an implementation of the reasoning procedures needs also to be predictable in the hard-real-time sense. The main mechanism used, continuous look-ahead, is based on the same basic principle as Real-Time A* [20], although its complexity is larger due to the fact that each step in predicting the future development of the world involves (in this case) non-monotonic reasoning in a suitable logic. Therefore, in order to provide predictability, one would need to give the worst-case timing estimates for proving theorems in those logics - an problem, if not hopeless, then at least far from being solved.

Given these constraints one can consider several alternative approaches to guaranteeing predictability of the GLA analysis layer. One of them may be the use of interruptible anytime algorithms for deduction. When the alloted reasoning time is over, then conclusions drawn so far are the only ones considered valid. This, of course, Immediately puts the question of validity of this approach: Is it formally correct that some sentences are sometimes false and sometimes true, depending only on the efficiency of the theorem prover? Can it happen that given the same amount of deduction time, the theorem prover will sometimes get an interesting conclusion and sometimes not (maybe depending on the state of the knowledge base or on the proof heuristics used in some particular case)? This raises the need of carefully choosing the granularity of the world description, the proof algorithms used and the time allocation policy. Probably the idea (presented e.g. by Zilberstein and Russell [48]) of using a number of representations in parallel, from coarse to fine-grained, is worth considering in this context.

Another possible line of work consists of pursuing the RTA* approach, as described earlier, but using some appropriately crafted logic for reasoning purposes. Such logic could be e.g. expressed in terms of a labelled deductive system [11], where an appropriate additive algebra on labels would limit the depth of proofs in a theory. However, such label systems would need to be studied in order to establish some correspondence between theories deducible with it and classical theories obtainable using standard logics of AI. The language of the logic itself would also need to be carefully chosen: a rich vocabulary may yield more expressiveness but usually for the price of longer or more complicated proofs.

However, in this case such richness might be beneficial, allowing one to use short proofs for non-trivial conclusions. A variation on this theme would be to limit the domain of discourse by considering essentially propositional languages with datalog properties and finite models.

The reason we have not extended the architecture with the deliberation tools earlier should be now obvious: we could not guarantee predictable temporal behaviour of such three-layered architecture. There is still much work to be done before we can announce that GLA fulfills the predictability requirement. In face of the alternatives: a purely reactive system with the necessity of compiling in all the possible reactions, but with guaranteed temporal behaviour, and the full-blown GLA, with rich deliberative capabilities, fast enough in most circumstances but without guarantees, we have to choose the first option as this is the only one that can be used without risk in safety-critical applications.

Of course, the approach described above makes only sense when predictability is accepted as the most important property of the developed system (which it is in case of hard-real-time applications). The important lesson that we have learned during recent years is that if one tries to first use a fast (in terms of development time) but dirty solution, hoping that the details would be fixed later, then the obtained result may happen to be completely useless, forcing the researcher to reconsider the whole theory from scratch. This was what indeed happened with the development of RL (the main formalism used in the middle layer of GLA) and this is what we would like to avoid now. Especially the predictability property has to be embedded in the theory from the very beginning, underlying every algorithm used and every control structure introduced - as we have learnt the hard way, reintroducing it into an existing architecture is virtually impossible.

4   Related Work

As mentioned above, a large number of layered agent architectures have been proposed for autonomous agent design and implementation. Chronologically, among the first ones were e.g. NASREM [1], synchronous control of [3], SSS [5], TouringMachines [8], and ATLANTIS [12]. Recently, a number of good overviews has appeared, e.g. chapter six of Arkin's textbook [2] (pointing to the fact that "the nature of the boundary between deliberation and reactive execution is not well understood at this time, leading to somewhat arbitrary architectural decisions", p. 207), Jennings, Sycara and Wooldridge's [18], Müller's [38] or Lee's [22], to mention just a few.

The other three-layered architectures differ from ours in several aspects. Gat [13] distinguishes the layers on the similar basis, i.e. the type of performed computations, but control in his system is located in the middle layer, with only occasional invocation of high-level (actually, path planning) procedures. As in our system, communication with the environment is done through the lowest (control) layer only. The language ALFA is a specialized programming language rather than a formalism for specification of system's abilities.

Connell's system SSS [5] has a similar decomposition of tasks as in our, or Gat's case. The lowest layer hosts control procedures, the middle one contains behavioural specification of system's reactions, and the highest layer is expected to perform path planning. However, in contrast to ours, his approach does not offer any tools for, nor even possibility of, analyzing the real-time performance of the implemented system.

Ferguson's TouringMachine architecture [8] is the most elaborate and complete of the three. It addresses both the real-time aspects and higher cognitive functions (including manipulation of system goals, intentions and beliefs about itself and other agents). The main difference is in the perceptory and effectory paths: TouringMachine layers are simultaneously fed with the sensory information and then compete for the right to control the actuators. Actually, neglecting the possibility of implementing complex continuous control algorithms in our process layer (TouringMachine has totally separated inputs and outputs), the two approaches are to a large extent similar, with our discrete response layer corresponding to the reactive layer of TM, and analysis layer performing the tasks divided between TM's planning and modeling layers.

Another example of a similar, and recently very popular, layered agent architecture is InteRRaP [39]. It can be seen as a more general solution than ours: yet another layer is introduced to provide multi-agent planning and cooperation ability. Another significant difference is that InteRRaP possesses a global knowledge base, accessible from all the processing layers, whereas our approach stresses the need of multiple models suited for the processing layer they are used by. In this way we can have inconsistencies between the models, but on the other hand the modeling is simpler and more realistic. However, the later versions of InteRRaP also allow separated world models, yielding this difference non-existent.

Only a few of the architectures mentioned in this section address the issue of real-time properties. Those that do, e.g., CIRCA [41]; usually adopt the "fast-enough" attitude combined with "anytime algorithms". A more recent architecture, explicitly addressing the hard-real-time requirements, is ARTIC [4]. It is a modification of a blackboard architecture, done in the spirit of GUARDIAN [14], i.e., the hard-real-time response is guaranteed by employing reflexes, while deliberation is performed without any guarantees.

Russell and coworkers have provided a useful theory for anytime algorithms [43,48], extending the original work by Dean and Boddy on this topic [6]. Thanks to their analysis it is exactly known what can and what cannot be expected from anytime algorithms in the context of real-time applications. The short answer is that soft real-time guarantees can be reasonably derived using probablistic approach, while hard real-time guarantees are much harder to achieve.

An approach ressembling anytime algorithms, but applied to the area of deduction, i.e. the second approach described in previous section, is the one by Fisher and Ghidini [10]. They provide a logical system capable of adapting its deductive power to the resource constraints. However, no useful (for us) bound can be derived for this approach - the only guarantee is that the number of theorems will be smaller in some cases, but the proofs can still be very long and no fixed limit in terms of the number of steps may be given.

The relevant issues of formal analysis of agent architectures has not attracted much attention until very recently. An example of correctness analysis of the classical PRS programs may be found in [46], in its turn based on an early work by Rao and Georgeff [42], while a more general look at the control structures of rule-based systems, relevant from the point of view of our approach, may be found in [16]. However, most literature on this topic needs to be traced in the database theory, where active real-time databases have been studied formally for a while.

Finally, the issue of comparing agent architectures, especially with respect to their effectiveness and suitability for intended applications, is an important topic worth attention and undoubtedly requiring further studies. An interesting preliminary dicussion may be found in [15] and [22].

5   Conclusions

In the paper we have presented the generic layered software architecture (GLA) and commented on the possibility of extending its reactive predictable behaviour with some deliberative capabilities, but in a controlled way. We have described the basic elements of the architecture and some of the tools available (although we have omitted the more advanced tools related to the correctness and timing verification). The we have mentioned Sandewall's theory of inhabited dynamical systems and discussed its usage in extending GLA into a predictable three-layered architecture. Finally we have mentioned a few other possibilities, based on the ideas of RTA* combined with labelled deductive systems.

Our future work on GLA software will be concentrated on guaranteeing the stability of the software engines and the associated tools. We expect to share the current GLA code with the scientific community as soon as a preliminary documentation is available. For more details please have a look at http://www.cs.lth.se/home/Jacek_Malec/.

As the last remark regarding the related work one might observe that "intelligent agent" is apparently the buzzword of the last decade. Intelligent software agents, intelligent robotic agents, intelligent real-time agents and intelligent autonomous agents seem ubiquitous in the recent literature in computer science (software engineering and artificial intelligence in particular) and in the systems and control area (especially intelligent control). However, not much attention is being paid to the very notion of an *intelligent agent*: it suffices for a system (either software-, or hardware-based, or both) to reveal a behaviour a bit more complex than just a simple input/output transformation, to be nicknamed intelligent agent. Even better if the behaviour is non-stationary.

What usually hides behind this name is a compound system consisting of several components performing time- and environment-dependent operations over extended periods of time, and composing the results of those operations in some (usually meaningful) way. One may ask though, what is the difference between an intelligent agent and a hierarchical, goal-seeking system, as described already in the 1960s (see e.g. [33]). The answer can be either "none", when it comes to the underlying principles, or "enormous" when we look at the scale of the systems created nowadays. However, the size of the delivered applications should not create an impression that we, agent researchers, are the originators of all the ideas in the field (although we might have rediscovered some of them if we did not read sufficiently much): most of what we discuss today has already been adressed one way or the other in some other area of science. Therefore an interesting research agenda would be to trace the issues underlying agent research back to their roots.

Acknowledgments. The author is indebted to Erik Sandewall and Patrick Doherty for the ideas underlying this paper, to Michael Fisher for a very useful reference and to the anonymous referees for their thorough comments on the earlier drafts of this paper. Probably any useful idea in this paper comes from them, while all the errors and unnecessary complications are, of course, the author's.

Moreover, the author would like to thank Markus for patience.

References

1. J. S. Albus, H. G. McCain, and R. Lumia. NASA/NBS Standard Reference Model for Telerobot Control System Architecture (NASREM). NIST Tecnical Note 1235, National Institute of Standards and Technology, Robot Systems Division, Center for Manufacturing Engineering, Gaithersburg, MD 20899, 1989.
2. R. C. Arkin. *Behaviour-Based Robotics*. MIT Press, 1998.
3. R. P. Bonasso. Integrating reaction plans and layered competences through synchronous control. In *Proceedings of the Twelvth International Joint Conference on Artificial Intelligence, Sydney*, pages 1225–1231. Morgan Kaufman, 1991.
4. V. Botti, C. Carrascosa, V. Julian, and J. Soler. Modelling agents in hard real-time environments. In *Proc. MAAMAW-99*, pages 63–76. 1999.
5. J. H. Connell. SSS: A hybrid architecture applied to robot navigation. In *Proceedings of the 1992 IEEE International Conference on Robotics and Automation*, pages 2719–2724, Nice, France, May 1992.
6. T. Dean and M. Boddy. An Analysis of Time-Dependent Planning. *Artificial Intelligence*, pages 49–54, 1988.
7. P. Doherty, G. Granlund, K. Kuchciński, E. Sandewall, K. Nordberg, E. Skarman, and J. Wiklund. The WITAS unmanned aerial vehicle project. In *Proceedings ECAI-00*, Berlin, Germany, 2000.
8. I. A. Ferguson. *TouringMachines: An Architecture for Dynamic, Rational, Mobile Agents*. PhD thesis, University of Cambridge, Computer Laboratory, Cambridge CB2 3QG, England, November 1992.
9. R. J. Firby. *Adaptive Execution in Complex Dynamic Worlds*. PhD thesis, Department of Computer Science, Yale University, 1989.
10. M. Fisher and C. Ghidini. Agents playing with dynamic resource bounds. In M. Hannebauer, J. Wendler, and E. Pagello, editors, *Proc. of the ECAI-00 Workshop on Balancing Reactivity and Social Deliberation in Multi-Agent Systems*, 2000.

11. D. Gabbay. *Labelled Deductive Systems, Volume I.* Oxford University Press, 1996.
12. E. Gat. *Reliable Goal-Directed Reactive Control of Autonomous Mobile Robots.* PhD thesis, Virginia Politechnic Institute and State University, 1991.
13. E. Gat. Integrating Planning and Reacting in a Heterogenus Asynchronous Architecture for Controlling Real-World Mobile Robots. In *Proceedings AAAI-92*, pages 809–816. AAAI Press, 1992.
14. B. Hayes-Roth. Architectural Foundations for Real-Time Performance in Intelligent Agents. *Journal of Real-Time Systems*, 2:99–125, 1990.
15. H. Hexmoor, M. Huber, J. P. Müller, J. Pollock, and D. Steiner. On the evaluation of agent architectures. In [19], pages 106–116.
16. K. V. Hindriks, F. S. de Boer, W. van der Hoek, and J.-J. Ch. Meyer. Control structures of rule-based agent languages. In [40], pages 381–396.
17. *Proceedings of the Thirteenth International Joint Conference on Artificial Intelligence.* Morgan Kaufman, 1993.
18. N. R. Jennings, K. Sycara, and M. Wooldridge. A roadmap of agent research and development. *Autonomous Agents and Multi-Agent Systems*, 1(1):7–38, 1998.
19. N. R. Jennings and Y. Lespérance, editors. *Intelligent Agents VI, Agent Theories, Architectures and Languages*, volume LNAI 1757 of *LNCS*. Springer, 2000.
20. R. E. Korf. Real-time heuristic search. *Artificial Intelligence*, 42:189–211, 1990.
21. J. Kvarnström, P. Doherty, and P. Hasslum. Extending TALplanner with concurrency and resources. In *Proceedings ECAI-00*, Berlin, Germany, August 2000.
22. J. Lee. Reactive-system approaches to agent architectures. In [19], pages 132–146.
23. M. Lin. *Formal Analysis of Reactive Rule-based Programs.* Licentiate thesis, Linköping University, 1997. Linköping Studies in Science and Technology, Thesis No 643.
24. M. Lin. *Analysis and Synthesis of Reactive Systems: A Generic Layered Architecture Perspective.* PhD thesis, Department of Computer Science, Linköping University, 1999. Linköping Studies in Science and Technology, Dissertation No 613.
25. M. Lin. Synthesis of control software in a layered architecture from hybrid automata. In F. W. Vaandrager and J. H. van Schuppen, editors, *Hybrid Systems: Computation and Control*, LNCS 1569, pages 152–164. Springer-Verlag, 1999.
26. M. Lin. Timing analysis of PL programs. In *Proc. 24th IFAC/IFIP Workshop on Real-Time Programming*, Schloss Dagstuhl, Germany, 1999.
27. M. Lin and J. Malec. Timing analysis of RL programs. *Control Engineering Practice*, 6:403–408, 1998. Also in: Real-Time Programming 1997, M. Maranzana (ed.), Pergamon Press, 1997.
28. M. Lin and J. Malec. Control of a manufacturing cell using a generic layered architecture. In *Proc. Int. Workshop on Robot Motion and Control*, Kiekrz, Poland, 1999.
29. J. Malec, M. Morin, and U. Palmqvist. Driver support in intelligent autonomous cruise control. In *Proceedings of the IEEE Intelligent Vehicles Symposium'94*, pages 160–164, Paris, France, October 1994. IEEE.
30. J. Malec. Applied knowledge representation. *CC-AI: The Journal for the Integrated Study of Artificial Intelligence, Cognitive Science and Applied Epistemology*, 9(1):9–41, 1992.
31. J. Malec. On implementing behaviours using a three-layered architecture. In A. Borkowski and J. L. Crowley, editors, *Proceedings of the 2nd International Symposium on Intelligent Robotic Systems*, pages 62–69, Grenoble, France, July 1994.
32. J. Malec. A unified approach to intelligent agency. In [47], pages 233–244.

33. M. Mesarovic, D. Macko, and Y. Takahara. *Hierarchical Multilevel Systems Theory.* Academic Press, New York, 1970.

34. M. Morin. Predictable cyclic computations in autonomous systems: A computational model and implementation. Licentiate thesis 352, Department of Computer and Information Sciences, Linköping University, 1993.

35. M. Morin. PLCL – Process Layer Configuration Language. Technical Report LAIC-IDA-91-TR10, Linköping University, 1991.

36. M. Morin. RL: An embedded rule-based system. Technical Report LAIC-IDA-94-TR2, Linköping University, 1994.

37. M. Morin, S. Nadjm-Tehrani, P. Österling, and E. Sandewall. Real-time hierarchical control. *IEEE Software*, 9(5):51–57, September 1992.

38. J. P. Müller. The right agent (architecture) to do the right thing. In Müller et al. [40], pages 211–225.

39. J. P. Müller, M. Pischel, and M. Thiel. A pragmatic approach to modeling autonomous interacting systems – preliminary report. In [47], pages 226–240.

40. J. P. Müller, M. P. Singh, and A. S. Rao, editors. *Intelligent Agents V, Agent Theories, Architectures and Languages*, volume LNAI 1555 of *LNCS*. Springer, 1999.

41. D. J. Musliner. CIRCA: The Cooperative Intelligent Real-Time Control Architecture. PhD Thesis, The University of Michigan, 1993.

42. A. S. Rao and M. P. Georgeff. A model-theoretic approach to the verification of situated reasoning systems. In IJCAI-93 [17], pages 318–324.

43. S. J. Russell and D. Subramanian. Provably bounded-optimal agents. *Journal of Artificial Intelligence Research*, 2:575–609, 1995.

44. E. Sandewall. *Features and Fluents.* Oxford University Press, 1994.

45. J. A. Stankovic. Real-time computing systems: The next generation. In *IEEE Tutorial on Hard Real-Time Systems*, pages 14–37. Computer Society Press, 1988.

46. W. Wobcke. On the correctness of PRS agent programs. In Jennings and Lespérance [19], pages 42–56.

47. M. J. Wooldridge and N. R. Jennings, editors. *Intelligent Agents, Agent Theories, Architectures and Languages*, volume LNAI 890 of *LNCS*. Springer, 1995.

48. S. Zilberstein and S. J. Russell. Anytime sensing, planning and action: A practical model for robot control. In IJCAI-93 [17], pages 1401–1407.

HAC: A Unified View of Reactive and Deliberative Activity

Marc S. Atkin, David L. Westbrook, and Paul R. Cohen

Experimental Knowledge Systems Laboratory
Department of Computer Science
140 Governor's Drive
University of Massachusetts, Amherst, MA 01003-4610, USA
{atkin,westy,cohen}@cs.umass.edu

Abstract. The Hierarchical Agent Control Architecture (HAC) is a general toolkit for specifying an agent's behavior. By organizing the hierarchy around tasks to be accomplished, not the agents themselves, it is easy to incorporate multi-agent actions and planning into the architecture. In addition, HAC supports action abstraction, resource management, sensor integration, and is well suited to controlling large numbers of agents in dynamic environments. Unlike other agent architectures, HAC does not conceptually distinguish reactive from deliberative, or single-agent from multi-agent behaviors. There is no pre-determined number of cognitive "levels" in the hierarchy—all actions share the same form and are implemented with the same functions. GRASP is a multi-goal partial hierarchical planner that has been implemented using the HAC framework. GRASP illustrates two points: Firstly, that the same HAC mechanisms used to write reactive actions can be used to implement a cognitive activity such as planning; and secondly, that the problem of integrating reactive and deliberative behavior itself can be viewed as having to simultaneously achieve multiple goals. Throughout the paper, we show how HAC and GRASP were applied to an adversarial, real-time domain based on the game of "Capture the Flag".

1 Introduction

In the Experimental Knowledge Systems Laboratory, we have developed a number of complex simulations. PHOENIX, a system that uses multiple agents to fight fires in a realistic simulated environment, is perhaps the best example [8]. We have also made efforts to write general simulation substrates [1,5]. Currently, we are working on creating a system which will allow army commanders to design and evaluate high level plans ("courses of action") in a land-based campaign.

It quickly became apparent that regardless of the domain, agent designers must face the same kinds of problems: processing sensor information, reacting to a changing environment in a timely manner, integrating reactive and cognitive processes to achieve an abstract goal, interleaving planning and execution, distributed control, allowing code reuse within and across domains, and

M. Hannebauer et al. (Eds.): Reactivity and Deliberation in MAS, LNAI 2103, pp. 92–107, 2001.

using computational resources efficiently. This led to the development of a general framework for controlling agents, called *Hierarchical Agent Control* (HAC). HAC has many unique features—the one we will be focusing on here is its ability to seamlessly integrate reactive and cognitive processes.

2   HAC: Hierarchical Agent Control

HAC can be viewed as a set of language constructs and support mechanisms for describing agent behavior. HAC takes care of the mechanics of executing the code that controls an agent, passing messages between actions, coordinating multiple agents, arbitrating resource conflicts between agents, and updating sensor values. Although our primary application has been a military simulation system called "Capture the Flag" [3] (see Fig. 1), HAC can equally well be applied to such domains as commercial games, multi-agent simulations, or actual physical

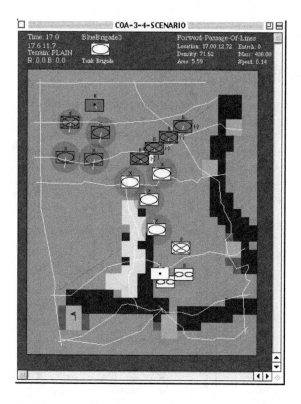

Fig. 1. The Capture the Flag domain (CtF). There are two teams; each has a number of movable units and flags to protect. They operate on a map which has different types of terrain. Terrain influences movement speed and forms barriers; terrain also affects unit visibility. A team wins when it captures all its opponent's flags

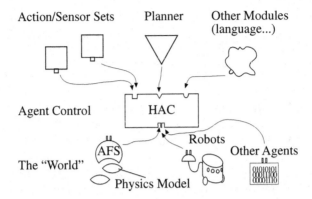

Fig. 2. The HAC system modules and organization. AFS is the "Abstract Force Simulator", a general simulator of forces and units in which CtF was implemented

robots [5]. Figure 2 shows how HAC relates to other system components we have developed.

2.1   The Action Hierarchy

HAC organizes the agent's actions in a hierarchy (see Fig. 3). The very lowest levels are the agent's effectors. The set of effectors will depend on the agent and the domain, but typically include being able to move the agent, turn it, or use a special ability such as firing a weapon. More complex actions are built from these primitive ones. An **attack** action, for example, may move to a target's location and fire at it. As one goes up the hierarchy, actions become increasingly abstract

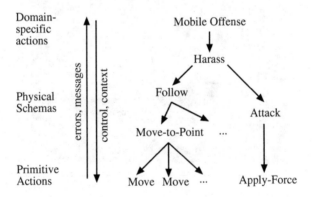

Fig. 3. Actions form a hierarchy; control information is passed down, messages are passed up. The lowest level are agent effectors; the middle layer consists of more complex, yet domain-general actions called *physical schemas* [4]. Above this level we have domain-specific actions

and powerful. They solve more difficult problems, such as path planning, and can react to a wide range of eventualities.

A hierarchy of sensors parallels the action hierarchy. Just as a more complex action uses simpler ones to accomplish its goal, complex sensors use the values of simpler ones. These are *abstract sensors*. They are not physical, since they do not sense anything directly from the world. They take the output of other sensors and integrate and re-interpret it. A low-level vision system (a physical sensor) produces a black and white pixel array. An abstract sensor might take this image and mark line segments in it. A higher level abstract sensor takes the line segments and determines whether there is a stretch of road ahead. A **follow-road** action can use this abstract sensor to compute where to go next. Abstract sensors are used throughout HAC and GRASP to notify actions and plans of unexpected or unpredictable events.

HAC executes actions by scheduling them on a queue. The queue is sorted by the time at which the action will execute. Actions get taken off the queue and executed until there are no more actions that are scheduled to run at this time step. Actions can reschedule themselves, but in most cases, they will be rescheduled when woken up by messages from their children. An action is executed by calling its **realize** method. The realize method does not generally complete the action on its first invocation; it just does what needs to be done on this tick. In most cases, an action's **realize** method will be called many times before the action terminates.

HAC is a *supervenient* architecture [20]. It abides by the principle that higher levels should provide goals and context for the lower levels, and lower levels provide sensory reports and messages to the higher levels ("goals down, knowledge up"). A higher level cannot overrule the sensory information provided by a lower level, nor can a lower level interfere with the control of a higher level. Supervenience structures the abstraction process; it allows us to build modular, reusable actions. HAC simplifies this process further by enforcing that every action's implementation (its **realize** method) take the following form:

1. React to messages coming in from children.
2. Update state.
3. Schedule new child actions if necessary.
4. Send messages up to parent.

Figure 3 shows a small part of an action hierarchy. The **follow** action, for example, relies on a **move-to-point** action to reach a specified location. **Move-to-point** will send status reports to **follow** if necessary; at the very least a completion message (failure or success). The only responsibility of the **follow** action is to issue a new target location if the agent being followed moves. HAC is an architecture; other than enforcing a general form, it does not place any constraints on how actions are implemented. Every action can choose what messages it will respond to. Parents can run in parallel with their children or only when the child completes.

2.2   An Example Action Definition

This section will elucidate the action-writing process using a concrete example. HAC provides a number of methods to make the process of writing actions easier. Across actions we must perform the same sorts of tasks: generating messages for the parent, advancing the action, etc. In HAC, actions are classes; each action defines a set of methods that address these tasks.

Figure 4 shows the implementation of a multi-agent action, **swarm**. It is a simple action that causes a number of agents to move around randomly within a circular region. We use the simpler action **move-to-point** to implement this; it is invoked with the construct **start-new-child**. When the agents bump or get stuck, they change direction. First, we define the **swarm** action to be a level-n-action. This means it can schedule children (as opposed to a primitive

```
(defclass* swarm (level-n-action)
  (area                          ;swarm area
  (agents nil)                   ;agents involved in swarm
  ;; storage
  (first-call t)))

(defmethod handle-message ((game-state game-state) (action swarm)
                            (message completion))
  (redirect game-state action (agent (from message))))

(defmethod handle-message ((game-state game-state) (action swarm)
                            (message afs-movement-message))
  (interrupt-action game-state (from message))
  (redirect game-state action (agent (from message))))

(defmethod redirect ((game-state game-state) (action swarm) agent)
  (start-new-child action game-state 'move-to-point
                   :agent agent
                   :destination-geom (make-destination-geom
                        (random-location-in-geom (area action)))
                   :messages-to-generate
                        '(completion contact no-progress-in-movement)
                   :speed nil
                   :terminal-velocity nil))

(defmethod check-and-generate-message ((game-state game-state)
                                (action swarm) (type (eql 'completion)))
  (values nil))       ;never completes

(defmethod realize ((game-state game-state) (action swarm))
  (when (first-call action)
    (setf (first-call action) nil)
    (loop for agent in (agents action) do
          (redirect game-state action agent)))))
```

Fig. 4. Implementation of a multi-agent "swarm" behavior in HAC

action which changes an agent's effector directly) and must handle messages from below as well as pass messages up. We define how we will react to messages from children using the **handle-message** methods. Message handlers specialize on the type of message that a child might send. In the example, we redirect an agent to a new location when the **move-to-point** action controlling it completes. If the **move-to-point** reports any kind of error (all errors relating to movement are subclasses of **afs-movement-message**), such as contact with another agent, we simply interrupt it and redirect the agent somewhere else.

These **handle-message** methods are invoked whenever a message of the specified type is sent to **swarm**. When this happens, the realize method is also called. In our example, the realize method is only used for initialization: the first time it is called, it sends all the agents off to random locations.

The set of **check-and-generate** methods define the set of messages that this action can send up to its parents. When the realize message is called, the **check-and-generate** methods are invoked. The swarm example never completes, and it doesn't report on its status, so it generates no messages.

The **swarm** action is invoked by creating an instance of it and giving it resources, i.e. agents, to work with.

2.3   Action Idioms

There are many commonalities in the way actions are constructed, and in the interest of streamlining the action design process, we have made more and more of these *action idioms* part of the HAC support mechanisms. Eventually, we would like writing actions in HAC to be like putting together a structure from building blocks.

Every action checks for messages from its children and generates messages to its parents. These functions are performed by the methods, **handle-message** and **check-and-generate-message**, respectively, which are specialized on the type of event to be processed. Typically these methods run before the main body of the **realize** method, but **check-and-generate** can take an optional argument to run afterwards. **Handle-message** handlers are also used to process messages sent by abstract sensors.

We often found that many **realize** methods did a lot of one-time initializations on the their first invocation, so we added a construct to deal with this. We also found that certain types of child–parent configurations were a lot more common than others. We introduced language features to support these common idioms: Child actions can be specified to execute sequentially or in parallel; an action can complete when any child completes, they all complete, or when some other condition is met; actions can use no, one, or multiple resources.

The issue of resource management quickly became paramount in the design of intelligent actions. HAC contains a number of mechanisms for managing resources and assigning resources to actions. When children are invoked, they are passed a specified subset of the parent's resources. Mechanisms exist to steal resources from one action and assign them to another, to notify an action when a resource is no longer available, or to find resources of a certain type. Some resources can only be used by one agent at a time, some are consumed, and some emerge only in the process of performing an action.

2.4   Deliberative vs. Reactive Behavior

Unlike the other architectures discussed in this volume, HAC does not define a clear dividing line between reactive and deliberative behaviors. In our view, reactive behaviors are those that execute quickly and do not require many of the agent's computational resources. Not only do they execute quickly, they are also activated very quickly. Reflexes such as ducking away from a looming object or spreading ones arms out when falling are good examples.

Deliberative behavior lies on the other end of the spectrum. Decisions on how to implement the behavior may take longer, as well as the behavior's execution. Planning is a perfect example for this: planning takes time—an agent will typically continue with other activities while the planning process executes.

Carpin [6] and Mavromichaelis [17] distinguish between reactive and deliberative systems by the amount of information used to make a decision. Our view is slightly different, we emphasize the cost of the decision (measured primarily in time). Naturally, one consequence of making a decision about what to do next quickly is that not as much information processing can be done.

Conceptually, every action in the HAC hierarchy is operating in its own time-frame, parallel with the others. Actions lower in the hierarchy tend to be more reactive, and those higher up tend to be more deliberative. The transition between them is smooth and completely up to the designer, and will depend on the domain. In physical systems, for example, issues of real-time performance are much more pressing[1]. Unlike other architectures, HAC does not prescribe a preset number of behavioral levels.

3   The GRASP Planner

This section will illustrate how a very deliberative action such as planning fits into HAC's action hierarchy. One way to look at planning is as a generalization of the process of scheduling a child action. Every action achieves some goal, even if this goal is not explicitly stated. The action **move-to-point** achieves the goal of getting to a specified location. Such goals are simple in that there is usually one good way to achieve them. As one goes up in the hierarchy, goals become a lot more complex: How should one go about achieving the goal **win-the-war**? Planning is necessary when there are several competing procedures for a achieving a goal, and when some form a search (as opposed to a simple test) is required to decide among them. So the purpose of a planner is to take a goal, and decide which child actions to schedule in order to achieve this goal.

---

[1]   The current HAC engine imposes no constraints on the CPU time used by an action. However, HAC could be made to work with real-time systems by replacing the centralized action queue by a more general mechanism that simply forwards events to the appropriate action, whether it is a local action running on the same piece of hardware or an action running remotely.

3.1   Multi-goal Partial Hierarchical Planning

HAC's planner is called GRASP (General Reasoning using AbStract Physics). GRASP is a least-commitment partial hierarchical planner [15]. Such planners are particularly well suited to continuous and unpredictable domains such as CtF, where the plan space branching factor can be very high. Partial hierarchical planners rely on a library of plan skeletons. Plan skeletons are plans that are not fully elaborated: they may contain unbound variables or subgoals which are not filled in until run-time. In HAC, plan skeletons are implemented as actions that explicitly state the goal they achieve.

GRASP is invoked by scheduling a specific action, **match-goal**, as a child. **Match-goal** takes as an argument a goal (or set of goals) to be satisfied. It then consults the plan library, checking which plans satisfy this goal. Using the algorithm outlined in Fig. 5, it chooses the best plan (or set of plans). During the matching process, unbound variables in the plan are instantiated—others are instantiated by the plan itself when it runs. When **match-goal** has selected a plan, it terminates, and schedules the best plan as a child action of the action that called it. This is completely transparent to the caller: the caller starts the planning process by posting a goal, and ends up with a child action that satisfies this goal. This child action can, in turn, post subgoals using the same process.

An action or a plan posts a set of goals $G = \{g_1, g_2, ...g_n\}$. This invokes the following process:

1. For every g_i:
   1.1 Search the list of plans for those that can satisfy g_i.
   1.2. Evaluate each potential plan's pre-conditions and only keep only those whose pre-conditions match.
   1.3. For each remaining plan, estimate it's required resources.
2. Sort G by the priority of g_i.
3. *candidate_plan_sets* := nil.
4. Loop over g_i in order of priority:
   4.1 If only one plan achieves g_i, instantiate it (bind unbound variables) and add it to every plan set in *candidate_plan_sets*; otherwise:
   4.2 If several plans achieve g_i, score each one based on:
       - how many resources it uses
       - how many other goals in G it (partially) satisfies
       - other plan-specific heuristics
   4.3 Choose m (m is rarely > 1 to limit combinatorics) of the highest scoring plans: $p_1, ..., p_m$
   4.4 Loop over remaining $g_j (j > i)$: if g_i partially satisfies g_j, merge g_j into $p_1, ..., p_m$
   4.5 Copy the plan sets in *candidate_plan_sets* m times; add p_k to copy k.
5. Loop over *plan_set* in *candidate_plan_sets*:
   5.1 Evaluate *plan_set* using forward simulation.
6. Execute the plan set (make them child actions of the goal poster) that in simulation, results in a world state with the highest score.

Fig. 5. The planning algorithm

If **match-goal** finds no appropriate plan, it fails just like any other action, sending an unsuccessful completion message to the goal poster. If a plan fails *during* its execution, it too can send a failure message to its parent. One way for the parent to react to this message would be for it to try calling **match-goal** again, in effect triggering a re-plan.

In HAC, actions run in parallel with each other. At every tick, the **realize** method of every scheduled action is called. Since planning is usually a time-consuming process, we have implemented **match-goal** so that it spreads its computations over several ticks.

GRASP extends the traditional partial hierarchical planning framework by allowing multiple goals to be associated with a resource or set of resources. These are not simply conjunctive goals; instead, goals are prioritized. GRASP uses heuristics in order to achieve the largest set of high priority goals possible.

In the Capture the Flag domain, winning involves coordinating multiple sub-goals: protecting your own flags, thwarting enemy offensives, choosing the most vulnerable enemy flag for a counter-attack, and so on. Each requires resources (units) to be accomplished. Sometimes one resource can be used to achieve several tasks. For instance, if two flags are close together, one unit might protect both. Or, advancing towards an opponent's flag might also force the opponent to retreat, thus relieving some pressure on one's own flags.

Figure 6 shows an example of the plan generation procedure. Each goal is prioritized, then plans are generated to achieve each one. Heuristics are used to generate a small number of possible plan sets. If resource problems arise during a plan's execution (because a resource was destroyed and the plan using it cannot succeed without it, for example), a resource error message is sent to the plan initiator using the HAC messaging mechanism, possibly causing resources to be re-assigned or a complete replan to take place.

When several plans apply, partial hierarchical planners typically select one according to heuristic criteria. GRASP instead performs a qualitative simulation on each candidate plan (or plan set). Potential plans are simulated forward, then a static evaluation function is applied to select the best plan [2]. The static evaluation function incorporates such factors as relative strength and the number of captured and threatened flags of both teams to describe how desirable the resulting world state is.

3.2   An Example Plan

Figure 7 shows a simplified version of the **block** plan, as implemented in CtF. **Block** protects units or flags; it is applicable when the enemy must travel via choke-points (referred to as "passes" in the plan) to reach the unit being protected. During the plan matching procedure (step 1.2 in Fig. 5), the passes necessary to protect the target are computed with the help of **init-plan** and stored in the plan's "passes" slot. The plan's **realize** method invokes the child action **block-pass** to send units to block each of the passes. Plans notify their parents if they have completed—just as actions do. The plan's **check-and-generate** methods aren't depicted here, but one failure condition for the **block** plan is

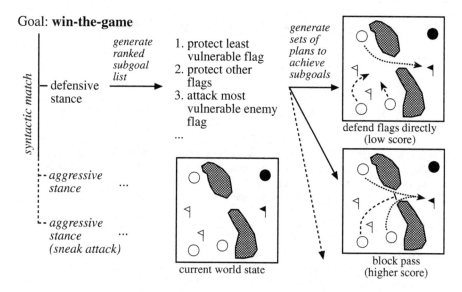

Goal: **win-the-game**

syntactic match

— defensive stance

generate ranked subgoal list

1. protect least vulnerable flag
2. protect other flags
3. attack most vulnerable enemy flag
...

generate sets of plans to achieve subgoals

defend flags directly (low score)

block pass (higher score)

current world state

-- *aggressive stance*   ...

-- *aggressive stance* ... *(sneak attack)*

Fig. 6. A planning example: White is trying to satisfy the goal **win-the-game**. Several top-level plans match this goal; the example explores what happens when **defensive-stance** is expanded. This plan emphasizes defense, which is reflected in the list of subgoals generated. There are several sets of plans that achieve these subgoals, and many ways to allocate resources to these plans. The planner uses heuristics to prune this set. In the first case, two units are allocated to flag defense, and one is sent out to attack. In the second case, only one unit is needed to block the mountain pass, thus protecting the flags, leaving two units for the attack. This plan set is more likely to succeed and is ranked higher

when any of the passes it's blocking is breached. The plan's precondition checks if any passes have already been breached before the plan even starts. If so, the plan is not considered further. The plan's resource estimation is actually a little more sophisticated than indicated by the figure, where **estimate-required-resources** simply returns a total mass value that depends on the number of passes. In the actual system, resource types and numbers are also taken into consideration.

The method **merge-plans** defines how this plan can be merged with others. In the case of **block**, we specify that **block** plans can only be merged with other **block** plans (all other combinations leave the original plans untouched). Merging occurs by creating one large plan that protects the union of the two pass sets. If the two plans share passes, this will result in a new plan that requires fewer resources to do the same job. The **goal-congruence** method also uses the set of common passes: it returns a number larger than 0 if both plans have at least one pass they are trying to protect in common.

```
(define-action block-ps-plan (plan protect-goal level n-action)
  (
   ;; storage
   (passes nil)    ;list of passes to block
   )
  :pre-conditions
    (not (passes-breached? passes)) ;; plan not applicable if any
                                    ;; passes already breached

(defmethod init-plan ((game-state game-state) (action block-ps-plan))
  "Any plan initializations that must occur after the plan's slot have
  been bound but before its pre-conditions are evaluated."
  (setf (passes action) (compute-passes-to-block)))

(defmethod realize ((game-state game-state) (action block-ps-plan))
  (when (first-call action)
    (dolist (pass (passes action))
      (setq blob (find-closest-blob (pass (resources action))))
      (setq resources (remove blob resourcess))
      (when blob
        (start-new-child action game-state 'block-pass
                         :blob blob
                         :resources (list blob)
                         :pass pass)))))

(defmethod estimate-required-resources ((action block-ps-plan))
  ;; determine passes that need blocking to protect this flag
  (setf (required-mass action) (* (length (passes action))
                                 *default-block-mass*)))

(defmethod merge-plans :after ((planA block-ps-plan)
                               (planB block-ps-plan))
  "Merge 'planB' into 'planA'."
  (setf (passes planA) (union (passes planA) (passes planB)))
  )

(defmethod goal-congruence ((planA block-ps-plan) (planB block-ps-plan))
  "To what degree (0..1) does 'planA's objectives also satisfy 'planB's?"
  (let ((common-passes-count (length (intersection (passes planA)
                                                   (passes planB))))
        (B-passes-count (length (passes planB))))
    (values (if (zerop B-passes-count)
                0.0
                (/ common-passes-count B-passes-count)))))
```

Fig. 7. Implementation of the "block" plan in CtF

3.3   Latent Goals

GRASP handles multiple goals. The issue of multiple goals was motivated in CtF when we found it important for agents to react opportunistically to unforeseen events. If an agent is moving to attack another unit, for example, and notices a flag along the way, it should in most cases interrupt its previous activity to capture the flag, then resume its attack.

As was stated previously, planning is the process of finding good solutions to explicitly stated goals. This section will address the problem of how to integrate solutions that have very different time scales. Put another way: How does one achieve multiple goals when some plans are reactive and some deliberative?

In GRASP, we handle this by introducing the concept of a *latent goal*. A latent goal is one that is not active all the time, but only when some condition holds. In order to prevent the planner from having to consider many goals, most of which are not applicable at any given time, we make these conditional goals latent. They are only considered by the planner when their triggering condition becomes true.

Let us introduce the following terms:

Goals Static symbols that a number of plans can satisfy.

Latent goals Goals that become active when a condition holds.

Sentinels An abstract sensor that monitors the world to check for the applicability of a latent goal.

When a latent goal is created for an agent (or group of agents), a sentinel is set up. When the sentinel activates, the associated latent goal is added to the set of goals these agents must consider. The latent goal now behaves exactly like a goal in a normal multi-goal set. When the triggering condition is no longer met, the latent goal is removed. A replan is triggered whenever an agent's goals change. If a latent goal should be achieved at any cost, even to the exclusion of other goals, the latent goal's priority can be set to a value higher than that of any other goal. Figure 8 illustrates this process.

Latent goals are not the same as conditional goals, used in many procedural languages. Conditional goals are created within a plan; the plan itself checks for their applicability and coordinates them with other goals being achieved. GRASP, on the other hand, places the burden of resolving latent goals on the *planner*. A plan need not know about the latent goals that may pop up during its execution.

Latent goals provide a mechanism for specifying the *context* under which an agent operates. The set of latent goals can be viewed as the set of common sense or implicit assumptions an agent should always be considering when trying to achieve the task at hand. In the same vein, reactive actions can be viewed as plans that achieve short-term goals. Frequently, these short-term goals arise unexpectedly (for example, an "obstacle avoidance" goal may be generated in the context of a **move-to-point** action). By extending GRASP to handle multiple goals, short-term goals can be reacted to without compromising the plans that are still executing to achieve the longer term ones.

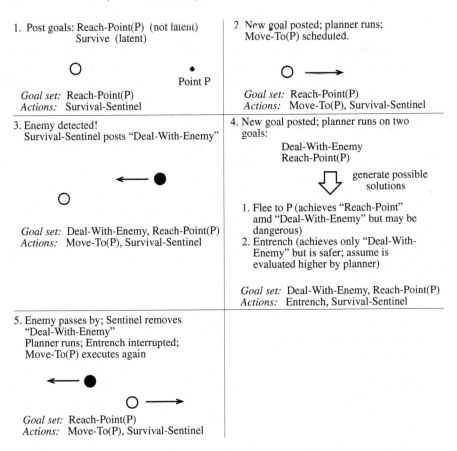

1. Post goals: Reach-Point(P) (not latent)
            Survive (latent)

Goal set: Reach-Point(P)
Actions: Survival-Sentinel

Point P

2. New goal posted; planner runs;
   Move-To(P) scheduled.

Goal set: Reach-Point(P)
Actions: Move-To(P), Survival-Sentinel

3. Enemy detected!
   Survival-Sentinel posts "Deal-With-Enemy"

Goal set: Deal-With-Enemy, Reach-Point(P)
Actions: Move-To(P), Survival-Sentinel

4. New goal posted; planner runs on two
   goals:
            Deal-With-Enemy
            Reach-Point(P)

   generate possible
   solutions

1. Flee to P (achieves "Reach-Point"
   amd "Deal-With-Enemy" but may be
   dangerous)
2. Entrench (achieves only "Deal-With-
   Enemy" but is safer; assume is
   evaluated higher by planner)

Goal set: Deal-With-Enemy, Reach-Point(P)
Actions: Entrench, Survival-Sentinel

5. Enemy passes by; Sentinel removes
   "Deal-With-Enemy"
   Planner runs; Entrench interrupted;
   Move-To(P) executes again

Goal set: Reach-Point(P)
Actions: Move-To(P), Survival-Sentinel

Fig. 8. Latent goal example, showing how an agent's goal and action sets change over time. The white agent has the goal of reaching point P (Step 1). Along the way, an enemy is sighted, prompting the agent's "survival" sentinel to post a goal to deal with the enemy (Step 3). The planner is invoked and attempts to achieve both these goals (Step 4). The solution that achieves both (fleeing) is considered too dangerous; instead, the agent entrenches. After the enemy has passed, the "Deal-With-Enemy" goal is removed, the planner runs again, and the agent resumes moving to P (Step 5)

4 Summary and Related Work

This paper has introduced HAC as a domain-general agent design tool. These are the issues we believe HAC addresses well:

- Agent control, action execution, planning, and sensing are all part of the same framework.
- Resources are explicitly modeled.

- Actions are not monolithic entities that always run to completion. Actions send messages about their status, completion (either successful or unsuccessful), or problems. They can be and often are interrupted or rescheduled.
- HAC is a modular system; supervenience enables us build re-usable action modules.
- Latent goals allow unforeseen events to be exploited.
- By organizing the hierarchy around *tasks that have to be accomplished*, it was very easy to incorporate multi-agent actions and planning into our architecture. Resources are the agents that implement actions.

The GRASP planner integrates a number of new and old ideas to deal with continuous and adversarial domains in real-time. It builds upon the established notion of a control hierarchy, used in many agent architectures and hierarchical task network planners (e.g., [22,9]). The idea of reasoning using procedural knowledge has also been used in a number of other systems, including PRS [14], PRS-Lite [19], RESUN [7], PHOENIX [8], the data analysis system AIDE [21], and in languages for reactive control such as RAP [10], XFRM [18] and PROPEL [16]. The APEX architecture also attempts to manage multiple tasks in complex, uncertain environments, placing particular emphasis on the problem of resolving resources conflicts [13].

Although many systems reason about multiple concurrent goals, GRASP is unique among partial hierarchical planners in that it places much of the burden of resolving these goals on the planner, using the availability of resources as its primary heuristic. Unlike PRS and RAP, for example, GRASP does not require the designer of actions (tasks) to anticipate every possible event interaction. Plans that react to unforeseen events can be kept conceptually separate from those that are implementing longer term goals.

Like PRS, HAC allows for the specification of blocking and non-blocking children (child actions that run in sequence with their parents or in parallel), and like later versions of RAP [11], success and failure are treated like any other message, and do not implicitly determine the flow of control between actions.

HAC and GRASP use the same representation for actions at all levels of the hierarchy, and also for plans and sensors. Contrast this with the majority of current agent control architectures, e.g. CYPRESS [23] and RAP [12], which distinguish between procedural low-level "skills" or "behaviors" and higher level symbolic reasoning. Different systems are often used to implement each level (CYPRESS combines SIPE-2 and PRS, for example). HAC does not conceptually differentiate between discrete actions and continuous processes, nor does it limit the language used to describe them. HAC provides a very general execution model that the designer must abide by, consisting of a hierarchy of actions, running in parallel, that send messages to one another. It attempts to simplify the process of writing actions by defining a language, in the form of macros and functions, that can be used in their implementation.

Acknowledgments. This research is supported by DARPA/USAF/ISO under contract numbers F30602-99-C-0061 and F30602-97-1-0289. The U.S. Government is authorized to reproduce and distribute reprints for governmental purposes notwithstanding any copyright notation hereon. The views and conclusions contained herein are those of the authors and should not be interpreted as necessarily representing the official policies or endorsements either expressed or implied, of the Defense Advanced Research Projects Agency/Air Force Materiel Command or the U.S. Government.

References

1. S. D. Anderson. *A Simulation Substrate for Real-Time Planning.* PhD thesis, University of Massachusetts at Amherst, February 1995. Also available as Computer Science Department Technical Report 95-80.
2. M. S. Atkin and P. R. Cohen. Using simulation and critical points to define states in continuous search spaces. In *Proceedings of the 2000 Winter Simulation Conference*, pages 464–470, 2000.
3. M. S. Atkin, D. L. Westbrook, and P. R. Cohen. Capture the Flag: Military simulation meets computer games. In *Proceedings of AAAI Spring Symposium Series on AI and Computer Games*, pages 1–5, 1999.
4. M. S. Atkin, D. L. Westbrook, and P. R. Cohen. Domain-general simulation and planning with physical schemas. In *Proceedings of the 2000 Winter Simulation Conference*, pages 1730–1738, 2000.
5. M. S. Atkin, D. L. Westbrook, P. R. Cohen, and G. D. Jorstad. AFS and HAC: Domain-general agent simulation and control. In *Working Notes of the Workshop on Software Tools for Developing Agents, AAAI-98*, pages 89–95, 1998.
6. S. Carpin, C. Ferrari, E. Pagello, and P. Patuelli. Bridging deliberation and reactivity in cooperative multi-robot systems through map focus. In M. Hannebauer, J. Wendler, and E. Pagello, editors, *Balancing Reactivity and Social Deliberation in Multi-agent Systems (this volume)*, pages 35–52. Springer, 2001.
7. N. Carver and V. Lesser. A planner for the control of problem solving systems. *IEEE Transactions on Systems, Man, and Cybernetics, special issue on Planning, Scheduling, and Control*, 23(6):1519–1536, November 1993.
8. P. R. Cohen, M. L. Greenberg, D. M. Hart, and A. E. Howe. Trial by fire: Understanding the design requirements for agents in complex environments. *AI Magazine*, 10(3):32–48, Fall 1989. also Technical Report, COINS Dept, University of Massachusetts.
9. K. Currie and A. Tate. O-Plan: The open planning architecture. *Artificial Intelligence*, 52:49–86, 1991.
10. R. J. Firby. An investigation into reactive planning in complex domains. In *Proceedings of the Sixth National Conference on Artificial Intelligence*, pages 202–206, Seattle, Washington, 1987.
11. R. J. Firby. Task networks for controlling continuous processes. In *Proceedings of the Second International Conference on Artificial Intelligence Planning Systems*, pages 49–54, 1994.
12. R. J. Firby. Modularity issues in reactive planning. In *Proceedings of the Third International Conference on Artificial Intelligence Planning Systems*, pages 78–85, 1996.
13. M. Freed. Managing multiple tasks in complex, dynamic environments. In *Proceedings of the Fifteenth National Conference on Artificial Intelligence*, pages 921–927, Madison, WI, 1998.

14. M. P. Georgeff and F. F. Ingrand. Decision-making in an embedded reasoning system. In *Proceedings of the Eleventh International Joint Conference on Artificial Intelligence*, pages 972–978, Detroit, Michigan, 1989. AAAI Press, Menlo Park, CA.

15. M. P. Georgeff and A. L. Lansky. Procedural knowledge. *Proceedings of the IEEE Special Issue on Knowledge Representation*, 74(10):1383–1398, 1986.

16. R. Levinson. A general programming language for unified planning and control. *Artificial Intelligence*, 76(1-2):319–375, 1995.

17. V. K. Mavromichalis and G. Vouros. Balancing between reactivity and deliberation in the ICAGENT framework. In M. Hannebauer, J. Wendler, and E. Pagello, editors, *Balancing Reactivity and Social Deliberation in Multi-agent Systems (this volume)*, pages 53–75. Springer, 2001.

18. D. McDermott. Transformational planning of robot behavior. Technical Report YALEU/CSD/RR #941, Yale University, New Haven, CT, December 1992.

19. K. L. Myers. A procedural knowledge approach to task-level control. In *Proceedings of the Third International Conference on Artificial Intelligence Planning Systems*, pages 158–165, 1996.

20. L. Spector and J. Hendler. The use of supervenience in dynamic-world planning. In Kristian Hammond, editor, *Proceedings of The Second International Conference on Artificial Intelligence Planning Systems*, pages 158–163, 1994.

21. R. St. Amant. *A Mixed-Initiative Planning Approach to Exploratory Data Analysis*. PhD thesis, University of Massachusetts, Amherst, 1996. Also available as technical report CMPSCI-96-33.

22. D. E. Wilkins. *Practical Planning: Extending the Classical AI Planning Paradigm*. Morgan Kaufmann, 1988.

23. D. E. Wilkins, K. L. Myers, J. D. Lowrance, and L. P. Wesley. Planning and reacting in uncertain and dynamic environments. *Journal of Experimental and Theoretical AI*, 7(1):197–227, 1995.

Part III

Enhanced Reactivity

Team Cooperation Using Dual Dynamics

Ansgar Bredenfeld and Hans-Ulrich Kobialka

GMD – Institute for Autonomous intelligent Systems (AiS)
Schloss Birlinghoven, D-53754 Sankt Augustin, Germany.
{bredenfeld,kobialka}@gmd.de
http://ais.gmd.de/be

Abstract. The design of autonomous mobile robots includes the design of team behaviors. We have extended the Dual Dynamics scheme for behavior design in order to let the designer specify team behavior. This approach comes with a tool suite for team behavior specification, simulation, and monitoring, and is used for the coordination of soccer playing robots.

1 Introduction

Teams of autonomous mobile robots present fascinating research perspectives for today, and likewise fascinating prospects for applications in the future. The challenge is to achieve team behavior that is both complex and robust. The main problems to be solved arise from the following communication requirements of a mobile robot team:

- The team is changing over time. Robots are added and removed.
- Team members have different control programs. They solve different tasks.
- Team cooperation has to be robust with respect to sensor noise and failures of the communication media.
- Autonomy and reactiveness of all team members has to be preserved.

Our testbed for research on robot team behavior is an uncompromising benchmark with severe demands on speed, complexity, and cooperation: the midsize league competition of the RoboCup [3]. In this application, teams of 4 autonomous mobile robots compete in a soccer game. In the last few years, the RoboCup has become an accepted benchmark, in which many robotics research institutes of international standing participate. Playing soccer involves many different kinds of actions, with complex relations and interactions between them. A hierarchical representation of actions and action selection control is a natural approach to handle this complexity [19].

The behavior description formalism that we develop is a mathematical model of a behavior control system, which to a certain degree integrates a behavior-based approach, robust control, a dynamical system's representation of actions and goals, and a hierarchical architecture. This is the Dual Dynamics (DD) scheme [15]. The development of behavior control systems according to the DD methodology is supported by a tool suite, the DD-Design Environment.

M. Hannebauer et al. (Eds.): Reactivity and Deliberation in MAS, LNAI 2103, pp. 111–124, 2001.

Dual Dynamics focuses on reactivity rather than planning. In fact, we intend to learn from human cognition where most capabilities are organized in a reactive fashion. This motivates us to look for reactive and decentralized solutions for problems which have been tackled by planning so far. Nevertheless, the integration of DD with a deliberative planner is investigated in another project (see Sect. 7).

As we searched for a team coordination concept for our soccer robots, we did it from a methodological perspective. We looked for a team coordination infrastructure

- that provides/enables appropriate solutions for the requirements listed above (team heterogeneity, dynamic team reconfiguration, robustness, and autonomy),
- that is smoothly integrated into the methodology and architecture of Dual Dynamics. For behavior designers, the additional learning effort regarding cooperation should be minimal.
- that is easy to use. The additional complexity introduced by distributed computing, unreliable communication, and dynamic team reconfiguration should be minimized.
- that does not restrict any reasonable cooperation policy. Examples of cooperation policies can be found in [1,6,10,11,12,18].

The paper is structured as follows. Section 2 gives a brief introductory overview of Dual Dynamics. Section 3 explains the approach we used to add communication to Dual Dynamics systems. It allows to specify reactive team behavior as a natural and orthogonal extension of a singular behavior system. Section 4 demonstrates our team behavior approach by an example taken from the team coordination of the GMD RoboCup robots. How team cooperation is specified, simulated, and tested by using the DD design environment is described in Sect. 5. In Sect. 6, we evaluate our approach with respect to our requirements and other related approaches. Dual dynamics and its design environment are also used for developing service robots in office environments (Sect. 7). In this project, we intend to demonstrate that our team cooperation infrastructure is well suited for many application areas beyond RoboCup.

2   Dual Dynamics

The Dual Dynamics (DD) theory combines ideas from self-organizing dynamical systems and hybrid control in order to mathematically specify/constrain the behavior of a robot.

The basic assumption on which DD rests is that a situated agent can work in different modes. Modes are coherent, relatively stable "frames of mind", which enable the agent to tune to different situations and tasks. Specifically, agents respond to sensory signals differently in different modes. The DD approach claims that transitions between modes can be formally captured by bifurcations of dynamical systems. A direct implication of casting mode changes as bifurcations

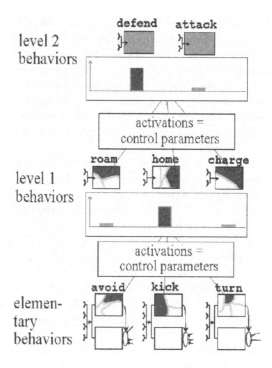

Fig. 1. Architecture of a Dual Dynamics behavior system

is that such changes are qualitative, discontinuous changes, not gradual ones. Our robots do not gradually change between modes. However, since these transitions are regulated by dynamical systems (in contrast to finite state machines), the decision point is dynamically and continuously tuned by the full wealth of incoming sensor information.

The main building blocks of a DD architecture are behavior modules, called *behaviors* for short.[1] Typical examples of behaviors are *kick* ("push the ball into the goal") or *turn* ("drive a curve to position behind the ball"). Behaviors are ordered in levels (Fig. 1). At the bottom level, there are elementary behaviors: motoric coordinations with direct access to incoming sensor data and actuators. Elementary behaviors are different from higher-level behaviors in that they are made from two parts which serve quite different purposes: target dynamics and activation dynamics. This has given the approach its name, "Dual Dynamics". The target dynamics define how the behavior interacts with the environment (i.e. how to react on sensor input) while the activation dynamics compute the activation of the behavior. The activation of a behavior modulates the effects of its target dynamics to the actuators (i.e. the motors).

---

[1] A behavior (module) has to be distinguished from the behavior of a robot which can be viewed by a human observer. A particular observed behavior may be influenced by several behavior modules.

An activation of a higher-level behavior acts as a control parameter for the activation dynamics of lower levels. The dynamical system which maintains a behavior's activation can undergo bifurcations; this is indicated by depicting these systems as stylized "phase diagrams" (boxes with irregular partitions in Fig. 1). At higher levels, there are increasingly comprehensive behaviors organized. Their task is to regulate modes. We emphasize that an elementary behavior is not "called to execute" from higher levels. The level of elementary behaviors is fully operative on its own and would continue to work even if the higher levels were cut off.

The effect of higher levels is neither to strictly "select", nor to softly "encourage" lower-level behaviors to become active but to change the overall, integrated dynamics of the entire elementary level, by inducing bifurcations in the activation dynamics on that level. This is the crucial distinction between DD and most other behavior-based architectures, e.g., the Saphira architecture [17] or the subsumption architecture [9]. In the Saphira architecture, low-level behaviors are explicitly activated from within a higher, symbolic reasoning control level; in the subsumption architecture, lower level behaviors can be inhibited by higher-level behaviors. In both instances, there is a direct influence on the activation of lower level behaviors from "higher up". In DD, the influence is not on the activation value itself, but on its regulation mechanism (i.e., the activation dynamics equation).

The DD architecture (Fig. 1) specifies the interplay of behaviors controlling a single robot. Such a set of behaviors is called a *behavior system*. In the next section, we show how behavior systems executing on different robots can cooperate.

3   Cooperation in Dual Dynamics

The need for team cooperation arises, since we have to design team behavior for our soccer playing robots. In a first approach, we implemented a central coordination agent which receives information from all robots and dominates them by sending them commands. This architecture conflicted with the autonomy of the robots, and so we looked for more suitable solutions.

Within a DD behavior system, all information (sensor readings and everything what is computed from it, like activations, actuator values) are stored in variables which are recomputed during each time step. This can be viewed as a kind of blackboard architecture. So a behavior system, which runs on a robot, has such a local blackboard where information is exchanged within the behavior system.

In order to connect local blackboards, we introduced so called *team variables* in the Dual Dynamics framework. A team variable is exported by a behavior system, so that other behavior systems can read its current value. Only the exporting behavior system is allowed to change the value of a team variable.

Conceptually, the set of team variables of all concurrently running behavior systems can be viewed as a global blackboard which is updated during each time

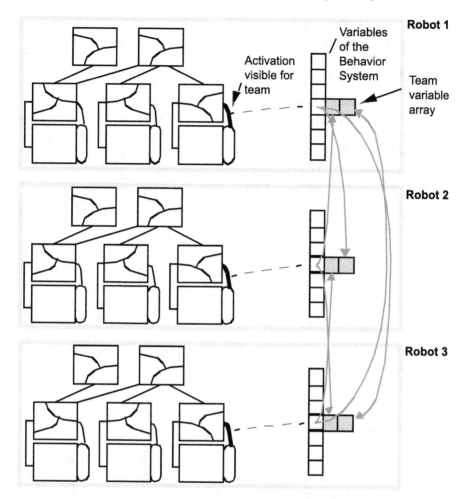

Fig. 2. A DD behavior system within which one variable is declared to be a team variable (the activation of the 3rd elementary behavior). This behavior system is executed concurrently on three robots. At runtime, the cooperation infrastructure detects that there are three robots publishing a team variable having the same name. The values are automatically distributed. At each site they are accessible in an array, one for each team variable. Array entries containing remote values are read-only (depicted as shaded)

step. Physically, the value of a team variable is transmitted to each robot (i.e. its behavior system) where a team variable *having the same name* is defined.

In a DD-model specification, the values of all remote team variables are accessible in an array. The size of the array corresponds to the number of robots which currently export team variable with the same name (see Fig. 2 for an example).

The characteristics of our solution are due to the flexibility which is needed in the RoboCup setting:

Heterogeneity. It can not be assumed that each robot in a soccer team uses the same behavior system. A goal keeper, for example, usually does not need knowledge about the internal states of an attack behavior. On the other hand, internal states of an attack behavior are essential for another striker in order to synchronize common actions targeted at the opponent's goal.

Dynamic Team Reconfiguration. Robots have to be replaced during a game: either robots are defect or they have to be removed from the field due to a referee decision after charging or any other rule violation. From a team variable point of view, this scenario requires to dynamically add or remove robots to a team and, consequently, to dynamically re-configure the team variable replication mechanism.

We tackled this problem by keeping track of all robots actually involved in a play situation. If a robot enters the field, it introduces itself to all active robots. As soon a connection between two robots is built up, they exchange information about the team variables whose values they intend to distribute or receive, respectively. This information is used to dynamically build mapping tables.

Behaviors should not be influenced by information of robots which have been taken off the field. Thus, the size of a team variable array grows and shrinks over time, depending on the number of active robots.

4   Team Behaviors in RoboCup

Cooperation in a team requires that the acting of a robot does not only depend on its state and sensor inputs, but also on the ones of its team mates. On the technical level, this means that the activation of a behavior (i.e. to which degree the behavior is active) is influenced by team variables. In the following, this should be illustrated by an example.

RoboCup robots usually try to go for the ball and kick it into the opponent's goal. This is quite trivial for a single robot on an empty field. Things get worse if several team mates are added: The robots crowd near the ball and disturb each other. In most cases the ball gets stuck between the robots, even they all want to move the ball to the same location, the opponent's goal.

Obviously only one robot should go for the ball. This should be the one which has the best chance to play the ball in a reasonable way. Each robot should decide if it makes sense to approach the ball, and, if yes, it has to calculate the chances and risks of several alternative behaviors. The rating of the most promising ball handling behavior is published via a team variable named GoForBallRating. A ball-handling behavior should only be active if the GoForBallRatings of all other robots are smaller than the own one. Similar approaches are used by other RoboCup teams, e.g., [6,11].

The rating of a ball handling behavior B depends on

- the chance C_B of getting to the ball before an opponent robot takes control of it (this is an important prerequisite). In particular, we use the length of the trajectory of the robot in order to get to the ball $L_{TrajSelf}$ and the distance between the ball and the nearest opponent robot D_{OpBall} to compute C as follows

$$C_B = \frac{1}{1 + e^{-80 \cdot (D_{OpBall} - L_{TrajSelf})}}$$

  C_B becomes zero if the ball position is not known.
- the value of its intention V_B (e.g., kicking the ball into the goal is more valuable then driving behind the ball),
- the probability P_B of achieving the intention (e.g. is there enough free space to drive with the ball), and
- the risk R_B implied by the execution of the behavior, e.g. will it cause any danger for the own goal.

The rating of behavior B is then

$$Rating_B = C_B \cdot V_B \cdot P_B \cdot R_B.$$

The ball handling behavior with the highest rating among all robots succeeds, i.e., this robot goes for the ball, while all other robots perform other (i.e. not ball handling) behaviors. Note that in this example (but also in general) we construct no global model of the "world" nor establish any consensus protocol. Each robot receives information from other robots and decides what to do.

Decisions (i.e. whether a behavior should be active or not) are computed by the activation dynamics. Figure 3 shows our way to compute the activation of a behavior using a canonical differential equation. Note that the activation is not computed in total, but only its change. In one time step, OnForces and OffForces increase/decrease the activation proportional to their time constants. In the example, if no force is on, the value of the activation remains the same (the equation is discussed with more detail in Fig. 4). These properties make activations robust with respect to noise on input variables, especially sensors, and disturbances, like delays, which typically occur in distributed systems.

Because the number and kind of concurrent behavior systems change over time (see Sect. 3), the example contains no assumptions regarding these. In general, team cooperation should perform in a reasonable way even if only one robot (i.e. behavior system) is currently active.

5   Realisation in the DD-Design Environment

The successful design of robot software requires means to specify, implement and simulate as well as to run and debug the robot software in real-time on a team of physical robots. We develop and utilize an integrated design environment [7,8] to specify Dual Dynamics models on a high-level of abstraction and to synthesize all

```
if ( Rating.... > GoForBallRatings of all other robots ) {
     OnFlag = 1;
} else{
     OnFlag = 0;
}
// the time constant of onForce (10) and offForce (5)
// determine how quick these forces can change the
// activation
onForce = 10 * OnFlag;
offForce = 5 * (1 - OnFlag);

decay = 3;
stability = 1;
bias = 0.5;

aKick' = - stability * aKick * (aKick - 1) * (aKick + 1 - bias)
         - onForce * (aKick + 0.1) * (aKick - 1)
         + offForce * (aKick - 1.1) * aKick
         - decay * aKick;

aKick = aKick + aKick' * deltaTime;
```

Fig. 3. The computation of the activation aKick of the ball handling behavior Kick depending on the team variable `GoForBallRating`. aKick ranges between 0 and 1 and determines to which degree the target dynamics of behavior Kick have influence on the motors

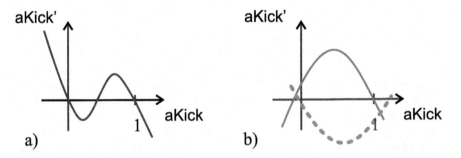

a)   b)

Fig. 4. The switching of a behavior's activation: The first line of the equation aKick' = ... in Fig. 3 is a cubic function which stabilizes aKick either in 0 or 1, see Fig. 4a). The OnForce drags the value towards 1 (upper curve in Fig. 4b)) and the OffForce towards 0 (lower curve). These forces influence aKick only when their conditions are fulfilled. Depending on the time constants, the forces need some time to switch aKick, i.e. there is some hysteresis

artifacts required to make DD models operative in practice: a detailed web-based documentation, a simulation model, a control program for a real robot, and a parameter set for real-time monitoring. At present, our environment consists of three interacting tools, the graphical specification and artifact generation tool

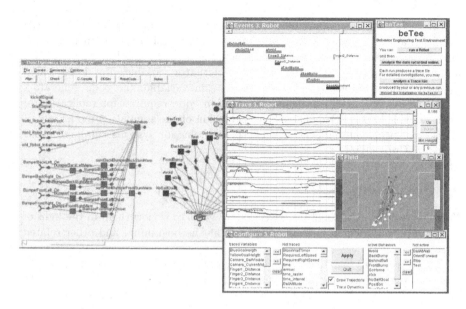

Fig. 5. Dual Dynamics Design Environment (*DD-Designer* + *beTee*)

Dual Dynamics Designer, the simulator *DDSim* and the real-time monitoring tool *beTee*.

DD-Designer is our specification and code generation tool. It comprises a graphical editor to enter the specification of a DD-model in terms of sensors, actors, sensor filters and behaviors. Sensor filters and behaviors are further detailed using the equation editor of *DD-Designer*. We use multi-target code generation to refine the DD-model to code artifacts required by the simulator *DDSim*, the real robot and the real-time monitoring tool *beTee*.

DDSim is a simulator to investigate a team of robots with different behavior systems on a RoboCup field. The simulation model is a generated Java class containing the implementation of a DD-model.

beTee is a real-time trace tool which allows to capture and analyze internal variable states of a DD-model either running on a robot or running in the *DDSim* simulator [16]. Both are connected to *beTee* via sockets. The configuration of *beTee* (i.e. how to interpret and visualize the data stream) is generated by the *DD-Designer*.

Figure 5 shows screen shots to give an impression of the designers view on robot behavior programming using Dual Dynamics. The left part shows *Dual Dynamics Designer* with a DD-model. Symbolic representations of sensors, sensor filters, behaviors and actuators are the main elements at the graphical interface. The right part shows *beTee* with a trajectory of the robot on a field and internal variables displayed either as lineplots in the middle or as event time traces in the upper left part of the screen shot.

Since we want to support team cooperation, we not only have to extend the Dual Dynamics framework, but also our behavior design environment. In the *DD Designer* this is done by adding a new feature to variables. Any variable, i.e., a sensor variable, an activation or an actuator variable, may be specified to be a team variable. If a variable is a team variable, the code generators of *DD-Designer* synthesize all implementation code required for replication of team variable values. This includes an extension of the simulation model and of course real-time communication between the behavior systems running on our real RoboCup robots.

6   Discussion

Now, as we have explained our concepts, we want to review them in the light of the requirements which have motivated us at the beginning, and other related approaches.

There are many particular concepts (or policies) of how robots should cooperate, for instance robots playing a soccer game [1,6,11,12]. Our aim was not to invent an additional one, but to create an cooperation infrastructure which can be used to implement any cooperation concept. It should be easy to use, robust (i.e. preserving autonomy while facing communication failures and breakdowns, and dynamic team reconfiguration), and integrated with the architecture of the behavior system which controls the robot.

6.1   Integration within a Methodological Framework or Architecture

There are not many papers discussing cooperation between autonomous robots while considering behavior based architectures. Still many control software for autonomous robots do not use behavior based architectures like the Subsumption Architecture [9], Saphira [17], 3T, Atlantis, motor schema [2], or Dual Dynamics. Instead the software is organized according to the preferences of the designer.

In [5], the motor schema architecture is used. The motor schema architecture was not extended, because the application (driving in a formation) did not require communication. Compared to this approach which has shown good results in simulations, our approach is based on mathematical techniques which increase the robustness of the behavior system when executing on real robots with noisy sensor input and communication delays.

We extended Dual Dynamics in a way that allows to express coordination within the DD scheme. We carefully avoided the introduction of additional powerful concepts, like messages or events. Compared to such a hybrid solution, the advantage of the extended DD scheme is its conceptual clarity.

6.2   Towards an "Easy to Use" Communication Paradigm

Many cooperation concepts define roles, their tasks, and policies of how robots obtain or switch between roles. Most approaches do not consider "low level" communication issues, like unreliable communication.

If we want to design a cooperation infrastructure, we need a paradigm for some language or interface which allows designers to implement their favorite cooperation concept in a quick and error-free way.

None the cooperation concepts we know in the context of robotics propose connection-based communication protocols (even they may use TCP on a lower level). This is because the design of such communication protocols is not a trivial job (especially if one wants to reach consensus while coping with unreliable communication) and carries the risk of delays and deadlocks.

More appropriate seem to be connection-less paradigms such as message-broadcasting or protocols known from bus-like communication, e.g. the CAN bus. In [11], all robot agents subscribe to a so-called team communication club and then receive all messages posted in this club.

The remaining open issue is how an incoming information is propagated to the control algorithm which drives the robot. For instance, if one uses the event-trigger paradigm (i.e. whenever a message arrives, an appropriate event is raised and some call-back procedures are invoked), this will lead to many asynchronous events and the designer has to care about how to get the "big picture" from that.

Another issue is the detection of outdated information and probably disconnected or "dead" team mates.

In our concept, these issues are handled "behind the curtains". The behavior system just operates on team variable arrays which may shrink or grow over time. The identity of robots is hidden. This facilitates the task of the designer, who has to implement a particular cooperation policy, a lot.

6.3   Robustness

Many approaches assume some reliable communication layer. In many cases, this may be a valid assumption. For instance, in the RoboCup small size league [6], the play has to stop when communication goes down because then the robots are disconnected from their main sensor, the camera mounted above the field. In the extended DD scheme, unreliable communication is considered at two levels:

1. The use of arrays containing the values of anonymous robots masks a lot of error conditions which are handled without tampering the designer.
2. In the extended DD framework, team variables can be handled (and in fact they are) like sensor data[2] (i.e. sensor variables). All available kinds of sensor filters can be directly applied to team data.

   In DD, all kind of variables can be made insensitive to sensor noise by using mathematical techniques like special kinds of differential equations. For example, the equation in Fig. 3 makes the robot robust with respect to communication failures and changing team mates.

Although the effects of unreliable communication and changing team mates can be limited, we suspect that these effects can not be totally excluded, even

---

[2] It is also feasible to have "remote" sensors (i.e. transmit sensor data from one robot to the other) within the extended DD scheme.

for "high level" cooperation concepts. So we expect some concepts to be not appropriate for real-time cooperation between robots, while in other concepts the handling of unreliability hopefully becomes "trivial".

7   Robot Cooperation in Office Environments

Service robots in office environments have requirements regarding a communication infrastructure which are similar to the ones for soccer robots. Service robots need to coordinate their activities as they come close to each other, for instance, when entering the same room. So, in order to stress the analogy, "teams" of communicating robots are built up dynamically and change over time. These robots can be very heterogeneous in terms of shape, capabilities, and goals. Each robot has to preserve its autonomy and has to cope with problems of sensor noise and unreliable communication. It is therefore reasonable to use the team cooperation concepts of Dual Dynamics also for service robots.

In another project at GMD, a service robot targeted to deliver mail is developed by using the DD methodology and the DD design environment. In this project, the DD approach — which currently focuses on the reactiveness of elaborated behavior systems in first place — is integrated with a deliberative planner which plans the routes of the robot through the office building. The concept has been first proposed in [13]; the current state is described in [14]. The main idea is that the planner updates its world model not only based on sensor input but also by observing the mode changes of the DD system. Although the focus of the project is on the integration of DD and planning, cooperation capabilities comes for free because the DD framework is used.

8   Conclusions

In this paper, we have presented a team coordination infrastructure which is integrated with the conceptual schema that we use for designing behavior based systems, the Dual Dynamics architecture. This enables the designer to implement cooperation policies in the same conceptual framework.

So far, Dual Dynamics has been successfully applied in robot projects inside GMD and for the behavior design of the "FU Fighters" team [6] which became vice world champion in the RoboCup small size league in Melbourne, September 2000.

The changes in the Dual Dynamics' concepts are quite small: a variable can be declared to be a team variable. At runtime, values of team variable are distributed only between those robots which have specified a team variable having the same name. Values of remote team variables are stored in arrays which may grow and shrink dynamically as robots are connected or disconnected (i.e. switched off) during a soccer game. We argue that this is a well-suited and easy-to-use paradigm for cooperation design in the context of robotics (see Sect. 6).

Besides this, the robustness of the mathematical concepts of Dual Dynamics offers additional capabilities in order to cope with noise of distributed sensors, and disturbances (e.g. communication delays, dynamic replacement of robots) occurring in a distributed setting.

We have shown that team behavior can be smoothly integrated with non team oriented behaviors. Our DD design environment supports the specification, simulation, and monitoring of team behaviors. Furthermore, a project is underway which integrates Dual Dynamics with a deliberative planner and establishes a platform to evaluate team cooperation in office applications.

References

1. G. Adorni, S. Cagnoni, M. Mordonini, and M. Piaggio. Team/goal-keeper coordination in the Robocup mid-size league. In *Proc. Fourth International Workshop on RoboCup*, Melbourne 2000.
2. R.C. Arkin. *Behavior-based Robotics*. MIT Press, 1998.
3. M. Asada and H. Kitano, editors, *RoboCup-98: Robot Soccer World Cup II*. LNCS 1604, Springer, 1999.
4. M. Asada, E. Uchibe, and K. Hosoda. Cooperative behavior acquisition for mobile robots in dynamically changing real worlds via vision-based reinforcement learning and development. *Artificial Intelligence*, 110:275-292, 1999.
5. T. Balch and M. Hybinette. Social potentials for scalable multi-robot formations. In *Proc. IEEE International Conference on Robotics and Automation (ICRA-2000)*, San Francisco, 2000.
6. S. Behnke and R. Rojas. A hierarchy of reactive behaviors handles complexity. In M. Hannebauer, J. Wendler, and E. Pagello, editors, *Balancing Reactivity and Social Deliberation in Multi-agent Systems (this volume)*, pages 125–136. Springer, 2001.
7. A. Bredenfeld, T. Christaller, W. Göhring, H. Günther, H. Jaeger, H.-U. Kobialka, P. Plöger, P. Schöll, A. Siegberg, A. Streit, C. Verbeek, and J. Wilberg. Behavior engineering with "Dual Dynamics" models and design tools. In *RoboCup-99: Robot Soccer World Cup III*, LNCS 1856, Springer, 1999.
8. A. Bredenfeld, T. Christaller, H. Jaeger, H.-U. Kobialka, and P. Schöll. *Robot Behavior Design Using Dual Dynamics*. GMD Report 117, 2000. (http://ais.gmd.de/BE/recent.html)
9. R. Brooks. The whole iguana. In M. Brady, editor, *Robotics Science*. pages 432–456. MIT Press, 1989.
10. S. Carpin, C. Ferrari, E. Pagello, and P. Patuelli. Bridging deliberation and reactivity in cooperative multi-robot systems through map focus. In M. Hannebauer, J. Wendler, and E. Pagello, editors, *Balancing Reactivity and Social Deliberation in Multi-agent Systems (this volume)*, pages 35–52. Springer, 2001.
11. C. Castelpietra, L. Iocchi, D. Nardi, M. Piaggio, A. Scalso, and A. Sgorbissa. Communication and coordination among heterogeneous mid-size players: ART99. In *Proc. Fourth International Workshop on RoboCup*, Melbourne 2000.
12. J.-S. Gutmann, W. Hatzack, I. Herrmann, B. Nebel, F. Rittinger, A. Topor, and T. Weigel. The CS Freiburg Team: Playing robotic soccer based on an explicit world model. *AI Magazine*, 21(1): 37-46, 2000.
13. J. Hertzberg, H. Jaeger, Ph. Morignot, and U.R. Zimmer. A framework for plan execution in behavior-based robots. In *Proc. of the 1998 IEEE Int. Symp. on Intell. Control (ISIC-98)*. pages 8–13. Gaithersburg, MD, 1998.

14. J. Hertzberg and F. Schönherr. Concurrency in the DD&P Robot Control Architecture. To appear in *Symposium Engineering of Natural and Artificial Intelligent Systems (ENAIS'2001)*, 2001.
15. H. Jaeger and T. Christaller. Dual dynamics: Designing behavior systems for autonomous robots. *Artificial Life and Robotics*, 2:108-112, 1998. (httpr://www.gmd.de/People/Herbert.Jaeger/Publications.html).
16. H.-U. Kobialka and P. Schöll. Quality management for mobile robot development. In *Proc. 6th International Conference on Intelligent Autonomous Systems (IAS-6)*. pages 698-703. IOS Press, 2000.
17. K. Konolige and K. Myers. The Saphira architecture for autonomous mobile robots. In D. Kortenkamp, R.P. Bonasso, and R. Murphy, editors, *AI-based Mobile Robots: Case Studies of Successful Robot Systems*. MIT Press, 1996.
18. P. Stone and M. Veloso. Layered approach to learning client behaviors in the RoboCup Soccer Server. *Applied Artificial Intelligence*, 12:165-188, 1998.
19. T. Tyrrell. The use of hierarchies for action selection. *Adaptive Behavior*, 1(4):387-420, 1993.

A Hierarchy of Reactive Behaviors Handles Complexity

Sven Behnke and Raúl Rojas

Free University of Berlin, Institute of Computer Science
Takustr. 9, 14195 Berlin, Germany
{behnke,rojas}@inf.fu-berlin.de
http://www.fu-fighters.de

Abstract. This paper discusses the hierarchical control architecture used to generate the behavior of individual agents and a team of robots for the RoboCup Small Size competition.

Our reactive approach is based on control layers organized in a temporal hierarchy. Fast and simple behaviors reside on the bottom of the hierarchy, while an increasing number of slower and more complex behaviors are implemented in the higher levels. In our architecture deliberation is not implemented explicitly, but to an external viewer it seems to be present.

Each layer is composed of three modules. First, the sensor module, where the perceptual dynamics aggregates the readings of fast changing sensors in time to form complex, slow changing percepts. Next, the activation module computes the activation dynamics that determines whether or not a behavior is allowed to influence actuators, and finally the actuator module, where the active behaviors influence the actuators to match a target dynamics.

We illustrate our approach by describing the bottom-up design of behaviors for the RoboCup domain.

1   Introduction

The "behavior based" approach has proven useful for real time control of mobile robots. Here, the actions of an agent are derived directly from sensory input without requiring an explicit symbolic model of the world [4,5,9]. In 1992, the programming language PDL was developed by Steels and Vertommen as a tool to implement stimulus driven control of autonomous agents [11,12]. PDL has been used by several groups working in behavior oriented robotics [10]. It allows the description of parallel processes that react to sensor readings by influencing the actuators. Many basic behaviors, like taxis, are easily formulated in such a framework. On the other hand, it is difficult and expensive to implement more complex behaviors in PDL, mostly those that need persistent percepts about the state of the environment. Consider, for example, a situation in a RoboCup [2] soccer game in which we want to position our defensive players preferentially on the side of the field where the offensive players of the other team mostly

M. Hannebauer et al. (Eds.): Reactivity and Deliberation in MAS, LNAI 2103, pp. 125–136, 2001.

concentrate. It is not useful to take this decision at a rate of 30Hz based on a snapshot of the most recent sensor readings. The position of the defense has to be determined only from time to time, e.g. every second, on the basis of the average positions of the attacking robots during the immediate past.

The Dual Dynamics control architecture, developed by Herbert Jäger [7,8], arranges reactive behaviors in a two-level hierarchy of control processes. Each elementary behavior in the lower level is divided into two modules: the activation dynamics which at every time step determines whether or not the behavior tries to influence actuators, and the target dynamics, that describes strength and direction of that influence. Complex behaviors in the higher level do not contain a target dynamics. They only compute an activation dynamics. When becoming active they configure the low-level control loops via activation factors that set the current mode of the primitive behaviors. This can produce qualitatively different reactions if the agent receives the same stimulus again, but has changed its mode due to stimuli received in the meantime.

We extended the Dual Dynamics approach by introducing a multi-level time hierarchy with fast behaviors on the bottom and slower behaviors towards the top of the control hierarchy. We don't restrict the target dynamics to the lowest layer, and add a third dynamics, the perceptual dynamics, to the system.

Dynamical systems have been used by others for behavior control. Gallagher and Beer, for instance, used evolved recurrent neural networks to control a visually guided walking agent [6]. Steinhage and Schöner proposed an approach for robot navigation formulated with differential equations [15]. Although planning and learning have been implemented in this framework [14], it is not clear how this non-hierarchical approach will scale to complex problems, since all behaviors interact pairwise with each other. Steinhage also proposed the use of nonlinear attractor dynamics for sensor fusion [13].

The remainder of the paper is organized as follows: In the next section we explain the hierarchical control architecture. Section 3 illustrates the design of behaviors using examples from the RoboCup domain.

2   Hierarchy of Reactive Behaviors

2.1   Architecture

Our control architecture is shown in Fig. 1. It was inspired by the Dual Dynamics scheme developed by H. Jäger [7,8]. In contrast to the two-level original proposal, the robots are controlled in closed loops that use many different time scales and that correspond to behaviors on different levels of the hierarchy. On the lowest level we have few simple and fast behaviors. While the speed of the behaviors decreases when going up the hierarchy, their number, as well as the number of sensors and actuators, increases. This allows to model complex systems.

We extended the Dual Dynamics concept further by introducing a third element, namely the perceptual dynamics, as shown on the left side of Fig. 1. Here, either slow changing physical sensors, such as the charging state indicators of the batteries, are plugged-in at the higher levels, or the readings of fast changing

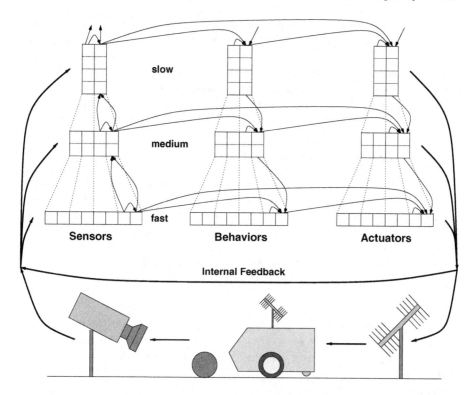

Fig. 1. Sketch of the control architecture

sensors, like the ball position in soccer, are aggregated by dynamic processes into slower and longer lasting percepts. The boxes shown in the figure are divided into cells. Each cell represents a sensor value that is constant for a time step. The rows correspond to different sensors and the columns show the time advancing from left to right.

A set of behaviors is shown in the middle of each level. Each row contains an activation factor between 0 and 1 that determines when the corresponding behavior is allowed to influence actuators.

The actuator values are shown on the right hand side. Some of these values are connected to physical actuators that modify the environment. The other actuators influence lower levels of the hierarchy when used as parameters of faster behaviors or generate sensory percepts in the next time step via the internal feedback loop.

Since we use temporal subsampling, we can afford to implement an increasing number of sensors, behaviors, and actuators in the higher layers without an explosion of computational cost. This leads to rich interactions with the environment, and therefore allows for complexity.

Each physical sensor or actuator can only be connected to one level of the hierarchy. One can use the typical speed of the change of a sensor's readings to decide where to connect it. Similarly, the placement of actuators is determined by the time needed to make a change in the environment. Behaviors are placed on the level that is low enough to ensure a timely response to stimuli, but high enough to provide the necessary aggregated perceptual information, and that contains actuators which are abstract enough to produce the desired actions.

2.2   Computation of the Dynamics

The dynamic systems of the sensors, behaviors, and actuators can be specified and analyzed as a set of differential equations. Of course, the actual computations are done using difference equations. Here, the time runs in discrete steps of $\Delta t^0 = t_i^0 - t_{i-1}^0$ at the lowest level 0. At the higher levels the updates are done less frequently: $\Delta t^z = t_i^z - t_{i-1}^z = f \Delta t^{z-1}$, where useful choices of the subsampling factor f could be 2, 4, 8, ... In Fig. 1 $f = 2$ was used.

A layer z is updated in time step t_i^z as follows:

$\mathbf{s}_i^z$ – *Sensor values:*
   The n_s^z sensor values $\mathbf{s}_i^z = (s_{i,0}^z, s_{i,1}^z, \ldots, s_{i,n_s^z-1}^z)$ depend on the readings of the n_r^z physical sensors $\mathbf{r}_i^z = (r_{i,0}^z, r_{i,1}^z, \ldots, r_{i,n_r^z-1}^z)$ that are connected to layer z, the previous sensor values $\mathbf{s}_{i-1}^z$, and the previous sensor values from the layer below $\mathbf{s}_{fi}^{z-1}, \mathbf{s}_{fi-1}^{z-1}, \mathbf{s}_{fi-2}^{z-1}, \ldots$.
   In order to avoid the storage of old values in the lower level, the sensor values can be updated from the layer below, e.g. as moving average.
   By analyzing the sensor values from the last few time steps, one can also compute predictions for the next few steps that are needed for anticipative behavior. If the predictions in addition take the last few actuator values into account, they can be used to cancel a delay between an action command and the perceived results of that action.

α_i^z – *Activation factors:*
   The n_α^z activations $\alpha_i^z = (\alpha_{i,0}^z, \alpha_{i,1}^z, \ldots, \alpha_{i,n_\alpha^z-1}^z)$ of the behaviors depend on the sensor values $\mathbf{s}_i^z$, the previous activations α_{i-1}^z, and on the activations of behaviors in the level above $\alpha_{i/f}^{z+1}$. A layer-$(z+1)$-behavior can utilize multiple layer-z-behaviors and each of them can be activated by many $(z+1)$-behaviors. For every behavior k on level $(z+1)$ that uses a behavior j from level z there is a term $\alpha_{i/f,k}^{z+1} T_{j,k}^z(\alpha_{i-1}^z, \mathbf{s}_i^z)$ that describes the desired change of the activation $\alpha_{i,j}^z$. Note that this term vanishes, if the upper level behavior is not active. If $\alpha_{i/f,k}^{z+1} > 0$, then the current sensor readings and the previous activations contribute to the value of the T-term. To determine the new α_i^z the desired changes from all T-terms are accumulated. A product term is used to deactivate a behavior, if no corresponding higher behavior is active.

$\mathbf{G}_i^z$ – *Target values:*
   Each behavior j can specify for each actuator k within its layer z a target value $g_{i,j,k}^z = G_{j,k}^z(\mathbf{s}_i^z, \mathbf{a}_{i/f}^{z+1})$.

$\mathbf{a}_i^z$ – *Actuator values:*

The more active a behavior j is, the more it can influence the actuator values $\mathbf{a}_i^z = (a_{i,0}^z, a_{i,1}^z, \ldots, a_{i,n_a^z-1}^z)$. The desired change for the actuator value $a_{i,k}^z$ is: $u_{i,j,k}^z = \tau_{i,j,k}^z \alpha_{i,j}^z (g_{i,j,k}^z - a_{i-1,k}^z)$, where $\tau_{i,j,k}^z$ is a time constant. If several behaviors want to change the same actuator k, the desired updates are added: $a_{i,k}^z = a_{i-1,k}^z + u_{i,j_0,k}^z + u_{i,j_1,k}^z + u_{i,j_2,k}^z + \ldots$

2.3 Bottom-Up Design

Behaviors are constructed in a bottom-up fashion: First, the control loops that should react quickly to fast changing stimuli are designed. Their critical parameters, e.g. a mode parameter or a target position, are determined. When these fast primitive behaviors work reliably with constant parameters, the next level can be added to the system. For this higher level, more complex behaviors can now be designed which influence the environment, either directly, by moving slow actuators, or indirectly, by changing the critical parameters of the control loops in the lower level.

After the addition of several layers, fairly complex behaviors can be designed that make decisions using abstract sensors based on a long history, and use powerful actuators to influence the environment.

3   Application to the RoboCup Small Size Competition

In the RoboCup [2] Small Size competition, five on five robots play soccer using an orange golf ball. The area of the robots is restricted to $180cm^2$, and the playground has the size of a table tennis field.

In the Small Size league, a camera is mounted above the field and is connected to an external computer that finds the position of the players and the ball and executes the behavior control software. The next action command for each robot is determined and sent via a wireless link to a microcontroller on the robot. The robots move themselves and the ball producing in this way visual feedback.

We designed the team FU-Fighters for the RoboCup'99 competition, held in Stockholm. We built robust and fast robots featuring a kicking device, as shown

Fig. 2. Kick-off and a FU-Fighters robot kicking the ball (photo: Stefan Beetz)

in Fig. 2. Local control is done using a Motorola HC05 microcontroller. The robots receive the desired motor speeds via a wireless serial link at a rate of up to 48Hz as commands. Each robot is marked with three colored dots that are tracked at 30Hz from an NTSC S-VHS video signal. Further details about the design of the FU-Fighters can be found at [1,3].

The behavior control was implemented using a hierarchy of reactive behaviors. In our soccer playing robots, basic skills, like movement to a position and ball handling, reside on lower levels, tactic behaviors are situated on intermediate layers, while the game strategy is determined at the topmost level of the hierarchy.

3.1   Taxis

To realize a Braitenberg vehicle that moves towards a target, we need the direction and the distance to the target as input. The control loop for the two differential drive motors runs on the lowest level of the hierarchy. The two actuator values used determine the average desired speed of the motors and the speed differences between them. We select the sign of the speed by looking at the target direction. If the target is in front of the robot, the speed is positive and the robot drives forward, if it is behind, then the robot drives backwards. Steering depends on the difference of the target direction and the robot's main axis. If this difference is zero, the robot can drive straight ahead. If the difference is large, it does not drive, but turns on the spot. Similarly, the speed of driving depends on the distance to the target. If the target is far away, the robot can drive fast. When it comes close to the target it slows down and stops at the target position. Figure 3 shows an example where the robot first turns around until the desired angle has been reached, accelerates, moves with constant speed to a target and finally decelerates. Smooth transitions between the extreme behaviors are produced using sigmoidal functions.

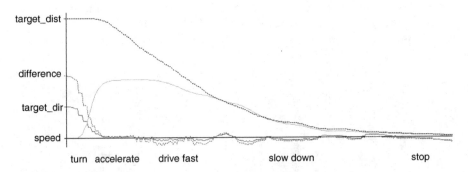

Fig. 3. Recording of two sensors (distance and direction of the target) and two actuators (average motor speed and difference between the two motors) during a simple taxis behavior. The robot first turns towards the target, then accelerates, drives fast, slows down, and finally stops at the target position

In addition to the coordinates of the target position, we include some parameters of the taxis behavior as actuators on the second level. This allows to configure the driving characteristics of the taxis. The parameters influence the maximal speed driven, the degree of tolerance to lateral deviations from the direct way, the desired speed at the target position, the directional preference (forward/backward), and the use of the brakes.

3.2   Goalie

This primitive taxis behavior can be used as a building block for the goal keeper. A simple goal keeper could be designed with two modes: block and catch, as shown in Fig. 4. In the block mode it sets the target position to the intersection of the goal line and a line that starts behind the goal and goes through the ball. In the catch mode, it sets the target position to the intersection of the predicted ball trajectory and the goal line. The goal keeper is always in the block mode, except when the ball moves rapidly towards the goal.

Since our goalie is equipped with a kicking device, it can actively reflect the ball. This usually moves the ball to the opposite half of the field. Additional behaviors ensure that the longer side of the goalie is faced towards the ball and that the goalie does not leave the goal, although it has been designed to move mostly parallel to the goal line.

3.3   Obstacle Avoidance

Since there are many robots and a ball that move quickly on the field, obstacle avoidance is very important for successful play. We implemented a reactive collision avoidance approach on the lowest level of the control hierarchy. The robots only avoid the closest obstacle, if it is between their current position and the taxis target. If such a situation is detected and a collision is likely to occur in the next second, then the obstacle avoidance behavior activates itself. This inhibits the normal taxis. The robot now decides whether it should avoid the obstacle by

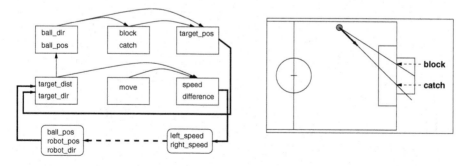

Fig. 4. Sketch of goal keeper behavior. Based on the position, speed, and the direction of the ball, the goalie decides to either block the ball or to catch it

going to the left or to the right. The position of the second closest obstacle, as well as the position of the closest wall point and the taxis target are taken into account for this decision. Since it is not useful to revise the avoidance direction frequently, it is made persistent for the next second. The robot drives on a circle around the obstacle until this is no longer blocking its way to the taxis target.

This fast reactive collision avoidance behavior should be complemented by path planning implemented on higher layers, such that a global view of the field is used and the activation of the collision avoidance behavior is minimized.

3.4   Field Player

The control hierarchy of the field player that wants to move the ball to a target, e.g. a teammate or the goal, could contain the alternating modes run and push. In the run mode, the robot moves to a target point behind the ball with respect to the ball target. When it reaches this location, the push mode becomes active. Then the robot tries to drive through the ball towards the target, pushing it into the desired direction. If the line of sight to the goal is free, we activate the kicking device before driving through the ball. This accelerates the ball such that it is hard to catch for the goalie. When the robot looses the ball, the activation condition for pushing is no longer valid and run mode becomes active again.

Figure 5 illustrates the trajectory of the field player generated in run mode. A line is drawn through the ball target, e.g. the middle of the goal line, and the ball. The target point for taxis is found on this line at a variable distance behind the ball. The position behind the ball for activating the push mode is chosen at a fixed offset from the ball. Half the distance of the robot to this position is added to the offset to determine the distance of the taxis target from the ball. The taxis behavior makes the robot always head towards the taxis target. As the robot comes closer, the taxis target moves to the push mode point. This dynamic taxis target produces a trajectory that smoothly approaches the line. When the robot arrives at the push mode point, it is heading towards the ball target, ready to kick.

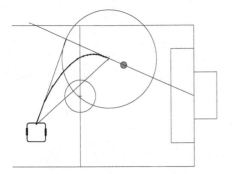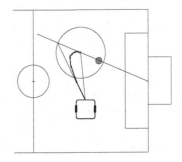

Fig. 5. Trajectories generated in the run mode of the field player. It smoothly approaches a point behind the ball that lies on the line from the goal through the ball

3.5   Team Play

Each of our robots is controlled autonomously by the lower levels of the hierarchy using a local view of the world, as indicated in Fig. 6. We present, for instance, the angle and the distance to the ball and the nearest obstacle to each agent. In the upper layers of the control system the focus changes. Now we regard the team as the individual. It has a slow changing global view of the playground and coordinates the robots as its extremities in order to reach strategic goals.

One simple strategy used to coordinate the four field players is that only one of them is allowed to go for the ball. The team evaluates the positions of the players relative to the ball and the goal and selects the one that gets the highest score. This player takes the initiative and tries to get behind the ball, dribbles and kicks it towards the goal. The robots not chosen in this selection do different things. If they are defenders, they cover the attacking robots of the other team. If they are offensive players, they position themself to be able to receive passes and then have a free path towards the goal. If the chosen robot is not able to get to the ball, the player with the second highest score is selected to take the initiative.

Although we did not implement explicit passes, some implicit passes have emerged during games. The most impressive ones are produced by a behavior that tries to free the ball from corners by quickly rotating the robot. If the direction of the rotation is chosen such that the ball is moved towards the goal, the ball frequently moved slowly across the field just in front of the goal. The offensive player waiting near the other corner of the goal area can now easily intercept the ball and kick it into the goal. These short distance kicks are extremely hard to catch for the goalie.

We also implemented a selective obstacle avoidance between the teammates. The player that goes for the ball does not avoid its teammates. They must avoid the active robot and move out of its path to the goal.

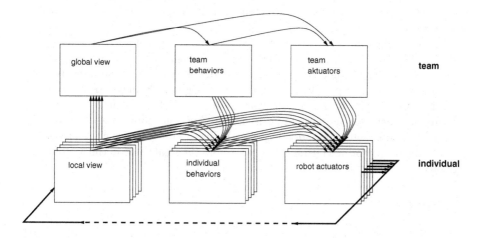

Fig. 6. Sketch of the relation between the team and the individual robots

The field players are assigned different roles, like left/right wing, offender, defender. We implemented a dynamic assignment of roles, depending on the actual positions of the robots, relative to home positions of the roles. This allows to have more roles than robots. Only those roles most important in a situation are assigned to players. This feature is needed when a robot detects that it does not reach it's target position for a longer time. Then the robot signals the team that is defect and the team does not assign further roles to this player until the next stoppage in play.

3.6   Complex Behaviors

We implemented some complex behaviors for the RoboCup competition. They include, for instance, dynamic homing, where the home positions of our defensive players are adjusted such that they block the offensive robots from the other team, and the home positions of our offensive players are adjusted, such that they have a free path to the goal. Another example is ball interception, where we predict the ball trajectory and the time it takes for the robot to reach successive points on this trajectory. We direct the robot towards the point where it can first reach such a point earlier than the ball. This results in an anticipative behavior. We also detect when a robot wants to move, but does not move for a longer time, e.g. because it is blocked by other robots or got stuck in a corner. Then we quickly rotate the robot for a short time, in order to free the player.

For presentations, we added an automated referee component to the system. It detects when the ball enters a goal and changes the mode of the game to kickoff. Then the robots move automatically to their kickoff positions. When the ball is detected in the middle of the field for some seconds, the game mode is changed back to normal play.

In our current system, the deliberation of common goals among the autonomous agents is not explicitly modeled. There is coordination among the robots. The highest level in the hierarchy, the team level, assigns each robot a role and keeps track of the robots. It is through their specific role that the robots collaborate.

One example can illustrate this. When the left wing player drives the ball through the field, the right wing player moves parallel to it. Once the left player reaches the corner of the field, it rotates in order to free the ball and produces a pass to the right. The pass will be taken by the right wing player or the central offensive player that is waiting in front of the goal. The result is a situation in which deliberation as bargaining is not present, but coordinated team play produces results that mimic deliberation. Figure 7 illustrates such a successful pass. It has been produced using the log-file from the final game in the Melbourne RoboCup competition.

4   Summary

In the paper we described a hierarchical architecture for reactive control. This architecture contains interacting behaviors residing on different time scales. These

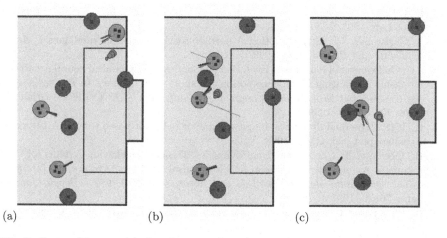

(a)   (b)   (c)

Fig. 7. Successful pass: (a) the player in the upper corner frees the ball and sends it towards the middle; (b) the center player receives the ball; (c) the center has kicked towards the goal

control loops are designed in a bottom-up fashion. Lower level behaviors are configured by an increasing number of higher level behaviors that can use a longer history to determine their actions.

We illustrated the design of behaviors using examples from the RoboCup domain. Our successful participation in the RoboCup'99 and '2000 F180 league competitions, where we finished second (next to Big Red, from Cornell University) and in the European RoboCup'2000, where we won, shows that the architecture can be applied to complex multi-agent control problems.

One remaining problem is the design complexity. The higher the design process advances in the hierarchy, the larger the number of sensors, behaviors, and actuators becomes. It is therefore increasingly difficult to determine the free parameters of the system. To design larger systems, automated design techniques, such as reinforcement learning, are needed.

References

1. P. Ackers, S. Behnke, B. Frötschl, W. Lindstrot, M. de Melo, R. Rojas, A. Schebesch, M. Simon, M. Sprengel, and O. Tenchio. The soul of a new machine. Technical Report B-12/99, Freie Universität Berlin, 1999.
2. M. Asada and H. Kitano, editors. *RoboCup-98: Robot Soccer World Cup II*. Lecture Note in Artificial Intelligence 1604. Springer, 1999.
3. S. Behnke, B. Frötschl, R. Rojas, P. Ackers, W. Lindstrot, M. de Melo, M. Preier, A. Schebesch, M. Simon, M. Sprengel, and O. Tenchio. Using hierarchical dynamical systems to control reactive bahaviors. In *Proceedings IJCAI'99 - International Joint Conference on Artificial Intelligence, The Third International Workshop on RoboCup - Stockholm*, pages 28–33, 1999.

4. R.A. Brooks. Intelligence without reason. A.I. Memo 1293, MIT Artificial Intelligence Lab, 1991.
5. T. Christaller. Cognitive robotics: A new approach to artificial intelligence. *Artificial Life and Robotics*, (3), 1999.
6. J.C. Gallagher and R.D. Beer. Evolution and analysis of dynamical neural networks for agents integrating vision, locomotion and short-term memory. In *Proceedings of the Genetic and Evolutionary Computation Conference (GECCO-99) – Orlando*, pages 1273–1280, 1999.
7. H. Jäger. The dual dynamics design scheme for behavior-based robots: A tutorial. Arbeitspapier 966, GMD, 1996.
8. H. Jäger and T. Christaller. Dual dynamics: Designing behavior systems for autonomous robots. In S. Fujimura and M. Sugisaka, editors, *Proceedings International Symposium on Artificial Life and Robotics (AROB '97) – Beppu, Japan*, pages 76–79, 1997.
9. R. Pfeifer and C. Scheier. *Understanding Intelligence*. MIT press, Cambridge, 1998.
10. E. Schlottmann, D. Spenneberg, M. Pauer, T. Christaller, and K. Dautenhahn. A modular design approach towards behaviour oriented robotics. Arbeitspapier 1088, GMD, 1997.
11. L. Steels. The PDL reference manual. AI Lab Memo 92-5, VUB Brussels, 1992.
12. L. Steels. Building agents with autonomous behavior systems. In L. Steels and R.A. Brooks, editors, *The 'Artificial Life' route to 'Artificial Intelligence': Building situated embodied agents*. Lawrence Erlbaum Associates, New Haven, 1994.
13. A. Steinhage. Nonlinear attractor dynamics: A new approach to sensor fusion. In P.S. Schenker and G.T. McKee, editors, *Sensor Fusion and Decentralized Control in Robotic Systems II: Proceedings of SPIE*, volume 3839, pages 31–42. Spie-publishing, 1999.
14. A. Steinhage and T. Bergener. Learning by doing: A dynamic architecture for generating adaptive behavioral sequences. In *Proceedings of the Second ICSC Symposium on Neural Computation NC2000 – Berlin*, pages 813–820, 2000.
15. A. Steinhage and G. Schöner. The dynamic approach to autonomous robot navigation. In *Proceedings of the IEEE International Symposium on Industrial Electronics ISIE'97*, pages SS7–SS12, 1997.

Reinforcement Learning for Cooperating and Communicating Reactive Agents in Electrical Power Grids

Martin Riedmiller[1], Andrew Moore[2], and Jeff Schneider[2]

[1] Computer Science Dept.
University of Karlsruhe
D-76128 Karlsruhe, Germany
[2] Robotics Insitute
Carnegie-Mellon-University
Pittsburgh, PA 15213, USA

Abstract. Social behaviour in intelligent agent systems is often considered to be achieved by deliberative, in-depth reasoning techniques. This paper shows, how a purely reactive multi-agent system can learn to evolve cooperative behaviour, by means of learning from previous experiences. In particular, we describe a learning multi agent approach to the problem of controlling power flow in an electrical power-grid. The problem is formulated within the framework of dynamic programming. Via a global optimization goal, a set of individual agents is forced to autonomously learn to cooperate and communicate. The ability of the purely reactive distributed systems to solve the global problem by means of establishing a communication mechanism is shown on two prototypical network configurations.

1 Introduction

Today, two main approaches of intellingent agent design are distinguished: reactive architectures are designed to quickly adapt to changing environment conditions in dynamically changing domains, giving an *immediate* response to a certain perceiptive input. On the other side, deliberative approaches typically implement a kind of 'in-depth reasoning', deriving appropriate acting by the use of knowledge deduction techniques [12]. The capability of any kind of social behaviour, e.g. cooperative capabilities in large systems of individual agents, is often considered a typical feature of deliberative system.

In this article we concentrate on purely reactive systems, and show, that they are able to show social behaviour. In particular, we focus on two important aspects of social behaviour, namely learning of cooperation and communication abilities. In contrast to knowledge based approaches, where the behaviour of the agent is determined a priori during the design phase, the reactive behaviour of the system proposed here is learned during execution. This allows to directly specify the behaviour of the entire multi-agent system in terms of a cost-function, which

M. Hannebauer et al. (Eds.): Reactivity and Deliberation in MAS, LNAI 2103, pp. 137–149, 2001.

evaluates the performance of the whole team in terms of fulfilling the overall team goal or not. This kind of specification of team behaviour is often a much more accessible and convenient way than the explicit programming of individual team members. Since learning here means learning autonomously from experience, the approach is based on refining agents' behaviour during repeated experiments. It therefore is especially suited for environments, where the agents repeatedly face similar situations.

1.1   Distributed Power-Grid Control

In general, there are two main reasons for the application of a distributed problem solving method instead of a centralized solution. One reason is the hope for a more efficient problem solution by the combination of locally valid solutions ('divide and conquer'), the other reason is the exclusion of a centralized solution by a restricted communication bandwidth. The control of the distribution of power in an electrical power-grid is an example of the latter type. Decisions about the existence and the characteristics of links between power-stations and customers have to be made by spatially distributed control agents, situated in distribution centers. These agents can only locally communicate with restricted bandwidth. Therefore, each decision making unit has only access to a local part of the complete system. Nevertheless, in a power-grid each local change does not only have some restricted local impact but typically influences the state of the complete network.

In the following we describe a reinforcement learning approach [6], [9] that learns to establish cooperation and communication between spatially distributed agents. The used simulation of a power-grid network covers some main effects occurring in real electrical power-grids and therefore allows to study the behavior of learning agents [5]. In contrast to a real power-grid network which is based on alternate current (AC), we here examine a direct current (DC) variant for the sake of a simpler and faster simulation – which is more appropriate for initial investigations. Whereas the physical behavior of AC power-grids is rather different from a DC one, we still expect the presented methods to be applicable as a general learning scheme for distributed control problems.

1.2   The Simulation Model

A simulation model of a direct current (DC) power-grid is examined. The grid is represented as a connected graph (Fig. 1). We distinguish between three node-types: A *producer node* provides power to the network. Due to its internal resistance, the voltage at its output varies with the connected load. The producer nodes are connected to *distributor nodes* which control the flow of current in the network by changing the resistances on their connecting links. Each distributor is connected to a *consumer node*. The consumer node models the customer in a power-grid network and has a certain demand of power represented by a desired voltage and a certain load. Connecting links may exist between producers and

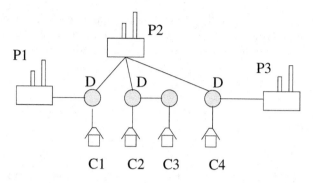

Fig. 1. Example of a power-grid with producers P, distributors D and consumers C

distributors, distributors and distributors and distributors and consumers. The links have a certain minimum resistance (a physical constraint) but otherwise the link resistance may be altered arbitrarily.

1.3   Control Task

The goal is to provide each customer with the requested power, defined by a time-varying load. This must be done by selecting the resistances on the network links appropriately. More formally, the state s of the power-grid is described by the voltages of the nodes and the resistances of the links, $s = (\bar{U}, \bar{r})$ and the task is to find an appropriate resistance vector $\bar{r}$, such that the customer part of the node voltages equals to the desired voltages $\bar{U}^c = \bar{U}_{desired}$. If the state of the power-grid was completely known to a centralized problem solver, then an appropriate resistance vector $\bar{r}$ could be computed directly (for example, by linear programming).

Here, instead, we are faced with a situation, where the control problem must be solved by a set of independent problem solvers, that only have a *local* view of the current system's state and can only perform local decisions. This has two important aspects:

- the cooperation aspect: an agent makes only local decisions, but only a co-ordinated policy can achieve the final goal
- the communication aspect: the agent can only recognize part of the world and thus depends on informative signals from other agents to act appropriately

1.4   A Distributed Reinforcement Learning (DRL) Approach

Each agent decides on the change of the resistances of its incoming and outgoing links. Since none of the agents knows what the other agents decide nor in which situation they are in, in general no one-step solution can be achieved. Instead, the determination of the final resistance vector $\bar{r}$ becomes an iterative search process. Therefore, we may formulate the search process for $\bar{r}$ as a deterministic

Markov Decision Process (MDP), where we are looking for a sequence of link resistance changes $\triangle R_0, \ldots, \triangle R_N$ that leads from an initial configuration s_0 of the power-grid to a situation s^*, where all customers are satisfied:

$$s_0 \overset{\triangle R_0}{\to} s_1 \overset{\triangle R_1}{\to} \ldots s^*$$

We now can formulate the control objective as the minimization of accumulated path costs

$$\min_{\triangle R_0, \triangle R_1, \ldots} \sum_t c(s_t)$$

where costs $c(s_t)$ depend on the satisfaction of all customers and are zero if and only if *all* customers are satisfied. The above MDP formulation makes it possible to apply reinforcement learning techniques based on the approximation of a value-function for the accumulated costs. In contrast to the common single agent approach, here we learn agent-dependant mappings of a *local* part of the state vector to costs, that depend on the behavior of the *entire* system. The learning rule is adapted from Q-learning [11] and has the following form:

$$Q_i^{new}(\sigma_i(s), a_t) \leftarrow c(s) + \min_a Q_i^{old}(\sigma_i(s'), a)$$

where $\sigma_i(s)$ denotes the local view of agent i in situation s. By considering global costs $r(s_t)$ (= the satisfaction of *all* customers) individual agents are forced to cooperate, since they can only get finite costs, if no consumer has unfulfilled demands. The agent policy is defined by the greedy exploitation of the Q-function.

The distributedness of the solution approach violates several assumptions required for the convergence of Q-learning. Currently, there is a growing amount of empirical evidence [2], [4], [3] that Q-learning can successfully work in such multi-agent domains. The results in Sect. 3 further stress this observation. An algorithm for reinforcement learning in deterministic multi-agent environments, for which convergence can be prooved, can be found in [7].

1.5   Learning to Communicate

Since an agent has only a local view of the state of the power-grid, some sort of communication must be allowed to inform him about the situation of its neighbors. Here, we only provide the ingredients for communication: An agent has the additional action of actively sending a message to its neighboring nodes and an incoming message is represented by an additional state variable. Within the proposed optimization framework this means, that the agent has two things to learn: First, there is the necessity to decide when to send a message, in order that the recipient has a real information gain from receiving this message, and second, the recipient must react in an appropriate way; otherwise, neither the sender nor the receiver can profit from the communication. Only the proper installation of both parts can eventually lead to achieving the ensemble goal, namely the improvement of the global cost function.

2   Control Policies

2.1   Sensing and Acting

The principal sensing and decision capabilities are the same for all of the tested control algorithms. All agents make one decision per time-step simultaneously. As a special action, each agent can send out a message which is distributed to all its connected neighbors. Each node (producers and distributors) checks its incoming messages every time-step. If a producer node gets an incoming message, it redistributes it to all its connected nodes. If a distributor node gets an incoming message, it becomes part of its local state. Therefore, the reaction of a distributor node to an incoming message depends on its current policy. The resistor to each connected consumer is adapted automatically in each time step, depending on the demand of the consumer and the voltage of the distributer.

State Information: The agent can consider four binary state features to make its decision:

- consumer request: true, if the power demand of the connected consumer is not fulfilled
- distributer message: true, if one of the connected distributors has sent a message
- producer message: true, if one of the connected producers has sent a message (meaning that the producer node itself has received a message of one of its connected distributors in the previous time-step)
- links at limit: true, if no link change is possible to get more current (e.g. all links have already reached their minimum resistance value)

Actions: all actions are implemented as 'intelligent meta-actions', which means that each abstract action may affect a whole group of link resistances and that additional computation may be used to determine the best possible values.

- get more current: decreases the resistors to all connected producers, if their voltage is higher than the current distributor voltage and the producer has not set the message bit. Additionally, if the voltage of the producer is lower than the current voltage of a distributor, then the resistor is increased.
- get less current: increases the resistors to all producers, if their voltage is higher then the current distributor voltage and if their message bit is set.
- send message: send a message to all connected nodes (distributors and producers)
- pause: do nothing

To consider the message bit in the implementation of the two actions 'get more/less current' in the above way gives a bias towards using the message bit as a power-request message. The reason why we must choose this implementation here is that we want to control the principle behaviour of all links with only one decision. Alternatively, when the control policy could modify each link individually, no such pre-wired behaviour was needed. However, the meaning of the message bit is not determined in a strong sense, which would mean that it is set every time a distributor needs current and/ or that the receiver of the message acts in a predetermined way. To learn when and how to use the message bit is still the task of the learning agent.

An agent can see an overall of $2^4 = 16$ different states. In each state, the policy can vary between 4 different actions, making an overall of $4^{16} \approx 4.2 \times 10^9$ different policies. If each of n agents has its individual policy, then the amount of different policies for the entire system is $(4^{16})^n$. Note that even in the case of a very high abstraction level from the original system's state, the search space for the agents' policies is extremely large.

2.2   Control Policies and Learning Algorithms

As an evaluation benchmark for the learning agents, we derived two versions of a conventionally designed control policy, one that uses communication, π_{hc}, and a communication-less variant π_h. The policies are the same for all the agents in the network.

For learning, the following approaches were tested:

- **Q shared:** Each agent does local Q-learning; the same Q-table (and therefore policy) is shared by all agents.
- **Q individual:** Each agent does local Q-learning and has its individual Q-table and policy.
- **Hill-climbing shared:** All agents share a common policy. After one sweep through all training examples, one entry in the policy table is randomly selected and changed. If the performance on all training examples did not get worse, then the change is retained, otherwise it is reversed again.
- **Hill-climbing individual:** Same as above, except that all agents have individual policies.

3   Empirical Evaluation

3.1   Experimental Settings

The performance of the different policies is measured in terms of accumulated costs per run, averaged over the number of occurring situations. The cost-function considered here is

$$C = \sum_t \sum_i c_i(t) \tag{1}$$

where $c_i(t) = 1$ if the consumer connected to distributor i gets less power than demanded in time-step t and $c_i(t) = 0$ otherwise. This cost-function is used both to learn and to compare the performance of the algorithms. For the Q-learning approach, each agent receives at every time-step the *global* reward signal $C(t) = \sum_i c_i(t)$.

A run lasts at most 20 time-steps for benchmark A and 30 time-steps for benchmark B. If within that period not all customers are satisfied, the run is considered to be a failure. In case of a failure, a Q-learning agent receives a final negative cost of $r^- = 100$ (as a very rough indication of the actual (infinite) costs that would occur in case of not fulfilling everyone's demand).

Since the size of the state and action space is limited through the choice of the features, a table can be used to store the Q-values. Alternatively, when continuous features are used, instead some sort of function approximation scheme such as neural networks could be applied, e.g. [1], [9].

3.2   The Cooperate and Communicate Benchmark

The *cooperate and communicate* scenario is based on a 2 producer, 2 distributer and 2 consumers network (left in Fig. 2). Distributor A is connected to both producers I and II, whereas distributor B is connected to only one producer, II. Therefore, situations may occur, in which distributor B gets too little power from its only producer II to satisfy its customer, whereas distributor A could be cooperative and take less current from the shared producer II and more from producer I. Therefore, A must be cooperative if required. Furthermore, since A cannot see the state information of B, A and B have to agree on a communication scheme, that allows B to tell A, when it needs more current.

For training and testing, we used 10 different power-demand scenarios which reflect typical situations that may occur in this kind of network structure. Without communication, the restricted local view makes it impossible for the agents to satisfy all the consumers for all varying demands. For the training scenarios, the communication-less hand-crafted policy π_h fails in 9 out of 10 cases and leads to high global costs $C = 18.2$ (row 1 in Table 1). On the contrary, the hand-crafted policy with communication satisfies all customer demands in all training cases (row 2 in Table 1).

Learning Behavior. Row 3 and 4 of Table 1 report the performance of the Q-learning agents for the case of shared Q-tables/ policies and individual Q-

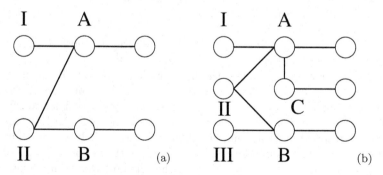

Fig. 2. Two typical grid structures used in the experiments (a) cooperate and communicate (benchmark A) (b) cooperate, communicate and take care (benchmark B)

Table 1. Performance on the training set for benchmark A

algorithm	costs	failures	no. of runs
π_h	18.2	9/10	-
π_{hc}	15.4	0/10	-
Q shared	14.0	0/10	300
Q individual	13.8	0/10	340
Hc shared	14	0/10	430
Hc individual	14.3	2/10	2140

table/ policies. The results show three remarkable things: First, the learned policies do much better than the communication-less policy π_h. This means, that the agents have successfully *learned* to cooperate and to install a communication mechanism that triggers the cooperation. Second, the successful policy was found after only 300 runs, which is surprisingly fast, considering the number of possible policies. Third, the learned policy leads to lower average costs (14.0) compared to the hand-crafted policy (15.4). Having a closer look at the two policies, hand-crafted and learned, we discovered that the better performance of the learned policy results from an optimized behavior in the cooperation case: Whereas the hand-crafted policy immediately increases the resistance to a shared producer to help a requesting agent and then tries to get more current from elsewhere, the learned policy first decreases its resistance to an alternative provider and then starts to cooperate by taking less current from the shared provider. This second policy helps to avoid useless circles and thus leads to lower costs.

Having a closer look at the learning behavior, we varied the learning parameter α for Q-learning (a fixed learning rate was used instead of a decaying one). Learning converged in the sense that the policies did not change any more after a certain amount of runs. The smaller the learning rate, the more runs were needed. Different learning rates lead to solutions with slightly varying but generally very low costs.

To compare the Q-learning approach to an alternative optimization technique, a hill-climbing algorithm was used to search for a policy. In case of a single shared policy for all agents, the hill-climbing approach did surprisingly well with respect to both the quality of the solution and the number of training runs needed (row 5 in Table 1). For hillclimbing, the best result found after at most 50,000 runs is reported. In the individual policies case, the hill-climbing approach got trapped in a local minimum, leading to two failures (row 6 in Table 1). In fact, getting stuck in local minima is one of the major problems of the hill-climbing approach (though in principle there is no theoretical reason that the distributed Q-learning approach might not get stuck, it empirically seems more robust).

Table 2. Performance on the test set for benchmark A

algorithm	costs	failures
π_h	9.648	20/1000
π_{hc}	9.525	0/1000
Q shared	9.498	0/1000
Q individual	9.498	0/1000
Hc shared	9.498	0/1000
Hc individual	9.672	8/1000

Generalization. Besides the ability of learning instead of design, another interesting aspect is the *generalization performance* of the acquired policy – how well does the policy behave on previously unseen situations? To test this, we randomly generated 1000 power demand scenarios. This was done by randomly setting the connection weights to real values in the grid and looking at the resulting power in the consumer nodes. This power profile then was used as a demand – therefore we are guaranteed that at least one solution exists. Table 2 shows the result. Even though the learning agents never saw the tested scenarios before, no failure occurred on the 1000 scenarios. The average costs per scenario are even lower than for the communicating hand-crafted policy π_{hc}. Two reasons contribute to this generalization performance: First, the state description is on a very abstract level and therefore each state describes a large amount of typical situations that may occur in the underlying power-grid. Second, the training examples are reasonably chosen, so that typical situations are contained.

3.3   The Cooperate, Communicate, and Take-Care Benchmark

In the second benchmark, additionally the ability to 'take care' of a depending agent is examined. It is based on a 3 producer, 3 distributer and 3 consumer power grid (right in Fig. 2). Here again, the distributors A and B share a common producer (II) and thus have to cooperate and communicate. Additionally, a third distributor C exists, which is only connected to distributor A. This means, that C has to get all its current via A, since there is no direct link to a producer. Therefore, in addition to the previous 'cooperate and communicate' capabilities, the policy of A now has to consider not only its direct consumer, but also the connected distributor. This is different, because in contrast to its connected consumer, A cannot see the local situation of C.

Again, the learning agents were trained on 10 typical scenarios that would require the above-mentioned capabilities. In this benchmark, a communicationless policy not only fails in 9 out of 10 training cases, but also results in high costs for not satisfying the customers (row 1 in Table 3). A communication policy can manage all the training examples (row 2 in Table 3).

Table 3. Performance on the training set for benchmark B

algorithm	costs	failures	no. of runs
π_h	29.5	9/10	-
π_{hc}	19.3	0/10	-
Q shared	19.7	0/10	27,000
Q individual	19.6	0/10	6,109
Hc shared	21.5	1/10	9,900
Hc individual	20.2	1/10	14,709

Learning. Using Q-learning with a shared Q-table (row 3 of Table 3), the agents were able to finally learn a successful policy for all 10 training scenarios in about 27,000 runs. Again, this number is small compared to the number of possible policies ($\approx 4 \times 10^9$). When the agents are allowed to learn individual policies, a successful policy can be learned much faster: about 6,000 runs were needed in this case (row 4 of Table 3). Both policies showed only slightly higher costs than the hand-crafted policy and no failure occurred. In this benchmark, learning turned out to be more complicated than in benchmark A. Two changes had to be made to get satisfying results. First, a modified cost-function

$$C' = \sum_t \min\{1, \sum_i c_i(t)\} \tag{2}$$

was used that does not extra punish situations, in which more than one consumer is unsatisfied. Therefore 'escaping' from a non-optimal policy by unsatisfying other customers is more likely than in case of the original cost-function. Second, we used a simple random exploration scheme: during training, approximately every tenth decision was made randomly (when testing the performance, the policy is strictly greedy with respect to the Q-table). As a result of this random exploration (and the violations of the MDP-assumptions of Q-learning), the policy did not converge to a final policy. The results thus reports the best policy found after at most 50,000 runs.

The hill-climbing agents also found quite successful policies in a reasonable amount of time, but both the shared policy and the individual policy agents failed to satisfy all customers in one of the 10 training cases.

Generalization. As in the first benchmark, the generalization abilities of the learned policies were tested against the hand-crafted policies (Table 4). On 1000 randomly generated scenarios, the communication-less hand-crafted policy failed in 9 cases. Using the hand-crafted policy π_{hc} with communication, all but one scenario could be solved (the problem with this scenario is caused by a non-defined responsibility for the link between two distributors. Whereas one distributor needs to increase the weight, the other needs to decrease it. A solution would be to exactly define in which situation which distributor may

Table 4. Performance on the test set for benchmark B

algorithm	costs	failures
π_h	15.006	9/1000
π_{hc}	14.947	1/1000
Q shared	14.947	1/1000
Q individual	15.587	1/1000
Hc shared	15.614	5/1000
Hc individual	17.936	10/1000

change the link. This would mean changing the implementation of the meta-actions and to have an additional state feature). The learned policy *Q-shared* did equally well on the test set, and failed only to solve the same scenario as π_{hc}. The individual Q-learned policies also only failed once, but the average costs per run where higher than in the single policy cases. A reason for this might be that in case of individual policies, more training examples were needed. Since the hill-climbing solutions already performed worse on the training examples, it is not surprising that the policies did not especially good on the test set.

3.4   Evaluation of the Results

The experiments confirm the usefulness of the proposed optimization framework to autonomously acquire good policies in distributed multi agents systems by learning from experience. The global reinforcement signal representing the global goal rather than the local benefit of a single agent, forces the agents to cooperate and to share their resources. The problems of a local restricted view can be overcome by the introduction of communication facilities. The agents were able to learn to communicate appropriately to fulfill their given global goal. It turned out that despite the violation of several assumptions, Q-learning can be used as an efficient learning mechanism for the agents. This point is subject to ongoing research. The learned policies generalized well to unknown situations. This shows, that from only a few characteristic examples very general policies can be learned. This might already be good enough for many real world applications where we are more interested in a good all-day performance than in the optimal response to some very rarely occurring situations. However, a learning system might even manage these cases, if the training set is incrementally enlarged every time the system faces a new yet unsolved situation.

4   Conclusion

Pure reactivity instead of deliberativeness does not mean to loose important problem solving capabilities like cooperation, coordination and communication.

If reactive behaviour is permanently improved in an optimization framework, then social interaction may emerge as a result of the endeavour of a team of agents, that is trying to achieve their shared optimization goal. Even communication mechanisms can be learned, if they provide a useful means to help to solve the optimziation goal.

The special features of a power grid network, especially the necessary need to cooperate in order to fulfill every demand in the network and the need of communication in case of locally restriced view make it an interesting benchmark to study social capabilities of agents. Clearly, at the current state, the proposed learning algorithms are not yet powerful enough to scale to large real world problems. On the theoretical side, it is not clear, how reinforcement based learning algorithms should be designed, that provably converge in distributed environments. An additional theoretical difficulty is posed, when the view of each agent is locally restricted. However, a growing amount of both theoretical and empirical work in the area of learning in distributed agent systems provides a basis for practical applications in the next few years. An interesting industrial application area is the field of production control, where reactive agents may take the part of (approximately) optimally scheduling jobs in large production systems [8], [10].

References

1. L. C. Baird. Residual algorithms: Reinforcement learning with function approximation. In *Machine Learning: Proceedings of the 12th International Conference*, 1995.
2. A. G. Barto and R. H. Crites. Improving elevator performance using reinforcement learning. In M. E. Hasselmo D. S. Touretzky, M. C. Mozer, editors, *Advances in Neural Information Processing Systems 8*. MIT Press, 1996.
3. C. Boutilier. Sequential optimality and coordination in multi agent systems. *Proceedings of 16.th Joint Conference on Artificial Intelligence, IJCAI*, pages 178–185, 1998.
4. W. Brauer and G. Weiss. Multi-machine scheduling – a multi-agent learning approach. In *Proceedings of the 3rd International Conference on Multi-Agent Systems*, pages 42–48, 1998.
5. W. Wong A. Moore J. Schneider and M. Riedmiller. Distributed value functions. In *Proceedings of International Conference on Machine Learning, ICML'99*, pages 371–378, Bled, Slovenia, 1999.
6. L. P. Kaelbling, M. L. Littman, and A. W. Moore. Reinforcement learning: A survey. *Journal of Artificial Intelligence Research*, 4:237–285, 1996.
7. M. Lauer and M. Riedmiller. An algorithm for distributed reinforcement learning in cooperative multi-agent systems. In *Proceedings of International Conference on Machine Learning, ICML '00*, pages 535–542, Stanford, CA, 2000.
8. S. Mahadevan and G. Theocharous. Optimization production manufacturing using reinforcement learning. In *Proceedings of the Eleventh International FLAIRS Conference*, pages 372 – 377. AAAI Press, 1998.
9. M. Riedmiller. Concepts and facilities of a neural reinforcement learning control architecture for technical process control. *Journal of Neural Computing and Application*, 8:323–338, 2000.

10. S. Riedmiller and M. Riedmiller. A neural reinforcement learning approach to learn local dispatching policies in production scheduling. In *Proceedings of International Joint Conference on Artificial Intelligence, ICJAI'99*, Stockholm, 1999.

11. C. J. Watkins. *Learning from Delayed Rewards*. PhD thesis, Cambridge University, 1989.

12. M. Woolridge. Intelligent agents. In G. Weiss, editor, *Multi Agent Systems*. MIT Press, 1999.

Being Reactive by Exchanging Roles: An Empirical Study

Olivier Sigaud[1] and Pierre Gérard[1,2]

[1] Dassault Aviation, DGT/DPR/ESA
78, Quai Marcel Dassault, 92552 St-Cloud Cedex, France
[2] AnimatLab-LIP6, 8, rue du capitaine Scott, 75015 Paris, France
olivier.sigaud@dassault-aviation.fr, pierre.gerard@lip6.fr

Abstract. In the multi-agent community, the need for social deliberation appears contradictory with the need for reactivity. In this paper, we
try to show that we can draw the benefits of both being reactive and
being socially organized thanks to what we call "social reactivity".
In order to defend this claim, we describe a simulation experiment in
which several sheepdog agents have to coordinate their effort to drive
a flock of ducks towards a goal area. We implement reactive controllers for agents in the Classifier Systems formalism and we compare the
performance of purely reactive, solipsistic agents which are coordinated
implicitly with the performance of agents using roles. We show that our
role-based agents perform better than the solipsistic ones, but because of
constraints on the roles of the agents, the solipsistic controllers are more
robust and more opportunistic. Then we show that, by exchanging reactively their roles, a process which can be seen as implementing a form
of social deliberation, role-based agents finally outperform the solipsistic
ones. Since designing by hand the rules for exchanging the roles proved
difficult, we conclude by advocating the necessity of tackling the problem
of letting the agents learn their own role exchange processes.

1 Introduction

Defining reactivity is difficult since the word has several meanings which are
closely related but not exactly equivalent. According to [13], reactivity is a matter
of responsiveness in time. In order to be reactive, an agent must do the right thing
at the right time. This view of reactivity has been one of the early leitmotives
of the rising field of behavior-based artificial intelligence [7,14] in reaction to the
endless planning processes used in classical artificial intelligence robotics. Since
the lack of reactivity of the planning robots prevented them from being used in
dynamic environments, it was claimed that doing the right thing was pointless
if it was not done in time.

Another definition of reactivity comes from a more formal background. In the
framework of Markov Decision Processes (MDP), the *Markov hypothesis* holds
when having any information about the past experience does not help an agent to
adopt a better behavior at the current time step. If the Markov hypothesis holds,

M. Hannebauer et al. (Eds.): Reactivity and Deliberation in MAS, LNAI 2103, pp. 150–172, 2001.

the problem faced by the agent is said to be a Markov problem. In this framework, an agent is said reactive if it selects its action according to its present situation without using any memory of the past. In a Markov problem, a reactive agent can act optimally. This view of reactivity, clearly presented in [8], is widespread in the reinforcement learning community. In this volume, [5] and [16] present a framework relying on that formalism.

Both views of reactivity differ in the fact that the second one does not imply anything about the time that the agent spends choosing its current action. But they are closely related since an agent which makes no use of its memory cannot make any prediction about the future. Hence, a reactive agent in the second sense does not spend any time in planning, it only reacts to its current situation. Since this notion of reactivity is very restrictive, it should allow any agent which verify it to be reactive in the first sense, *i.e.* to decide what to do very fast, then to react in time to events in its environment.

Now, if an agent is reactive in the second sense, it can be proven formally that there are situations where it will not be able to adopt an optimal behavior. These problems are called *non-Markov problems*. Each time the Markov hypothesis does not hold, relying only on the current perception does not allow to select the best action. Hence it is clear that adopting a reactive behavior means selecting short-sighted actions, which may not be suitable when long-term strategies are necessary.

Collective tasks are full of such situations where looking for an immediate reward or pursuing an immediate goal is not the best thing that an agent may do. For instance, in the ROBOCUP domain [1], if an agent has the ball and is close to the goal, it may shoot reactively even if an opponent is likely to catch the ball, whereas it might be more appropriate to give the ball to a teammate who is better located. The second behavior could be seen as deliberative rather than reactive because it seems to imply that the agent knows that after it passes the ball, its teammate will shoot and score. This example seems to support the view according to which deliberative social behaviors and reactivity are two opposite requirements which should be balanced in a multi-agent architecture.

In this paper we want to challenge this view. We will show through an empirical study that social behaviors can be as reactive as solipsistic behaviors. In our previous example, giving the ball to a teammate is a behavior which can be fired as reactively as shooting to the goal. The fact that giving the ball allows to score in the long term does not imply that social agents have to plan in order to find that such a behavior is more efficient than merely shooting. Our purpose is to show that giving roles to the agents and applying reinforcement learning schemes that take into account long-term rewards allows them to adopt some behaviors which an external observer would consider as exhibiting social deliberation abilities, whereas these behaviors are implemented reactively. In particular, we will show that giving to the agents the ability to exchange their roles is both something which helps finding better strategies and something which can be done straight-forwardly.

The paper is organized as follows. In the next section, we describe our simulated problem and the multi-agent strategy we designed to solve it. In Sect. 3, we present the Learning Classifier Systems (LCS) [1] framework and how we used it in order to implement the controller of our agents. In Sect. 4, we present the solipsistic controller which we designed and some obvious drawbacks of this design. In Sect. 5, we show how our first hand-crafted controller was significantly improved by an explicit use of roles, resulting in a new architecture involving a set of behaviors devoted to the fulfillment of each role, and we present the benefits which can be drawn from such an architecture. In Sect. 6, we compare the results obtained with both hand-crafted controllers through a first empirical study. In particular, we compare their robustness to changes in parameters of the simulation. In Sect. 7, we discuss these results and show that the lack of robustness of the role-based controllers is due to the incapability of the agents to exchange their roles. Then we present further evidence for the necessity of letting the agents exchange their roles. In Sect. 8, we present a new role-based controller which takes this necessity into account and show that the robustness problem is solved. In Sect. 9, we discuss our architecture from a more multi-agent oriented stance, and highlight what would be necessary to apply it to more complicated problems. Since designing by hand the rules for exchanging the roles proved difficult, we conclude in Sect. 10 by advocating the necessity of tackling the problem of letting the agents learn their own role exchange processes.

2   The Problem and Its Representation

The necessity of having good benchmarks to test and compare algorithms and architectures is now central in the multi-agent research community. The ROBO-CUP [1] is such a benchmark seeming both general and complicated enough to act as a representative testbed for the entire field. In this volume, [3] and [6] illustrate their concepts in the ROBOCUP domain. But, if one uses machine learning techniques and adaptive capabilities to solve the complete task, the problem seems too difficult. In the particular case of reinforcement learning techniques, the agents do not get enough feedback to learn everything from scratch. The researchers may either use these techniques at one particular level of the game, or use them to solve particular subtasks (for instance, the pass to a teammate [2]).

Therefore, the tendency in adaptive multi-agent simulations is to study much simpler application domains. The Prey/Predator pursuit domain involving several predators [20] is such a benchmark and illustrates this trend. But in these latter cases, the problem is often oversimplified: the agents move in a grid-world, they have few possible actions. Hence, the problem lacks the continuous dynamics characterizing most industrial applications. Since our focus is on adaptive

---

[1] In order to make clear that we sometimes use the Classifier Systems formalism without applying learning algorithms, we will distinguish Classifier Systems (CS) as a formalism and Learning Classifier Systems (LCS) as a technique throughout this paper.

techniques and we have industrial applications in mind, we have chosen to design an original application which appears as a good compromise between the too complex ROBOCUP problem and the oversimplified Prey/Predator problem. We draw inspiration from [23], who have presented the Robot Sheepdog Project, involving a robot driving a flock of ducks towards a goal position. The algorithm controlling the robot was first tested in simulation and then implemented on a real robot driving a real flock of ducks.

In this paper, we present a simulated extension of the task to the case where several agents share the goal mentioned above. Since it is neither oversimplified nor too complex, we believe that this experiment is a good case-study to meet and tackle the difficulties arising when one tries to combine adaptive capabilities and multi-agent coordination schemes.

2.1 Description of the Problem

Our simulated environment is shown in Fig. 1. It includes a circular arena, a flock of ducks and some *sheepdog agents* who must drive the flock towards a goal area. We tested all controllers in simulations involving at least three sheepdog agents and six ducks. The ducks and the sheepdog agents have the same maximum velocity. The goal is achieved as soon as all the ducks are inside the goal area.

The behavior of the ducks results from a combination of three tendencies. They tend:

- to keep away from the walls of the arena [2];
- to join their mates when they see them, *i.e.* when they are within their visual range;
- to flee from the sheepdog agents which are within their visual range.

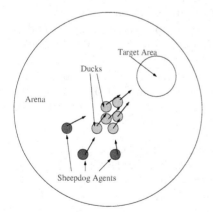

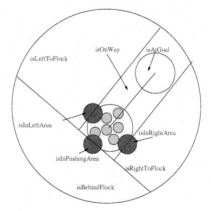

Fig. 1. The arena, ducks and sheepdogs   **Fig. 2.** Description of the situation

---

[2] Therefore, if they are left on their own, they tend to go to the center of the arena

Once the behavior of the ducks is implemented, we must design the controllers of the sheepdog agents so that they drive the flock towards the goal area. A first step of this design process consists in finding which features of the simulated environment are relevant to achieve the goal of the sheepdog agents. This is what we present in the next section.

2.2 Description of the Pre-conceived Strategy

When one programs the sheepdog agents as simply being attracted by the center of the flock, it appears that, when a sheepdog agent is close to the flock and follows it, the flock tends to scatter because each duck goes away from the sheepdog along a radial straight line.

In order to solve this scattering problem, the strategy we adopted was to design the behavior of the agents so that at least one agent should push the flock towards the target area from behind, while at least one other agent should follow the flock on its left hand side and another one on its right hand side so that the flock would not scatter while being pushed.

2.3 Description of the Inputs of the Sheepdogs

As a result of this design, the description of the situation given to the agents consists of a set of tests on their position, as shown in Fig. 2. This gives us a first set of conditions:

- isAtGoal
- isLeftToFlock
- isInLeftArea
- isBehindFlock

- isOnWay
- isRightToFlock
- isInRightArea
- isInPushingArea

The important point is that all these position tests are relative to the position of the flock rather than absolute positions with coordinates. But the agents always know where they are with respect to the flock center, which would not be the case with an actual robot having a limited vision field. Thus these inputs might be thought of as delivered after treatments from a camera watching from above. Furthermore, there is no noise on them, which prevents us from drawing any conclusion on the applicability of our framework in the real world.

In order to coordinate the actions of the agents, we also added the following tests on the situation of other agents:

- nobodyBehindFlock
- nobodyInLeftArea
- nobodyLeftToFlock
- nobodyOnWay

- nobodyPushing
- nobodyInRightArea
- nobodyRightToFlock
- isFlockFormed

Here again, the information is always perfectly accurate, while it would require a complicated communication protocol or a top-level manager to ensure this in an actual robotic experiment.

Our choices might appear surprising to multi-agent systems designers. But they are sound in our industrial context. Our focus is on adding adaptive behaviors capabilities in complex simulations where engineers do not want to take care about constraints on the availability of the information if this information is actually computed in the simulator [3]. Our choice would be different if we had to design a multi-robot system or to meet the constraining requirements of the ROBOCUP simulation league.

2.4   Description of the Behaviors of the Sheepdogs

All the behaviors of the sheepdog agents consist in going towards a certain point. In general, when the flock is formed, the sheepdog agents react to the center of the flock. But, when the flock is scattered, they can also react to the duck which is closest to them or the one which is the further from the center of the flock. The name of each behavior can be interpreted straight-forwardly. In the case of the *"driveXtoY"* behaviors, it consists in going behind X with respect to Y so as to push X towards Y. The overall behavior set is the following:

- doNothing
- goToFlockCenter
- goBehindFlock
- goToLeftGuidingPoint
- goToRightOfFlock
- driveOutmostDuckToFlock
- driveClosestDuckToGoal
- goToOutmostDuck

- goToGoalCenter
- followFlockToGoal
- goToPushingPoint
- goToRightGuidingPoint
- goToLeftOfFlock
- driveClosestDuckToFlock
- goToClosestDuck
- goAwayFromFlock

The controllers of our sheepdog agents involve 16 conditions and 16 basic behaviors. Designing the controller involving these sensori-motor capabilities consists in finding a good mapping between the conditions and the behaviors.

3   Implementing Controllers as Classifier Systems

3.1   Elements of the Learning Classifier System Framework

As we have some industrial applications in mind, we want to use a formalism into which we can put some expert control knowledge. But we also want to use adaptive techniques. In this context, the Learning Classifier Systems (LCS) formalism appears as a natural candidate.

The LCS framework designed by [12] gave rise to popular adaptive algorithms. Since the work of [24] who simplified this first framework, a classical LCS can be seen as composed of a population of rules, or *classifiers*, containing *conditions* as a set of observations and *actions*:

$$[Condition] \rightarrow [Action](Strength)$$

---

[3] See [18] for more information on the industrial side of this work

The different parts of the classifier are strings of symbols in $\{0, 1, \#\}$, where $\#$ means "either 0 or 1". The population of classifiers was generally evolved thanks to a *genetic algorithm* (GA) – see [11] – using the strength of the classifiers as a fitness measure. When several classifiers could be fired in the same state, the strength was also used to select the one which would be fired. In these early versions of LCSs, the quality of the classifiers was modified by the *Bucket Brigade* algorithm according to the estimated reward received by the agent for firing the classifier.

A major improvement of the LCS framework was acheived by [25] in designing XCS, replacing a *strength-based* LCS by an *accuracy-based* one.

Recently, a new way of using the LCS framework has received a growing interest [19]. Based on ideas of [17], it consists in adding in the classifiers an [*Effect*] part which allows the system to use the classifiers for anticipating rather than merely reacting to the environment. It uses direct experience in order to build new classifiers, instead of relying on a genetic algorithm. The classifiers of such LCSs contain the following components:

$$[Condition][Action] \rightarrow [Effect] \ (quality\,parameters)$$

The learning process of such LCSs can be decomposed into two complementary processes:

• *latent learning* consists in building a reliable model of the dynamics of the environment, by ensuring that the [*Effect*] part of all classifiers are correct. This new part stores information about state transitions and allows lookahead planning. The latent learning process can take place at each time step without any reward, hence it is very efficient. In particular, as [26] has shown, the quality of anticipation of every classifier which can be fired at a time can be updated according to the subsequent input message, even if the classifier has not actually been fired;

• *reinforcement learning* consists in improving a policy using the experience of the system, so that it becomes able to choose the optimal action in every state. This process takes advantage of latent learning to converge faster.

These new approaches can be seen as replacing the blind search performed by the GA by an heuristic search which takes advantage of the previous experience to improve the classifiers. As a result, they are less general since, for instance, they are devoted to tackling multi-steps problems whereas GA-based LCS can also tackle single-step problems, but they are also more efficient in what they are designed for.

3.2   Our Algorithm

Our own classifiers contain the following components:

$$[Condition][Action] \rightarrow [Effect] \ R$$

where R estimates the immediate reward received by the system when the classifier is fired.

The latent learning process creates and deletes classifiers. The creation process can be split in two main parts:

- the effect covering mechanism adjusts the effect parts by comparing successive observations and correcting mistakes;
- the condition specialization process identifies the most general of relevant conditions.

A classifier which sometimes anticipates well and sometimes not is such that its [Condition] part matches several distinct states. It is too general and must be replaced by new classifiers with more specialized [Condition] parts.

These mechanisms allow the system to converge towards a set of accurate classifiers anticipating correctly. We use this information about the state transitions in order to improve the reinforcement learning process.

The first part of this process consists in estimating the immediate reward resulting from the firing of each classifier. At each time step, we use the received reward to update an estimation of the immediate reward (R) of every classifier involving the last action and the last state, even if it has not actually been fired. The state transition informations and the immediate reward estimations allow to use a Dynamic Programming algorithm [4] to compute a policy. A more detailed description of this algorithm can be found in [9].

Rather than initializing a LCS with random classifiers or completely general ones, we first tried to use the CS formalism for implementing expert classifiers without using its adaptive capabilities. The methodological issues of our work are discussed in detail in [18].

4   A "Basic" Controller

In Table 1, we present the first controller that we designed in order to implement the solution described in Sect. 2.2. It can be seen that we only use 13 of the 16 available inputs. Each line in the table is a classifier telling to the agent what to do in a particular situation. For instance, the first line says that if the agent is in the pushing area and if there is nobody on the way of the flock towards the goal and if the flock is formed, then the agent should go towards the goal center.

From Table 1, it can be seen that this representation of the controller is not very compact: there are a lot of "#", which means that each classifier uses very few of the available inputs. As a result, the controller is difficult to design, since any change in the input set involves reconsidering all the lines in the table. As it will appear in Sect. 6, the controller could also be more efficient.

Of particular interest are the five last classifiers, which are devoted to the case when the flock is scattered. Since we had no idea of how to organize the behaviors in such a case, we only gave five possible behaviors to deal with that situation and let the controllers pick one of them at random at each time step. As we will show in Sect. 6, this is not an efficient design, even though it still allows the sheepdogs to reach their goals. But this inefficient design also lets room for improvement by using adaptive algorithms. Though this is not the focus of this

Table 1. A hand-crafted controller

isBehindFlock	isInPushingArea	isLeftToFlock	isRightToFlock	isInLeftArea	isInRightArea	isOnWay	nobodyBehindFlock	nobodyPushing	nobodyLeftToFlock	nobodyRightToFlock	nobodyOnWay	isFlockFormed	Action
#	1	#	#	#	#	#	#	#	#	#	1	1	goToGoalCenter
#	1	#	#	#	#	#	#	#	#	#	1	1	goToFlockCenter
1	#	#	#	#	#	#	#	1	#	#	#	#	goToPushingPoint
#	#	1	#	#	#	#	1	#	#	#	#	#	goBehindFlock
#	#	1	#	#	#	#	#	1	#	#	#	#	goBehindFlock
#	#	#	1	#	#	#	1	#	#	#	#	#	goBehindFlock
#	#	#	1	#	#	#	#	1	#	#	#	#	goBehindFlock
#	#	1	#	1	#	#	0	0	#	#	1	1	followFlockToGoal
#	#	#	1	#	1	#	0	0	#	#	1	1	followFlockToGoal
#	#	1	#	0	#	#	#	#	#	#	1	1	goToLeftPushingPoint
#	#	#	1	#	0	#	#	#	#	#	1	1	goToRightPushingPoint
#	#	#	#	#	#	1	#	#	#	1	#	#	goToRightPushingPoint
#	#	#	#	#	#	1	0	#	#	0	#	#	goToRightPushingPoint
#	#	#	#	#	#	1	#	#	#	1	#	#	goToLeftofFlock
#	#	#	#	#	#	1	0	#	#	0	#	#	goToLeftofFlock
#	#	#	#	#	#	1	#	#	1	#	#	#	goToLeftPushingPoint
#	#	#	#	#	#	1	0	#	0	#	#	#	goToLeftPushingPoint
#	#	#	#	#	#	1	#	#	1	#	#	#	goToRightofFlock
#	#	#	#	#	#	1	0	#	0	#	#	#	goToRightofFlock
#	#	#	#	#	#	#	#	#	#	#	#	0	driveClosestDuckToFlock
#	#	#	#	#	#	#	#	#	#	#	#	0	goToOutmostDuck
#	#	#	#	#	#	#	#	#	#	#	#	0	goToClosestDuck
#	#	#	#	#	#	#	#	#	#	#	#	0	driveOutmostDuckToFlock
#	#	#	#	#	#	#	#	#	#	#	#	0	goAwayFromFlock

paper, in Sect. 6 we will breifly mention that, by specializing these classifiers, *i.e.* by adding new conditions on them, and by giving them different probabilities of being selected, our learning algorithm was able to obtain very quickly a better controller than the one we designed by hand.

5   A Role-Based Controller

The notion of role appears naturally in the strategy we presented in Sect. 2.2. In our solution, at least one agent must push the flock from behind (playing a PUSHER role) and at least one agent must guide the flock on its left hand side and another one on its right hand side (playing LEFTGUIDE and RIGHTGUIDE roles respectively). Therefore we tried to modify the architecture of the controller used

Table 2. The role table (F. stands for Future)

isInPushingArea	isInLeftArea	isInRightArea	isFlockFormed	Former Role	New Role
1	#	#	1	F.Pusher	Pusher
#	1	#	1	F.LeftGuide	LeftGuide
#	#	1	1	F.RightGuide	RightGuide
1	#	#	0	F.Pusher	F.Pusher
#	1	#	0	F.LeftGuide	F.LeftGuide
#	#	1	0	F.RightGuide	F.RightGuide
1	#	#	0	Pusher	F.Pusher
#	1	#	0	LeftGuide	F.LeftGuide
#	#	1	0	RightGuide	F.RightGuide
0	#	#	#	Pusher	F.Pusher
#	0	#	#	LeftGuide	F.LeftGuide
#	#	0	#	RightGuide	F.RightGuide

in Sect. 3 so as to make an explicit use of roles. Our new architecture contains two kinds of components:

• The *role table* is a CS stating under which conditions on the situation a agent changes its role into another role. If no observation matches, the role remains the same. The roles are initialized so that each agent chooses between FUTUREPUSHER, FUTURELEFTGUIDE and FUTURERIGHTGUIDE randomly, but in such a way that each role is assigned to at least one agent. Then the role of the agent evolves between FUTUREX and X, where X is either PUSHER, LEFTGUIDE or RIGHTGUIDE. But with this controller, a pusher cannot become a lateral guide nor vice versa. Our *role table* is shown in Table 2.

• The *behavior tables* are CSs which fire actions of the agent according to conditions on the situation. There is one table for each role. Hence, there is only one *behavior table* active at a time in the controller of each agent, the one which corresponds to the role played by the agent.

We have six behaviors, each one corresponding to the fulfillment of one particular role, *i.e.* FUTUREPUSHERBEHAVIOR, PUSHERBEHAVIOR, FUTURELEFT-GUIDEBEHAVIOR, LEFTGUIDEBEHAVIOR, FUTURERIGHTGUIDEBEHAVIOR and RIGHTGUIDEBEHAVIOR. All these *behavior tables* are shown in Tables 3–8.

Introducing roles in our architecture brings several benefits.

• It is easier to design a *behavior CS* devoted to fulfill one particular role, since a particular role corresponds to a specialized part of the global behavior. Hence, each *behavior table* is much smaller than the Table 1 presented in Sect. 3.

Table 3. FuturePusherBehavior

isInPushingArea	isFlockFormed	isBehindFlock	Action
0	1	#	goToPushingPoint
1	1	#	goAwayFromFlock
#	0	0	goBehindFlock
#	0	1	driveClosestDuckToFlock

Table 4. PusherBehavior

isInPushingArea	isBehindFlock	nobodyOnWay	nobodyLeftToFlock	nobodyRightToFlock	isFlockFormed	Action
1	#	1	0	0	1	goToGoalCenter
0	1	#	#	#	1	goToPushingPoint
#	0	#	#	#	1	goBehindFlock
#	0	#	#	#	0	driveOutmostDuckToFlock
#	1	#	#	#	0	goToOutmostDuck

Table 5. FutureLeftGuideBehavior

isLefttoFlock	isInLeftArea	isFlockFormed	isBehindFlock	Action
1	0	1	#	goToLeftArea
0	#	1	#	goToLeftofFlock
#	#	0	0	goBehindFlock
#	#	0	1	driveClosestDuckToFlock

Table 6. LeftGuideBehavior

isLefttoFlock	isInLeftArea	nobodyPushing	isFlockFormed	Action
1	#	0	1	followFlockToGoal
#	1	0	1	followFlockToGoal
0	0	#	1	goToLeftArea
#	#	#	0	goToOutmostDuck

Table 7. FutureRightGuideBehavior

isRighttoFlock	isInRightArea	isFlockFormed	isBehindFlock	Action
1	0	1	#	goToRightArea
0	#	1	#	goToRightofFlock
#	#	0	0	goBehindFlock
#	#	0	1	driveClosestDuckToFlock

Table 8. RightGuideBehavior

isRighttoFlock	isInRightArea	nobodyPushing	isFlockFormed	Action
1	#	0	1	followFlockToGoal
#	1	0	1	followFlockToGoal
0	0	#	1	goToRightArea
#	#	#	0	goToClosestDuck

• It is easier to deal with the case where the flock is scattered. Since each agent can fire different actions according to its role, it is easier to find a good coordination scheme between all actions, with respect to the case of the reactive controller where we had no control on which action would be fired by which agent.

- From a reinforcement learning research perspective, it is easier to design an internal reinforcement signal policy when we use roles. Generally, fulfilling a role corresponds to reaching a particular situation which can be detected by the agent, and/or to insure that some validity conditions hold. Then the agents can be rewarded or punished if the first condition holds or the second one is broken. In our flock control simulation, for example, playing a FUTURELEFTGUIDE role involves reaching the *leftArea* while playing a LEFTGUIDE role involves keeping the flock formed. Hence, an agent in charge of the left side of the flock can be rewarded when it reaches the *leftArea*, becoming a LEFTGUIDE, and punished if the flock is scattered, coming back to FUTURELEFTGUIDE. We think that this is a good way of introducing intermediate reinforcement signals, in a more natural framework than in [15], for instance.

6   Empirical Study

We first ran 2000 experiments to get a statistically significant view of the results obtained with these controllers. Although the hand-crafted role-based controllers appeared more efficient than the ones without roles with three sheepdogs, we did want to check whether it would be more or less robust with respect to the size of the population of agents, since the role-based controllers are designed for a group of three sheepdogs.

Therefore, we decided to test the robustness of both control policies by testing them with various sets of parameters, and particularly by changing the size of the population of sheepdogs.

6.1   Robustness to an Increasing Number of Sheepdogs

We first tested the robustness of the controllers when the number of sheepdog agents was increased from three to twenty.

The results are shown on Fig. 3. Each point in the curves represents an average performance over 100 trials, and each set of 100 trials starts with the same 100 random initial positions. We must also mention that the goal is never reached in less than 95 time steps, which is the minimum number of time steps for the sheepdog agents to surround the flock and drive it to the goal from a lucky initial situation.

If a trial lasts more than 4000 time steps, it is stopped and counted as a failure. Failures are not taken into account in the computation of the average, since their duration is arbitrary. Since there are very few failures, we do not devote a figure to show them. Indeed, the worst case was four failures over the 100 trials that give one point on the figures. It appears that the role-based controller failed ten times on the $18 \times 100 = 1800$ trials, while the basic and learned basic controllers only failed respectively five times and two times over the 1800 trials. The failures happen more often with more than twelve sheepdogs in the role-based case, which supports our diagnosis of a lack of robustness of this solution.

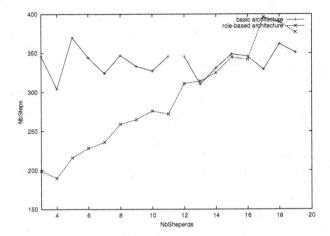

Fig. 3. Robustness of basic and role-based controllers to 3 to 20 sheepdogs

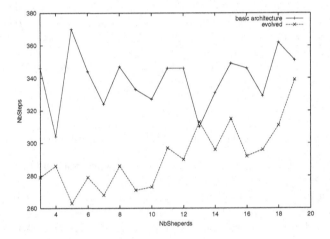

Fig. 4. Robustness of basic and evolved controllers to 3 to 20 sheepdogs

It can be seen in Fig. 3 that the role-based architecture performs better with three sheepdogs than the basic one, but that the basic architecture is more robust to an increasing number of sheepdogs. It can also be seen in Fig. 4 that the controller obtained from applying adaptive algorithms to the basic architecture during two trials performs better than the hand-crafted basic one, and is still robust.

6.2 Robustness to a Change in the Behavior of the Ducks

In order to understand better the phenomena observed in Sect. 6.1, we also tried to modify the behavior of the ducks so as to modify the dynamics of the environment of the sheepdogs. We tuned the sensitivity of the ducks with respect to the walls of the arena so that they would keep away from these walls only when getting too close to them. As a result, the flock tends to form anywhere in the arena rather than only in the center as in the previous case. However, the repulsiveness of the walls is sensed far before the ducks reach the target area. As a result, it is not easier for the sheepdogs to drive the flock to the target area. We also lowered the tendency of the ducks to go towards each other so that the flock would scatter more often. These two modifications makes the job harder for the sheepdogs.

The relative performance of the basic and role-based controllers with both kinds of ducks can be seen on Fig. 5. It can be seen that, as expected, the performance of the basic controller is very sensitive to the change of the behavior of the ducks. The performance is much worse with the new ducks, and tends to be much less robust to an increase of the number of sheepdogs. On the contrary, the performance of the role-based controller is nearly unaffected by the change of ducks, both curves are nearly identical.

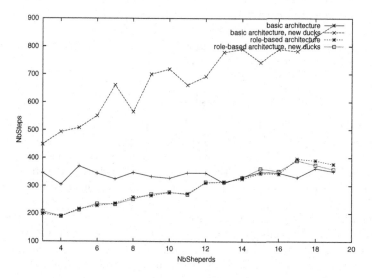

Fig. 5. Robustness of both controllers to a new behavior of ducks

7 Discussion of the Results

7.1 Explaining the Results

The reduced performance of the basic architecture when applied to the new ducks can be explained by the fact that the flock is scattered more often. We have shown that it was more difficult to design an efficient strategy with the basic controller to deal with the case where the flock was scattered, since the behavior of the different agents could not be specialized.

In contrast, the performance of the role-based controllers is not degraded, their efficiency is not affected by the increasing tendency of the flock to scatter.

But why is this that the role-based controllers are less robust to an increasing number of sheepdogs than the basic one? From a closer look at a lot of simulation runs, it appeared that this comes from a longer time spent in the initial messy situation before the flock can get formed. At the beginning of each trial, indeed, all the sheepdogs and ducks are scattered at random in the arena. Hence, the more sheepdogs there are among the ducks, the longer it takes to the ducks to form a flock.

This is particularly true for the role-based agents. Since each agent has its own role at the beginning, it must reach its pushing or guiding area, even if it is by the wrong side of the flock. As a result, it may cross the flock and scatter it or at least delay the movement of the ducks towards each other. Therefore, the more role-based agents there are, the more they tend to prevent the ducks from forming a flock.

The basic agents, on the contrary, organize themselves more opportunistically with respect to their initial positions. Each agent goes to the closest pushing or driving area. Since there are more agents, these areas are reached faster and this compensates for the longer time spent in forming the flock.

We can summarize this finding in asserting that the basic controllers are less tightly designed, but result in more opportunistic behaviors than the one obtained with the role-based controllers.

7.2 Good Reasons for Exchanging the Roles

We have shown in Sect. 6 that our role-based controller was less robust than the basic one because the role of the agents were assigned from the start and the agents were not allowed to re-organize themselves opportunistically.

The lack of opportunism of the role-based architecture comes from the fact that our hand-crafted role table specifies too narrowly the situations into which one role should be exchanged with another one. More precisely, as we have said, one agent which has started with a FUTUREX role can only switch to a X role and back, where X stands for PUSHER, LEFTGUIDE and RIGHTGUIDE.

Three different considerations convinced us that the agents should be able to exchange their roles in order to solve their task more efficiently.

- The first one is that a good way of improving the performance of our role-based solution would be to let the agents choose their initial role according to their initial position: they would choose the role driving them to the closest guiding or pushing area. But if we do so, nothing guarantees that there will be at least one agent to play each role. Then it is necessary that they exchange their roles in order to coordinate their efforts.

• The second evidence in favor of letting the agents exchange their roles has been found by examining some particular trials. To our surprise, we discovered that the controllers without roles were often manifesting an unexpected strategy more efficient that the one we had in mind. This strategy is shown in Fig. 6.

It happens that two sheepdog agents are able to drive the flock to the target area. This strategy seems very robust since the ducks seldom escape from the chase of the sheepdog agents. It can be seen as a different distribution of the roles, where two agents play new roles between pusher and guide, and the other ones may help to form the flock again when necessary.

• The last one was also revealed by a closer examination of the behavior of the agents. In the situation depicted in Fig. 7, both guides are by the same side of the flock while the pusher is ready to push. If the agents cannot exchange their roles, the agent which is behind the flock will start pushing it and the flock will scatter, since there is no guide on one side. But if the agents can exchange their roles, the best solution here is that the PUSHER becomes a RIGHTGUIDE while one of the LEFTGUIDES becomes PUSHER and comes behind the flock in order to push. This is the kind of social reorganization which we will present in the next section.

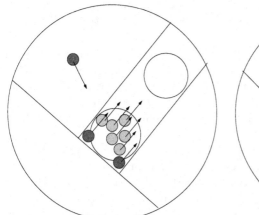

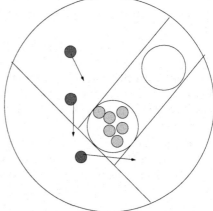

Fig. 6. An emergent strategy   **Fig. 7.** Two guides by the same side

8   A Further Inquiry

8.1   The New Role Table

In order to check that exchanging the roles would allow our controllers to be both more efficient than the basic ones and more robust than the first role-based ones, we designed by hand the new role table shown in Table 9. The corresponding behavior tables are the same as in Sect. 5.

The task was more difficult than what we expected. The difficulty comes from the fact that nothing guarantees anymore that there will be at least one agent to play each role, while this condition is necessary for success. Thus, the classifiers must be designed in such a way that each change of role from one agent is balanced quickly by another change of role from another agent which will play the dropped role. In order to do this, it appeared necessary to add new inputs to coordinate more efficiently the roles. These input state respectively whether there is already an agent which plays a PUSHER, a LEFTGUIDE and a RIGHTGUIDE role or not, without taking into account whether it is a FUTURE one or not. This gives an argument in favor of distinguishing only three roles and two behaviors per role, as we will discuss in Sect. 9.

Once again, these informations about the role played by other agents are considered as available through the simulation platform while it would require complicated communication mechanisms to be maintained among a team of robots. We didn't tackle any team state maintenance, as [21] or [22] do, for instance.

The classifiers shown in Table 9 can be split into four groups.

• The first group, up to classifier 8, deals with the starting situation. Each agent is initialized with the START role, and will only play it during one time step. The classifiers tell which role the agent should choose according to their initial location with respect to the pushing and guiding areas. In the case when the agent is within the flock of ducks or on its way to the goal, it chooses at random to become either FUTURELEFTGUIDE or FUTURERIGHTGUIDE. Since the roles are chosen according to the initial position and these positions are random, nothing guarantees that the roles will be equally distributed between the agents.

• The second and third groups of classifiers do the job which was done in Table 2 by our former role table. The second group, from classifier 9 to classifier 11, deals with the case when a FUTUREX has reached its intermediate goal and becomes an X, while the third group, from classifier 12 to classifier 17, deals with the case when an X has failed playing its role and comes back to the FUTUREX role.

• The last group of classifiers is devoted to the exchanges of roles. The classifiers 18 and 19 tell that if a guiding agent is by the wrong side of the flock with respect to its role, it should change its role rather than try to cross the flock and scatter it. The classifiers from 20 to 27 describe what the guides should do in the situation described in Fig. 7. Classifiers 20 to 23 are fired if there is no guide to deal with the other side, while classifiers 24 to 27 are fired if there is no pusher. This last situation can occur either if the pusher went to the other side

Table 9. The new role table (F. stands for Future)

	isBehindFlock	isLefttoFlock	isRighttoFlock	isInPushingArea	isInLeftArea	isInRightArea	isFlockFormed	isTherePusher	isThereLeftGuide	isThereRightGuide	Former Role	New Role
1	0	0	0	#	#	#	#	#	#	#	Start	F.RightGuide
2	0	0	0	#	#	#	#	#	#	#	Start	F.LeftGuide
3	1	0	0	#	#	#	#	#	#	#	Start	F.Pusher
4	#	1	#	#	#	#	#	#	#	#	Start	F.LeftGuide
5	#	#	1	#	#	#	#	#	#	#	Start	F.RightGuide
6	#	#	#	1	#	#	1	#	#	#	Start	Pusher
7	#	#	#	#	1	#	1	#	#	#	Start	LeftGuide
8	#	#	#	#	#	1	1	#	#	#	Start	RightGuide
9	#	#	#	1	#	#	1	#	1	1	F.Pusher	Pusher
10	#	#	#	#	1	#	1	1	#	1	F.LeftGuide	LeftGuide
11	#	#	#	#	#	1	1	1	1	#	F.RightGuide	RightGuide
12	#	#	#	1	#	#	0	#	1	1	Pusher	F.Pusher
13	#	#	#	0	#	#	#	#	1	1	Pusher	F.Pusher
14	#	#	#	#	1	#	0	1	#	#	LeftGuide	F.LeftGuide
15	#	#	#	#	0	#	#	1	#	#	LeftGuide	F.LeftGuide
16	#	#	#	#	#	1	0	1	#	#	RightGuide	F.RightGuide
17	#	#	#	#	#	0	#	1	#	#	RightGuide	F.RightGuide
18	#	1	#	#	#	#	#	#	#	#	F.RightGuide	F.LeftGuide
19	#	#	1	#	#	#	#	#	#	#	F.LeftGuide	F.RightGuide
20	#	#	1	#	#	#	#	#	0	#	RightGuide	F.Pusher
21	#	1	#	#	#	#	#	#	#	0	LeftGuide	F.Pusher
22	#	#	1	#	#	#	1	#	0	#	F.RightGuide	F.Pusher
23	#	1	#	#	#	#	1	#	#	0	F.LeftGuide	F.Pusher
24	1	#	0	#	#	#	1	0	#	#	F.LeftGuide	F.Pusher
25	1	0	#	#	#	#	1	0	#	#	F.RightGuide	F.Pusher
26	#	#	1	#	#	#	#	0	#	#	RightGuide	F.Pusher
27	#	1	#	#	#	#	#	0	#	#	LeftGuide	F.Pusher
28	#	#	#	#	#	#	#	#	0	1	Pusher	F.LeftGuide
29	#	#	#	#	#	#	#	#	0	1	F.Pusher	F.LeftGuide
30	#	#	#	#	#	#	#	#	1	0	F.Pusher	F.RightGuide
31	#	#	#	#	#	#	#	#	1	0	Pusher	F.RightGuide

as described in Fig. 7, or in the initial situation if there was no agent choosing the FUTUREPUSHER or the PUSHER role at the beginning. At last, the four last classifiers tell what the pusher should do in the situation described in Fig. 7.

The empirical study of the robustness of this new controller gave the results shown in Fig. 8. We used the first kind of ducks under the conditions described

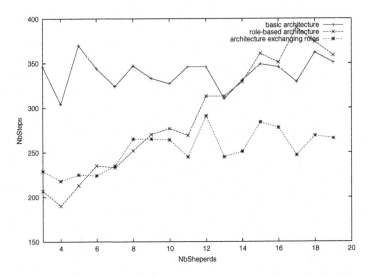

Fig. 8. Robustness of the new controller to an increasing number of sheepdogs

in Sect. 6.1. Two curves were already given in Fig. 3, we present them again for comparison with the new one.

It can be seen that we have acheived what we were trying to. Even if there is still a slight rising slope and if the performance with three to five robots is not as good as the one of the former role-based controller, the new controller is both more robust than this former controller and more efficient than the basic one. There are only three failures over 1800 trials with this controller, one with three sheepdogs, one with five and one with eighteen of them.

We also checked the number of times when each classifier of Table 9 was fired. It appears that the classifiers for exchanging from LEFTGUIDE to RIGHTGUIDE and vice versa are fired 23 times in average on 100 trials, while all the other classifiers for exchanging the roles are fired less than 5 times. This shows that, while these classifiers are used very seldom, much less than once per trial, they result in a very significant improvement of the controllers.

Now, we can claim that the case depicted on Fig. 7 is particularly representative of the discussion we raised in the introduction. The results we obtained show that being reactive and solipsistic is inefficient in that particular situation. It is the kind of situation where the agents must reorganize with each other in order to be more efficient. We have shown that this reorganization can be dealt with in our reactive, CS-based framework, just by designing roles and by letting the agents exchange their roles. Our point was that this seemingly deliberative social behavior can be written as classifiers in the role table of our agents in such a way that they *react socially* to the situation depicted in Fig. 7 just by exchanging their roles. This does not take more time than any other reactive behavior. Here, our agents are clearly reactive in the first sense given in the introduction, *i.e.* they are responsive in time, but not in the second sense, since they use a memory of their former role.

9   Discussion from a Multi-Agent Perspective

We have already said that our research goals are directed towards adaptive behaviors more than towards multi-agent architecture. But having adaptive multi-agent systems also implies to design general architecture providing flexibility and abstraction. Thus, we must improve our work with that respect too. Henceforth, we discuss here some obvious limitations of our architecture from a multi-agent perspective.

First, another way to look at our role-based architecture would be to consider that there are only three roles (PUSHER, LEFTGUIDE and RIGHTGUIDE), and that the fulfillment of each role involves two behaviors (FUTUREX and X). In the case of our example, implementing this way to articulate roles with several behaviors would give rise to an unnecessary complication of the architecture. But in more complicated examples, if more behaviors are necessary to fulfil one role or if the fulfillment of two different roles involves some common behaviors, distinguishing roles and behaviors by binding to each role a set of behaviors and a way to sequentialize their activation would provide a higher degree of flexibility and abstraction.

Such a mechanism can be found in architectures devoted to solve ROBOCUP problems both in [22] and in [21]. The first shares closer goals with our work since some of the behaviors are learned. But the second introduces a higher level of organization, namely the articulation between roles and formations, which might also help improve our work.

Indeed, the fact that having more sheepdogs to drive the flock results in poorer performance unless we design a very robust controller is rather counter-intuitive. The key point here is that our agents use the same strategy whatever their number. This strategy relies on the assumption that the flock will get formed fast, which is no more valid when the number of agents increases. Thus, a major way for improvement would be to let the agents change their strategy when their number increases. For instance, as soon as they are as numerous as ducks, each agent could take care of one particular duck, rather than wait for the flock to be formed. Now, using different formations according to the number of agents would be a good way to implement different strategies.

There is no technical nor theoretical obstacle to improve our architecture in that way. But the reader must keep in mind that our research goal is the bottom-up building of a control architecture thanks to learning processes, which is more difficult than just hand-crafting correct and flexible multi-agent controllers.

10   Future Work and Conclusion

Even if we have shown in a preliminary study that applying adaptive algorithms to our hand-crafted controllers results in a significant improvement of the performance, we have not defended yet our claim that agents can find by themselves the coordination schemes presented in Table 9. Our claim that our system is still reactive can be refuted because all the anticipation necessary to find such a good coordination scheme has been given by the expert, rather than learned by the system.

Our first focus was on the improvement of hand-crafted solutions because, from an engineering perspective, an automated improvement of an expert controller means that the expert who designed the controller can rely on adaptive algorithms to optimize it. Hence he spends less time in this design, which is very appealing in an industrial context. Our first results have shown that the classifier systems formalism is good for coding controllers both because some knowledge of the expert can be easily represented in it and because applying optimization algorithms is straight-forward in the formalism.

But now we will have to start studying whether our algorithms are able to learn similar role-based controllers from scratch. This is not the case yet with the algorithm used here and presented in detail in [10]. Obtaining such a result would be all the more interesting that designing by hand the role exchange strategy presented in Sect. 8.1 proved difficult and time consuming.

It is clear that the performance of the role exchange architecture heavily depends on the definition of the controller, and that this controller was difficult to design by hand. The point is that the behavior tables were designed first and the role exchange table afterwards, whereas they are highly interdependent. Maybe, a different set of behavior tables would have resulted in a simpler role exchange table. This fact supports the claim that both the behavior tables and the role exchange table should be built by an automated learning process in a unified framework.

Therefore, we are now extending the scope of our algorithms towards the ability to build an architecture reflecting the one we designed in order to implement the use of roles in our flock control experiment. Our algorithm will be able to create internal states when necessary and to let evolve the mapping between these internal states and some conditions on the situation. Implementing roles as internal states should give us a control system for an agent able to create and evolve its own roles. Furthermore, the agents team should be able to globally reorganize their behaviors thanks to the adaptive processes.

To summarize, we presented a simulation testbed into which several agents had to solve a common task and we have shown how giving roles to the agents was an efficient way to design a control strategy. We have shown how these roles could be represented in the CS framework, and that such a way of using them gives an ability to react socially to multi-agent situations.

At last, we believe that the experimental testbed presented in this paper, though it is quite simple, is rich enough to raise most of the issues that we will meet in our industrial applications. As a conclusion of our study, it appears that the framework exposed here can be reused for more complicated multi-agent tasks, but it would require improvements by the multi-agent side, for instance if we would want to use it in the ROBOCUP domain. We did not try to do it because it would be too much time consuming while we are expected to work on our industrial problems. But we can already infer that obstacles to apply our framework to the design of a ROBOCUP team are that an organizational level would be necessary both to ensure the correct computation of all team information that we considered as directly available in our work, and to bring all the necessary flexibility and abstraction capabilities which are not present today in our architecture.

Acknowledgements. The authors want to thank the anonymous reviewers of an early version of this paper who gave valuable advices to improve it and all the attendees of the ECAI 2000 workshop on "Balancing Reactivity and Social Deliberation in Multi-Agent Systems" who raised interesting points which have been beneficial to the continuation of this work.

References

1. M. Asada and H. Kitano, editors. *Robocup-98: Robot Soccer World Cup II.* Lectures Notes in Artificial Intelligence 1604, Springer-Verlag, 1999.
2. M. Asada, E. Uchibe, and K. Hosoda. Cooperative behavior acquisition for mobile robots in dynamically changing real-worlds via vision-based reinforcement learning and development. *Artificial Intelligence*, 110(2):275–292, 1999.
3. S. Behnke and R. Rojas. A hierarchy of reactive behaviors handles complexity. In M. Hannebauer, J. Wendler, and E. Pagello, editors, *Balancing Reactivity and Social Deliberation in Multi-agent Systems (this volume)*, pages 125–136. Springer, 2001.
4. R. E. Bellman. *Dynamic Programming.* Princeton University Press, Princeton, NJ, 1957.
5. M. Bouzid, H. Hanna, and A.-I. Mouaddib. Deliberation levels in theoretic-decision approaches for task allocation in resource-bounded agents. In M. Hannebauer, J. Wendler, and E. Pagello, editors, *Balancing Reactivity and Social Deliberation in Multi-agent Systems (this volume)*, pages 198–216. Springer, 2001.
6. A. Bredenfeld and H.-U. Kobialka. Team cooperation using dual dynamics. In M. Hannebauer, J. Wendler, and E. Pagello, editors, *Balancing Reactivity and Social Deliberation in Multi-agent Systems (this volume)*, pages 111–124. Springer, 2001.
7. R. A. Brooks. Intelligence without reason. A.I. Memo 1293, Massachusetts Institute of Technology, Artificial Intelligence Laboratory, 1991.
8. M. Colombetti and M. Dorigo. Training agents to perform sequential behavior. Technical Report TR-93-023, International Computer Science Institute, Berkeley, 1993.
9. P. Gérard and O. Sigaud. YACS: Combining dynamic programming with generalization in classifier systems. In W. Stolzmann, P.-L. Lanzi, and S. W. Wilson, editors, *LNAI 1996 : Advances in Classifier Systems.* Springer-Verlag, to appear, 2001.
10. P. Gérard, W. Stolzmann, and O. Sigaud. YACS: a new learning classifier system with anticipation. *Journal of Soft Computing*, to appear, 2001.
11. D. E. Goldberg. *Genetic Algorithms in Search, Optimization, and Machine Learning.* Addison Wesley, 1989.

12. J. H. Holland. *Adaptation in Natural and Artificial Systems*. The University of Michigan Press, 1975.

13. L. P. Kaelbing. An architecture for intelligent reactive systems. In J. Allen, J. Hendler, and A. Tate, editors, *Readings in Planning*, chapter 11, pages 713–728. Morgan Kaufmann Publishers, Inc., 1990.

14. M. J. Matarić. *Interaction and Intelligent Behavior*. PhD thesis, MIT AI Mobot Lab, 1994.

15. M. J. Matarić. Rewards functions for accelerated learning. In W. W. Cohen and H. Hirsch, editors, *Proceedings of the Eleventh International Conference on Machine Learning*, San Francisco, CA, 1994. Morgan Kaufmann Publishers.

16. M. Riedmiller, A. Moore, and J. Schneider. Reinforcement learning for cooperating and communicating reactive agents in electrical power grid. In M. Hannebauer, J. Wendler, and E. Pagello, editors, *Balancing Reactivity and Social Deliberation in Multi-agent Systems (this volume)*, pages 137–149. Springer, 2001.

17. R. L. Riolo. Lookahead planning and latent learning in a classifier system. In *From Animals to Animats: Proceedings of the First International Conference on Simulation of Adaptive Behavior*, pages 316–326, Cambridge, MA, 1990. MIT Press.

18. O. Sigaud and P. Gérard. Using classifier systems as adaptive expert systems for control. In W. Stolzmann, P.-L. Lanzi, and S. W. Wilson, editors, *LNAI 1996 : Advances in Classifier Systems*. Springer-Verlag, to appear, 2001.

19. W. Stolzmann. Anticipatory classifier systems. In J. R. Koza, W. Banzhaf, K. Chellapilla, K. Deb, M. Dorigo, D. B. Fogel, M. H. Garzon, D. E. Golberg, H. Iba, and R. Riolo, editors, *Genetic Programming*. Morgan Kaufmann Publishers, Inc., San Francisco, CA, 1998.

20. P. Stone and M. Veloso. Multiagent systems: A survey from a machine learning perspective. Technical Report CMU-CS-97-193, School of Computer Science, Carnegie Mellon University, Pittsburg, PA 15213, 1997.

21. P. Stone and M. Veloso. Task decomposition, dynamic role assignment, and low-bandwidth communication for real-time strategic teamwork. *Artificial Intelligence*, 110(2):241–273, 1999.

22. M. Tambe, J. Adibi, Y. al Onaizan, A. Erdem, G. A. Kaminka, S. C. Marsella, and I. Muslea. Building agent teams using an explicit teamwork model and learning. *Artificial Intelligence*, 110(2):215–239, 1999.

23. R. Vaughan, N. Stumpter, A. Frost, and S. Cameron. Robot sheepdog project achieves automatic flock control. In R. Pfeifer, B. Blumberg, J.-A. Meyer, and S. W. Wilson, editors, *From Animals to Animats 5: roceedings of the Fifth International Conference on Simulation of Adaptive Behavior*, pages 489–493, Cambridge, MA, 1998. MIT Press.

24. S. W. Wilson. ZCS, a zeroth level classifier system. *Evolutionary Computation*, 2(1):1–18, 1994.

25. S. W. Wilson. Classifier fitness based on accuracy. *Evolutionary Computation*, 3(2):149–175, 1995.

26. C. M. Witkowski. *Schemes for Learning and behaviour: A New Expectancy Model*. PhD thesis, Department of Computer Science, University of London, England, 1997.

Part IV

Controlled Social Deliberation

Situation Based Strategic Positioning for Coordinating a Team of Homogeneous Agents

Luís Paulo Reis[1], Nuno Lau[2], and Eugénio Costa Oliveira[1]

[1]LIACC – Artificial Intelligence and Computer Science Lab., University of Porto, Portugal
{lpreis,eco}@fe.up.pt, http://www.ncc.up.pt/liacc/
Tel.: 351-22-5081315, Fax: 351-22-5081315
[2]DET – Electronics and Telecommunications Department, University of Aveiro, Portugal
lau@det.ua.pt, http://www.ua.pt
Tel.: 351-234-370524, Fax: 351-234-370545

Abstract. In this paper we are proposing an approach for coordinating a team of homogeneous agents based on a flexible common Team Strategy as well as on the concepts of Situation Based Strategic Positioning and Dynamic Positioning and Role Exchange. We also introduce an Agent Architecture including a specific high-level decision module capable of implementing this strategy. Our proposal is based on the formalization of what is a team strategy for competing with an opponent team having opposite goals. A team strategy is composed of a set of agent types and a set of tactics, which are also composed of several formations. Formations are used for different situations and assign each agent a default spatial positioning and an agent type (defining its behaviour at several levels). Agent's reactivity is also introduced for appropriate response to the dynamics of the current situation. However, in our approach this is done in a way that preserves team coherence instead of permitting uncoordinated agent behaviour. We have applied, with success, this coordination approach to the RoboSoccer simulated domain. The FC Portugal team, developed using this approach won the RoboCup2000 (simulation league) European and World championships scoring a total of 180 goals and conceding none.

1 Introduction

In the last decades, there has been a growth on the popularity and amount of research in the field of Multi-Agent Systems (MAS). This growth came together with the increasing degree of complexity of the requirements induced by the analyzed application domains. In the last years, MAS research has been focused on more realistic environments that are becoming more and more real-time, continuous, non-deterministic, partially inaccessible, dynamic and noisy [20,21]. These kinds of scenarios include search and rescue-like scenarios as it is the case of RoboCup-Rescue domain [11], public transport coordination, mine clearance, land exploration and hospital/ factory maintenance [4]. The complexity of these scenarios is even greater when they become multi-objective, simultaneously collaborative as well as adversarial environments as it is found in the simulated RoboSoccer [3,15,16] and robotics do main [27],

M. Hannebauer et al. (Eds.): Reactivity and Deliberation in MAS, LNAI 2103, pp. 175–197, 2001.

as well as war scenario domains like battlefield combat [26]. In this kind of domains, coordination must be achieved first, before the competition (game, rescue or battle) starts, through the definition of a flexible team strategy that all the agents know in advance and, second, during the competition, through communication and reactive reasoning based in the sensed information [20]. A good trade-off between social deliberation and reactivity is essential in most of these multi-agent systems applications. Reactivity is usually needed in order to enable the agents to react quickly to the events in the environment, while social deliberation is required for appropriate decision-making processes and to coordinate the agents enabling them to perform as a coherent team despite their own autonomy.

Several authors have proposed general models for flexible teamwork and ways to balance reactive behavior with the social deliberation. However, most of the approaches either are not sufficiently reactive to perform efficiently in real time and very dynamic domains or do not endow agents with sufficiently developed social behavior to perform intelligently as a member of a team in continuous, multi-objective and complex multi-agent environments. Some notable exceptions may be recognized, like Stone and Veloso work [21] that has been applied with success to RoboCup soccer and network routing, Tambe's STEAM [25] successfully applied in virtual battlefield simulations and Jennings' GRATE* [13] also applied in dynamic domains.

Peter Stone et al have proposed the use of "locker room agreements" [20,21] as a mechanism for defining pre-determined multi-agent protocols available for all the elements in the team [20]. They have used that mechanism to define a flexible team-work structure including task decomposition and dynamic role assignment [20,21]. Their approach was implemented in the simulated robotic soccer team CMUnited [22] that won RoboCup world championships [8,9] RoboCup98 [1] and RoboCup99 [28]. Their team strategy is composed of formations using very simple protocols for switching between them (based on the result and time at each stage of the competition). Each formation assigns each agent a given role and protocols are suggested for enabling role exchange between the agents. The teamwork structure also includes set-plays, e.g. multi-step, multi-agent plans for execution in some situations. In this approach, roles may either be rigid or they may be somewhat flexible [21]. In their approach to robotic soccer roles correspond to a specific positioning in the field, like, for example a central defender.

Most implementations of multi-agent cooperation frameworks, rely on domain specific coordination. However, some relevant exceptions may be identified. ARCHON project [29], proposes a multi-agent cooperation system, in the domain of electricity transportation management, based on joint-intentions and on a general model of teamwork. Other example is Jennings' [13] joint responsibility framework, which is based on a joint commitment to the team's joint goal. His framework is implemented in the GRATE* system. GRATE* is a layered architecture in which the behaviour of an agent is guided by its mental attitudes, beliefs, desires, intentions and joint intentions. Agents are composed of two individual layers: a domain level system and a cooperation and control layer. In GRATE*, teamwork is executed when an organizer agent detects the need for joint action, becoming then the responsible for establishing the team and ensuring all member's commitments [13].

Other general model for teamwork is STEAM (simply, a Shell for Team-work) [25]. STEAM is based in the joint intentions theory [14] but also on the SharedPlan theory [6,7]. STEAM uses joint intentions as the basis for teamwork but team members also build up a hierarchical structure of joint intentions, individual intentions and beliefs about the teammates intentions [25]. STEAM has been applied in several domains like the attack and transport domains that use an interactive commercial simulator developed for military training and RoboCup soccer server [3], in the context of the ISIS team. Although being far from a complete model of teamwork, STEAM attempt to bridge the gap from cooperation theory to its implementation is a remarkable one.

The trade-off between reactivity (essential to cope with the real-time, dynamic, noisy environment) and cooperation (needed to enable team joint behavior and to achieve overall team goals in the adversarial environment) is very difficult to achieve in the context of a general cooperation framework. In this paper we introduce a new approach to the coordination of a team of agents together with a method to balance reactivity and social behavior. The main innovations of our approach are:

- Balancing social behavior and reactivity through the distinction between active and strategic situations;
- Situation based strategic positioning – a policy used to position the agents in situations classified as strategic situations;
- Dynamic role and positioning exchange – enabling agents to switch roles (that define agent behaviors) and positionings (that define the places in a given formation);
- Formalization of what is a team strategy for a competition in partially cooperative and adversarial domains based on the concepts of tactics, formations and roles;
- A new agent architecture including a specific high level decision module capable of implementing the team strategy and supporting very flexible and efficient team performance.

The proposed approach is based on the definition of a team strategy using the concepts of tactics, formations and roles. Agents' decision making is based on a clear distinction between strategic and active situations. Based on this distinction, agents use, for strategic behaviour, Situation Based Strategic Positioning and, for active behaviour, domain specific high-level and low-level skills. To improve the flexibility of the team, agents are also able to switch their positions and specific behaviours (roles), at run-time, in the field. This mechanism called Dynamic Positioning and Role Exchange (DPRE) is based on previous work by Peter Stone et al [20,21] who suggested the use of flexible agent roles with protocols for switching among them. We have extended this concept and suggested that agents may exchange their roles (that correspond to agent types in our formulation) and their positionings in the current formation if the utility of that exchange is positive for the team. Moreover we propose a method to calculate that utility. Including DPRE in our robot soccer team implementation has significantly improved the overall team performance for teams of homogeneous agents and it may also be applied to heterogeneous agents.

This paper is organized as follows: Section 2 presents a formalization of a team strategy based on tactics, formations, positionings and agent types. The same section also describes Situation Based Strategic Positioning (SBSP) and Dynamic Positioning and Role Exchange (DPRE) mechanisms. Section 3 describes our agents' architecture and presents our high-level decision module control flow. Section 4 describes the application of our team strategy, SBSP and DPRE to the robotic soccer domain. The next section gives some experimental results. Finally, we present some conclusions as well as an outlook to future research we intend to do.

2   Team Strategy Formal Description

In our team coordination development we use the concepts of team strategy, role (agent behavior type), tactic, formation and positioning inside a formation.

Definition 1. *Team Strategy* is given by a set of *Tactics, Tactic Activation Rules,* a set of possible agent *Roles* and information concerning *Opponent Modeling Strategy, Teammate Modeling Strategy* and *Communication Protocols.*

$$TeamStrategy = (Tactics, TactActivationRules, Roles, OppModStrategies,$$
$$TeammateModStrategies, CommunicationProtocols)$$

$$Tactics = \{Tactic_1, Tactic_2, ..., Tactic_{nTactics}\}$$
$$\qquad a \ set \ of \ tactics \ possibly \ applicable \ to \ the \ team$$

$$Roles = \{Role_1, Role_2, ..., Role_{nroles}\}$$
$$\qquad a \ set \ of \ roles \ (agent \ types) \ that \ define \ different \ agent \ behavior \ types$$

$$OppModStrategies = \{OppModStrat_1, OppModStrat_2, ..., OppModStrat_{nOppModStrategies}\}$$
$$\qquad a \ set \ of \ Opponent \ modeling \ strategies$$

$$TeammateModStrategies = \{TeamModStrat_1, TeamModStrat_2, ...,$$
$$TeamModStrat_{nTeamModStrat}\}$$
$$\qquad a \ set \ of \ Teammate \ mod \ eling \ strategies$$

$$CommunicationProtocols = \{ComProtocol_1, ComProtocol_2, ..., ComProtocol_{nComProtocols}\}$$
$$\qquad a \ set \ of \ communication \ Pr \ otocols$$

Tactics are used to supply the team with a set of *Formations* (see definition 3) that give the agents general strategic *Positioning* and *Role* information (agent individual characteristics). Tactics are selected according to *Tactic Activation Rules* that use *Global* information. For example if the competition is near the end, our team is losing it, but it is clear that it still has a chance of winning, then a more risky and aggressive tactic should be used. If it is clear by the competition statistics and opponent model information that the competition is surely lost then, a more defensive tactic, that tries to minimize the damage, may be the best one. For each *Tactic* a set of *Formations* and a set of *Preset Plans* are defined. These *Formations* and *Plans* are used in adequate situations.

Definition 2. A *Tactic* is defined by a set of *Formations, Formation Activation Rules,* and a set of *Predefined Plans.*

$$Tactic_i = (Formations_i, FormationActivRules_i, PresetPlans_i) \quad \forall i = 1..ntactics$$

Definition 3. A *Formation* is defined by the *Positioning* (which includes the *Reference Position*, *Role* and *Importance*) of the agents inside the *Formation*.

$$Formations_i = \{Formation_{i,1}, Formation_{i,2},..., Formation_{i,nformations_i}\}$$
$$\forall i = 1..ntactics$$
$$Formation_{i,j} = (AgentPositioning_{i,j,1}, AgentPositioning_{i,j,2},..., AgentPositioning_{i,j,nAgents})$$
$$\forall i = 1..ntactics, \quad \forall j = 1..nformations_i$$

Definition 4. A *Preset Plan* is defined by its *Plan Activation Information*, and the agents *Positioning evolution, Role evolution* and *Actions* along the time.

$$PresetPlans_i = \{PresetPlan_1, PresetPlan_2,..., PresetPlan_{nplans_i}\}$$
$$\forall i = 1..ntactics$$
$$PresetPlan_{i,k} = (PlanActInfo_{i,k}, PlanAgentPositioningEvolution_{i,k},$$
$$PlanAgentRolesEvolution_{i,k}, PlanAgentActionsEvolution_{i,k})$$
$$\forall i = 1..ntactics, \quad \forall k = 1..nplans_i$$

Definition 5. The *Positioning* of an agent inside a formation is defined by its *ReferencePosition*, *PositioningRole* and *PositioningImportance*.

$$Positioning_{i,j,p} = (ReferencePosition_{i,j,p}, PositioningRole_{i,j,p}, PositioningImportance_{i,j,p})$$
$$\forall i = 1..ntactics, \quad \forall j = 1..nformations_i, \quad \forall p = 1..nplayers_{i,j}$$

For each positioning inside a given formation, a reference position is defined:

$$ReferencePosition_{i,j,p} = (ReferencePositionX_{i,j,p}, ReferencePositionY_{i,j,p})$$
$$ReferencePositionX_{i,j,p} \in \{-field\_length..field\_length\}$$
$$ReferencePositionY_{i,j,p} \in \{-field\_width..field\_width\}$$

This reference position is adjusted using the agent type and situation information to give that agent's strategic position at each time. Each positioning inside a formation has a *PositioningImportance*. For example, in the robosoccer domain, the central defenders are very important in defensive situations while the central forwards are very important in attacking situations. In a war scenario the home base last defenders are very important. This position importance is defined using a qualitative scale:

$$PositioningImportance_{i,j,p} \in \{VeryLow, Low, Medium, High, VeryHigh\}$$

Definition 6. *PositioningRole* defines the *Characteristics* of a given agent that occupies a positioning inside a given *Formation*. The *Roles* used as *PositioningRoles* in the *Formation* must be defined in the *TeamStrategy*.

$$PositioningRole_{i,j,p} \in \{1..nroles\}$$
$$\forall i = 1..ntactics, \quad \forall j = 1..nformations_i \quad \forall p = 1..nplayers_{i,j}$$

Roles may be used, for example in the RoboSoccer domain, to give agents specific characteristics like *Aggressive_Defender*, *Positional_Defender*, *Positional_Attacker*, etc.

Definition 7. A *Role* of the *Team Strategy* is defined by its *Active Characteristics, Strategic Characteristics* and by the *Critical Situation Rules*. The strategic state is abandoned to enter an active state if one of the *Critical Situation Rules* is true at a given time.

$$Role_i = (ActiveCharacteristics_i, StrategicCharacteristics_i, CriticalSituationRules_i)$$

$$\forall i = 1..nroles$$

Contrary to all the other concepts, *Role Strategic Characteristics* and *Active Characteristics* are domain dependent and must be defined accordingly. Figure 1 shows an example of this team strategy definition for an arbitrary domain.

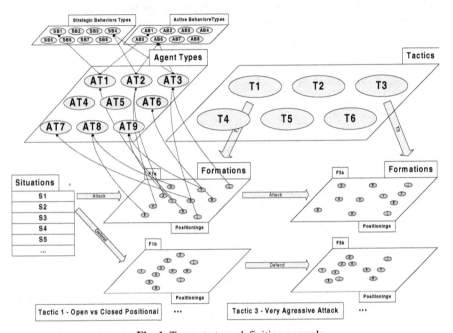

Fig. 1. Team strategy definition example

In Fig. 1, the team strategy is very simple. It is composed by 6 tactics, each composed by several formations to be used in different situations (like attack, defend, etc.). Each formation uses different agent types for each of the different positionings. Each agent type is defined by its active and strategic characteristics.

3   Agent Architecture

We have chosen an agent architecture suitable for implementing our team strategy. This agent architecture is shown in figure 2. Agents include the traditional main control loop using perception interpretation and action prediction to update the world state, then deciding the appropriate action and finally executing the selected action. A high-level decision module is used to decide agent's current tactic, formation, role (agent behavior) and action at a given moment. Domain knowledge is structured in tactics, formations, agent roles, communication protocols, preset plans and game situations. These structures are predefined by the strategy designer according to the domain. Moreover, they are flexible enough to be fully instantiated before each competition by the team manager, according to each specific competition conditions, team capabilities and the opponent team foreseen characteristics. They may also be learned through both a training process and from other previous competitions.

Our agents build up a world model by interpreting the sensed information and predicting the results of the actions selected for execution. The main difficulties associated with this process are updating the world state effectively and choosing the appropriate action [20]. Communication also plays an important role here, and our agents use it for:

- Communicating their internal world states and situation information - keeping world representations more accurate;
- Communicate useful events (like a pass or a positioning exchange) in order to improve coordination.

3.1 Multi-Level World State Representation

World state representation includes information regarding several objects in the world and other high-level information like estimations about the final result of the competition, current time, opponent behavior, competition statistics, etc. We can separate this information in four levels of abstraction:

Global Information. High-level information needed to decide about the possible best team's tactic in a given moment. This information includes opponent team global behavior (quality, capabilities, aggressiveness, etc.) and high-level statistics from the competition (team's losses and successes while performing each specific collective action, etc);

Situation Information. Information that is relevant to the selection of the appropriate formation and for the situation based strategic positioning mechanism. This information is mostly concerned with the present and includes the formations of each team, field conditions, etc;

Action Selection Information. Information that is relevant to select an appropriate action like attacking and defending possibilities, moving options, interception possibilities, etc;

Physical State. Low level information, including the agent's state and the positions and velocities of the objects in the world.

Regarding the low-level information, there usually are several objects in the world which remain stationary, whose position is known and can be used for agents self-localization and there are several mobile objects whose localization must be continuously tracked. Each agent's internal world state stores an instantiation of all stationary as well as moving objects known. Sometimes, since world information is only partial, some objects although visible cannot be accurately identified. All moving objects have a representation of their locations and velocities stored with associated degrees of confidence values within interval [0,1]. The confidence values are needed because of the large portion of hidden world, which implies that the objects' positions stored are only estimations [20]. It is obviously a mistake to remember only objects that are currently in view, but it is also incorrect to assume that a mobile object will stay static (or continues moving with the same velocity) indefinitely. By decaying the confidence in unseen objects over time, agents can determine whether or not to rely on the current position and velocity values [2].

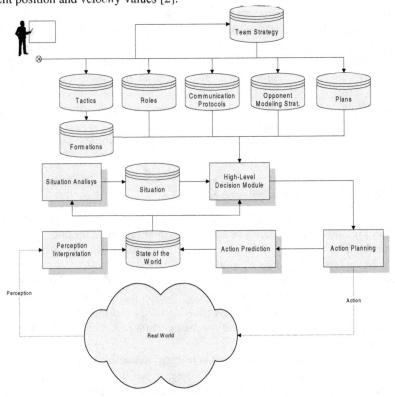

Fig. 2. Agent architecture

3.2 Situation Based Strategic Positioning with Dynamic Positioning and Role Exchange

We will now describe the two main agents positional coordination methods supplied by our strategy enabling the agents to cooperatively follow a given tactic and formation:

Situation Based Strategic Positioning (SBSP): This mechanism uses the situation information to select the best strategic position for each one of the players in the team. This strategic position depends on the current tactic and formation, the player role and positioning in the formation and the current situation.

Dynamic Positioning and Role Exchange (DPRE): This enables the agents to switch their positioning or their roles inside a given tactic and formation whenever that action leads to an improvement of the team global utility.

Each agent has an allocated positioning inside the current formation that changes dynamically with the competition specific situation. Due to the dynamic positioning and role exchange mechanism agents do not have fixed positioning inside the formation. For example, agent 2 can be at positioning 2 at a given time and at positioning 9 a few moments later. Also, positionings determine the agent's role (within the roles defined in the team strategy). Each role gives the agents different characteristics like tendency to be either positional or aggressive, tendency to be more offensive or defensive, etc. Changing positioning inside the formation also implies changing role. Of course in real applications this is not totally possible because a large part of the agent role characteristics depend on the physical and psychological characteristics of that agent. But if we have homogeneous agents in our team, it is rather straightforward and very useful to do this. For heterogeneous agents role adequacy must be also considered.

3.3   Situation Based Strategic Positioning

Our approach to building a cooperative team uses Situation Based Strategic Positioning enhanced with Dynamic Positioning and Role Exchange. As it was said before, this coordination policy for a team of agents is based on the distinction of Strategic and Active situations.

Definition 8. An *Active Situation* is a situation in which at least one *Critical Situation Rule* is fired for a given agent.

Critical Situation Rules are defined using Action Selection Information and take in account the present *Situation* (attack, defend, etc.).

Definition 9. A *Strategic Situation* is a situation in which an agent doesn't have any *Critical Situation Rule* fired.

If an agent is not involved in an active situation then it tries to occupy its strategic positioning that changes according to the situation of the game. Game information includes the competition time and result, opponent modeling information, competition mode, several statistics, attack and defensive information, positions, states and velocities of the objects in the world, etc. This information is complemented with other situation-based information like the plan currently in execution. Predefined strategic information includes several tactics, formations (for game situations), and agents' behaviors inside formations. Strategic behaviors, used in strategic situations, enable the team with a social behavior by allocating different tasks to different agents using a global perspective. Strategic behaviors provide the team with an efficient coverage of the whole field. The positions of agents in strategic mode maximize the options for cooperation with the agents in active mode. While agents in active mode use their specific domain knowledge to decide their action in a reactive decision mechanism, players in strategic mode fulfill the tasks allocated by the formation in use, by covering different sections of the field in the best possible way.

Definition 10. The *Situation Based Strategic Positioning of each agent* is a function of the current *Tactic*, *Situation* (that define the *Formation* in use) and *Agent Type* (that define the Agent Strategic Characteristics).

The situation information associated with the predefined strategic information is used to estimate the agent's own strategic position for each situation. It is also used to estimate his teammates strategic position for each situation. Knowing its own strategic position and the teammates strategic position, agents may decide if an exchange of positioning with a teammate is beneficial or not to the team and, therefore, if it is useful or not to perform dynamic positioning and role exchange.

3.4   Dynamic Positioning and Role Exchange

Our proposal includes the use of utility functions in order to evaluate usefulness of a positioning or role exchange.

Definition 11. A *Dynamic Positioning and Role Exchange* consists of the exchange (inside a given tactic and formation) of the *Positioning* and *Role* (including all agent behavior characteristics) between two agents.

As part of the world state representation, each agent has an estimate of the other agent's positions in the field:

$$AgentPositions = \{AgentPos_1, AgentPos_2, ..., AgentPos_{nplayers}\}$$

$$\forall p = 1..nplayers$$

$$AgentPos_p = (AgentPosX_p, AgentPosY_p)$$

Dynamic Positioning and Role Exchange aims to improve the performance of a homogeneous team of cooperating agents. At each time in the course of the competition, each agent has a positioning (place in the formation) and a role (behavior characteristics) inside the current active formation. Each agent keeps track of his positioning but also of the positioning allocated to each of the other agents in the team:

$$AlocAgentPositionings = \{AlocPositioning_1, AlocPositioning_2, ..., AlocPositioning_{nplayers}\}$$

$$AlocPositioning_p \in \{1..nplayers\}$$

If the team is composed of homogeneous agents each agent can carry out another role and occupy other positioning without any additional problem. Since the team is composed of cooperative agents, this positioning and role exchange takes place only when the agents can improve the global team utility by doing so. This utility is computed through the following formula:

$$DPREUtility(tact, form, p_a, p_b) =$$

$$+ Utility(Position_{p_a}, Positioning_{tact,form,p_b}, PlayerRole_{tact,form,p_b})$$

$$+ Utility(Position_{p_b}, Positioning_{tact,form,p_a}, PlayerRole_{tact,form,p_a})$$

$$- Utility(Position_{p_a}, Positioning_{tact,form,p_a}, PlayerRole_{tact,form,p_a})$$

$$- Utility(Position_{p_b}, Positioning_{tact,form,p_b}, PlayerRole_{tact,form,p_b})$$

$$\forall p_a = 1..nplayers_{tact,form}, \forall p_b = 1..nplayers_{tact,form}, p_a < p_b$$

If the DPRE Utility for a given pair (p_a, p_b) is positive, then the Dynamic Positioning and Role Exchange takes place, that is, each player assumes other one's positioning and role:

$$\begin{cases} AlocatedPlayerPositioning_{tact,form,p_a} = AlocatedPlayerPositioning_{tact,form,p_b} \\ AlocatedPlayerPositioning_{tact,form,p_b} = AlocatedPlayerPositioning_{tact,form,p_a} \end{cases}$$

The utility functions for each player positioning and role are concerned with the players' current position distance to his strategic position, the positioning importance, agent's states (physical conditions, objects carried, etc.) and the role characteristics. For heterogeneous agents the utility function must also take into account the agent's adequacy to perform each of the roles.

Because agents have local perspectives, their own utilities for a given DPRE exchange may be different and so, one of the agents may believe that the exchange is useful while the other believes the opposite. To deal with this problem, communication between the agents shall be used to synchronize the exchange. This situation is not very problematic because when one of the agents believes that a possible exchange has a positive utility, he will try to perform the exchange and communicate the teammate that fact. Meanwhile, the agent will go to the teammate position, which tends to increase the value of the estimated utility for this exchange for both agents.

3.5   High-Level Decision Module Control

We are not particularly concerned with the low-level skills and world state accuracy available to the individual agent but first and foremost we are concerned with its high-level intelligent decision capabilities and social abilities (coordination and communication). Therefore, the main features of our agents are included in the high-level decision module. Fig. 3 depicts control flow inside that module which will be explained next.

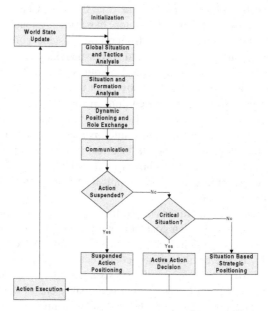

Fig. 3. Control flow of the high-level decision module

After the initialization of some internal structures that includes reading several configuration files, the agent enters the main control loop. This loop starts by running the tactic decision module in which the agent uses global situation information to decide the current tactic. This module is directly connected to the second module of the main control loop, which is concerned with situation analysis and formation selection. The control loop follows with dynamic positioning exchange and communication analysis.

If the competition is stopped (for example after a foul in a soccer game or a cease fire in a battlefield scenario), stopped action positioning is performed; if not, then if a critical situation is not identified, meaning that the agent does not need to get immediately into active behavior, global situation based strategic positioning is performed. Whenever the situation is critical, then an appropriate action is selected. The loop closes with internal activities not directly connected with decision-making, that is, action execution and world state updating.

4   Application of the Team Strategy to RoboCup

4.1   RoboCup Simulation League and the Soccer Server

Our formalization has been applied to the RoboSoccer simulated domain in the context of the FC Portugal simulated soccer team [17]. The application domain is based on the RoboSoccer server [3,15,16] that has been used as the basis for the RoboCup international competitions and for several associated research challenges [10]. The soccer server is a very complex and realistic domain. Unlike many discrete and accessible traditional Artificial Intelligent domains (like Chess or Checkers), soccer server comprises several real world complexity factors like asynchronous sensing and acting. The simulation comprises characteristics from robotic systems combined with characteristics from real human soccer players and soccer matches. The server's sensor and actuator noise models are inspired by typical robotic systems [20], while many other characteristics, such as limited stamina, movement and vision, are motivated by human limitations. This is indeed a very rich domain for the study of multi-agent real-time coordination and communication. Each team is composed of eleven software agents that must act autonomously, with limited perception, action and communication abilities and that have to collaborate in a real-time, noisy, adversarial environment to achieve common goals. Teams have two contradictory goals:

To score on the opponents goal. To accomplish this, players shall advance in the field towards that goal line;

To prevent the opponent's from scoring in their own goal. To achieve this, players must cover the way to their own goal and shall not advance too much in the field.

Reactive behavior is essential in RoboCup games because of the real-time dynamics of the environment. However, the agent's contradictory goals and the complexity of the environment, also demand an intelligent social behavior. Balancing both these approaches however it is not an easy task but is probably one of the major challenges in the RoboCup simulation league. To be successful teams must react very fast to changes in the environment (like ball velocity changes) but on the other hand, must also perform very complex collective moves (like organized joint attacks, keep a defensive line, etc.).

4.2 Team Strategy for the RoboSoccer Domain

To apply our team strategy formalization and SBSP to the RoboSoccer domain, we need to define specific *Critical Situation Rules*, *Agent Strategic Characteristics* and *Agent Active Characteristics*. *Critical Situation Rules* (CSRs) are used to identify situations in which strategic positioning must be abandoned and an active mode must be entered. Each *Role* that an agent can play has associated a set of *Critical Situation Rules*.

$$CriticalSituationInfo_i = \{CriticalSituationRule_{i,1}, CriticalSituationRule_{i,2}, ...,$$

$$CriticalSituationRule_{i,ncriticalrules}\} \quad \forall i = 1..nroles$$

For each agent role, its Strategic Characteristics include Ball Positional Attraction that is used to adjust player's strategic positions towards the region where the ball is, and a positional rectangle that strategically the players should not leave (although they may leave it in active situations). For some roles (namely defenders and goal keeper) it is needed to stay always behind the ball x-coordinate. In some specific field regions, the players' strategic positions should be more attracted towards the position of the ball. This is the case of the forward players when the ball is near the opponent's goal line, or the defenders when the ball is near their own penalty area.

$$StrategicCharacteristics_i = (BallPositionalAttraction_i, PositionalRectangle_i,$$

$$BehindBall_i, BallAttraction_i, BallAtractionRegion_i) \quad \forall i = 1..nroles$$

Active Characteristics are concerned with ball possession and ball recovery functionalities. Ball possession functionalities rely on characteristics that are divided into four main groups dealing respectively with passing, forwarding, shooting and dribbling. Ball recovering functionalities depend on the abilities for intercepting the ball, marking an opponent that has the ball, marking an opponent without ball, covering the goal from an opponent, obstructing an opponent, covering a pass line, get free to receive a pass and prepare the reception of a pass. Each ball possession and ball recovery ability is composed of an evaluation rule and a behavior. Evaluation rules are used in order to choose the best possible ability to use at a given moment.

As it was said before, information is used at different levels of detail. *Global Information* refers to high-level information of the game and is used to decide the appropriate *Tactic* to use. In the RoboSoccer specific application, this information may include: information about time, current result, game statistics (number of shoots, corners, successful passes, ball possession time, etc.) and opponent modeling information (which includes the opponent team tactic, formation and players' roles, positions and characteristics).

Situation Information is used (along with *Global Information*) for a dynamic selection of the *Formation* to use. This information includes *Ball Possession Information* (ball possessor, confidence, team in possession, time of possession, etc.), bll information (position, velocity) and player's information (teammates and opponents).

$GlobalSituation = (Time, Result, StatisticsInfo, OppModInfo)$

$Situation = (BallPossesionInfo, BallInfo, TeammateInfo, OpponnentsInfo)$

$StatIsticsInfo = (BallPossessionInfo, ShootInfo, PassInfo, DribbleInfo, CornersInfo,$
$\qquad OffSideInfo, FreeKickInfo, KickInInfo, GoalieKickInfo)$

$PositionalInformation = (BallLowLevelInfo, OffSideLines, TeammateLowLevelInfo,$
$\qquad OpponentLowLevelInfo, InterceptionInfo, CongestionInfo,$
$\qquad DangerInformation)$

$ActionInformation = (PassInformation, ForwardInformation, ShootInformation,$
$\qquad DribbleInformation,...)$

Statistics Info is concerned with game statistical information. This includes, for each one of the teams, statistics concerning ball possession time by field region (for each team), shooting statistics (number of shoots, their characteristics and results), statistics about passing (number of passes, their characteristics and results) and the same type of statistics for forwards and dribbles. Statistics for stopped game situations are also included for corner, offside, free kick, kick in and goalie kick.

4.3 Situation Based Strategic Positioning for RoboSoccer

Based on the player allocated positioning and on the role allocated by the formation to that specific positioning, the player's strategic position in each situation is calculated using the following process:

$AlocRole_p = PlayerRole(AlocPositioning_p)$

$PlayerStrategicPosition_p =$

$\qquad AdjustedPosition(ReferencePosition(AlocPositioning_p) +$

$\qquad\qquad BallPosAttraction(AlocRole_p, BallPos, BallPosAttrac, PosRectangle) +$

$\qquad\qquad BallAttraction(AlocRole_p, BallPos, BallAttraction, BallAttractionlRegion)),$

$\qquad BehindBall(AlocRole_p),$

$\qquad OffsideConversion(AlocRole_p))$

The player strategic position is calculated as an adjusted position (using the *behind ball* and *offside* conditions) of the sum of the reference position (that depends on the tactic and situation) with the ball positional attraction and ball attraction in specific regions of the field. The factors used to adjust this reference position depend on the agent type and their definition consists basically in defining the agent type strategic characteristics.

Contrarily to other positional mechanisms that do not use tactics or agent types, like Stone's SPAR [20], SBSP enables a very flexible positioning of soccer players. SBSP enables the team to have completely different shapes for different situations. For example, the team may have a very compact shape in a defend situation and spread in the field on an attack situation (just like a real soccer teams). It also enables the team to be correctly positioned in situations like goal scoring opportunities (in which players must assume possible shooting positions inside the opponent's area). Finally it enables different players (that have different agent types) to have completely different positional behaviors.

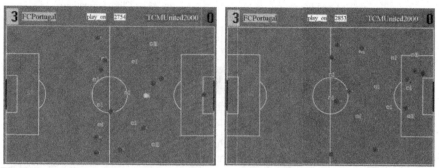

Fig. 4. Situation Based Strategic Positioning in an attack situation and in a goal scoring opportunity situation in RoboCup 2000 game against ATTCMU2000

SPAR [20] is based on attractions (to active teammates, ball and opponent's goal) and repulsions (from opponents and passive teammates) and does not consider situations or different positional behaviors for different player types. Thus players are unable to have this flexibility. This difference is quite visible in games between FC Portugal and CMUnited99 and was also quite visible in the game between FC Portugal and ATTCMU2000 in RoboCup2000 (Fig. 4).

Strategically players should keep the position determined by situation based strategic position. But because agents are also involved in active behaviors, their real positions in the field may differ considerably from the strategic positions. For these situations the DPRE mechanism is very useful to keep the formation shape.

4.4 Team Strategy Practical Application

A team strategy includes several different tactics and conditions for the activation of those tactics. An example is a very simple team strategy that uses only three tactics: Normal 433, Aggressive 442 and Very Aggressive 235. The rules for selecting the appropriate tactic could be that in the beginning of the game or if winning, the 433 tactic would be selected. If the game is a draw after the game interval or if losing by 1 goal, the Aggressive 442 would be selected. If the game is a draw near the end or if losing by more than one goal, the Very Aggressive 235 tactic would be selected.

Each one of the tactics uses several formations composed of different players with different roles. Typical formation types are used for defending (when the opponents have control of the ball) and for attacking (when the team has ball possession). Other types of formations could be used for transporting the ball from defense to attack, for goalie free kick, corners, etc. A simple example for the first tactic is the use of only two formations: a simple 433 closed formation for defending and a simple 433 open formation for attacking (as illustrated in Fig. 5).

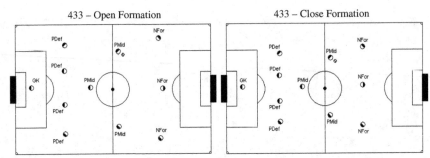

Fig. 5. Typical 433 Formations: In the open formation, the players are more spread over the field. In the close formation (used for defending) players are more concentrated in the middle of the field. Player roles are also represented (GK-Goal Keeper, PDef-Positional Defender, PMid – Positional Midfielder and NFor –Normal Forward)

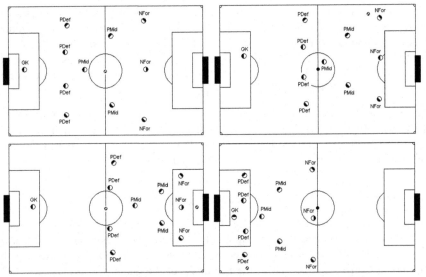

Fig. 6. Illustration of the Situation Based Strategic Positioning concept, considering only the ball positional attraction and ball attraction parameters. In the top left figure, the ball is in the center of the field, on the top right figure the ball formation positional attraction is shown. In the bottom left figure, the formation is attracted by the ball but also, since the ball is in a ball attraction region, forwards and two of the midfielders are directly attracted by the ball. The bottom right figure shows a similar situation with the ball on the defensive side of the field

Positions of the players inside the formations and their respective roles are different depending on the tactic and on the game current situation. The formations shown in Fig. 5 assume that the ball is on the middle of the field and that all players are in a strategic behavior. But, like it was said before, the strategic positioning of the players is "situation based" and depends on the tactic and formation in use (and the player role in that formation as well) plus several situation parameters (Fig. 6).

As one can see in figure 6, the ball represents a crucial part of the situation in the SBSP mechanism. The formation is attracted by the ball, adjusting itself to the game situation. If the ball is in a Ball Attraction Region (like the opponents area), several players are attracted directly towards the ball as it is illustrated in the bottom left image in Fig. 6. Besides the ball attraction, players, depending on its role definition, may stay always behind the ball and may avoid staying in an offside position. Using this formation definition mechanism, we can define players with totally different behaviors. For example, giving a player a high positional attraction in the x-axis makes the player perform long runs along the field accompanying the ball movement along the field. Giving the player a role with a very high ball attraction and setting the ball attraction region for that role to be the whole field, configures a player that always goes towards the ball position. This kind of players can be very annoying to some opponents.

5   Experimental Results and Discussion

Our agents' coordination proposal has been implemented in the FC Portugal RoboCup simulation league team. The team was implemented using a world state update model and low level skills based on CMUnited99 publicly available source code [22]. Modifications were performed on the interception, kicking and dribbling abilities of the players [17]. FC Portugal also uses intelligent perception and communication [17] and integrates soccer knowledge in the high-level decision modules for ball possession and ball recovery [17,18].

FC Portugal defeats very easily all the teams that have competed in Stockholm for RoboCup99. Table 1 summarizes the results achieved[1] in a series of 10 games against eight of the most well known teams that competed in Robocup99. The results were achieved using always a simple team strategy based on a 433 positional tactic (used when the team is wining or drawing the game) and a 442 aggressive tactic (used when the team is losing). Both tactics included only two situations (defending and attacking) and used open formations for attacking and closed formations for defending. The team used "positional agent types" very similar to the ones used by FC Portugal in Melbourne RoboCup 2000.

Table 1. FC Portugal scores against RoboCup99 teams

Teams	Wins	Draws	Losses	Score	Mean
CMUnited99 (U.S.A)	10	0	0	113-0	11.3-0.0
Magma Freiburg 99 (Germany)	10	0	0	144-0	14.4-0.0
Essex Wizards99 (England)	10	0	0	161-0	16.1-0.0
11 Monkeys 99 (Japan)	10	0	0	238-0	23.8-0.0
Mainz Rolling Brains99 (Germany)	10	0	0	209-0	20.9-0.0
Brainstormers99 (Germany)	10	0	0	146-0	14.6-0.0
Cyberoos99 (Australia)	10	0	0	254-0	25.4-0.0
Zeng99 Acamp (Japan)	10	0	0	244-0	24.4-0.0
Total	100	0	0	1509-0	18.9-0.0

---

[1] The results were achieved using three separate machines running Linux RedHat 6.1 (one for each team and one for the server) connected through a 10Mbit network. Pentiums 550MHz, 128 MB were used for the server and for FC Portugal team and a Pentium 550MHz with 256MB of memory was used for the opponent team.

The results clearly show that FC Portugal could easily beat all those opponents. The team was capable of scoring an average of more than 11 goals to the previous undefeated champions CMUnited 99 [23]. Also against other very good teams, like the second (Magma Freiburg [5]) and third (Essex Wizards [12]) places of RoboCup 99, FC Portugal team was able to score many goals.

In the RoboCup 2000 European and World championships, these results were confirmed. Although competing with well established teams, and being a very recent team, FC Portugal won the European RoboCup 2000, held in Amsterdam (May 29-June 2), and the World RoboCup 2000, held in Melbourne (August 28 - September 3). In these two competitions, FC Portugal scored a total of 180 goals, without conceding a single goal. Table 2, summarizes the results achieved by FC Portugal in both competitions.

Table 2. Scores of FC Portugal in EuroRoboCup2000 (Amsterdam) and RoboCup2000 (Melbourne)

Euro RoboCup – Amsterdam	Score	RoboCup 2000 - Melbourne	Score
Essex Wizards (England)	3 – 0		
Lucky Luebeck (Germany)	13 – 0	Oulu2000 (Finland)	33 - 0
Cyberoos (Australia)	4 – 0	Zeng2000 (Japan)	18 - 0
Pizza Tower (Italy)	22 – 0	Robolog (Germany)	20 - 0
Polytech (Russia)	19 – 0	Essex Wizards (England)	7 - 0
PSI (Russia)	6 – 0	Karlsruhe Brain. (Germany)	3 - 0
Wroclaw (Poland)	13 – 0	YowAI (Japan)	6 - 0
Essex Wizards (England)	5 – 0	ATTCMU2000 (U.S.A)	6 - 0
Karlsruhe Brain. (Germany)	2 – 0	Karlsruhe Brain. (Germany)	1 – 0
Total Score	86 – 0	Total Score	94 - 0

In Amsterdam FC Portugal used almost unchanged CMUnited99 basic skills [22] (kicking, dribbling, interception, etc.) but the team was able to beat other teams with much better low-level skills (e.g. Essex Wizards [11] with a better dribbling ability, Karlsruhe Brainstormers [19] with a more powerful kick). The main reasons for this (apparently strange) success were, at the social behavior level:

Team strategy based on very flexible tactics with well-conceived formations for different game situations and flexible player types;

Situation based strategic positioning that enabled the team to move in the field as a real soccer team;

Dynamic positioning and role exchange mechanism that enabled the team to keep higher levels of stamina and a reduced number of useful positions uncovered;

Associated with this, the individual decision capabilities of the agents (ball possession and ball recovery decision modules) were also very important.

In Amsterdam FC Portugal used the SBSP mechanism combined with the DPRE and individual decision modules to explore the free space on the field to attack and to cover that same free space while defending. Against teams that had good positional systems this playing type revealed to be less effective and FC Portugal could not score many goals.

In Melbourne, several teams used positioning mechanisms similar to SBSP, (mostly the ones that competed in Amsterdam, with whom FC Portugal played half of its games). This way, the positional advantage, FC Portugal had in Amsterdam, was only totally decisive in games against not very strong teams. In the games against very good teams, FC Portugal superiority was also related, not only with the team strategy, SBSP and DPRE but also with the intelligent perception and communication mechanisms [17], strong kick based on optimization techniques [17], marking techniques and debugging tools used [17].

Table 3. Scores of FC Portugal in series of 10 games against some of the best RoboCup 2000 teams. Place indicates the ranking of these teams in RoboCup 2000, while W, D and L, stand respectively for wins, draws and lost games. Score represents the combined score of 10 games

Teams	Place	W	D	L	Score
Brainstormers2K (Germany)	2nd	10	0	0	24-0
ATTCMU2000 (U.S.A)	3rd	10	0	0	71-0
CMUnited99 (U.S.A)	4th	10	0	0	113-0
Essex Wizards2000 (England)	7th	10	0	0	68-0
Cyberoos2000 (Australia)	9th	10	0	0	234-0
Robolog2000 (Germany)	13th	10	0	0	168-0
Total		60	0	0	678-0

Table 3, shows FC Portugal scores against six of the best teams in RoboCup 2000[2] [24] and Table 4 shows FC Portugal results turning off the SBSP or/and the DPRE mechanisms. Turning off the SBSP mechanism makes the agents assume always an active behavior. To implement this, a new critical rule that selects the best ball recovery behavior to perform in a given situation was added. This way, if no other critical situation rule is activated, the agent selects between the available ball recovery behaviors and executes the best one. Ball recovery behaviors considered include interception, passive interception, prudent interception, mark opponent, mark pass line, go to ball position, and get free from opponents.

The results show that turning off the SBSP mechanism makes the team perform much worse. The team is unable to win all the games and the games against Karlsruhe Brainstormers are now very tied (although Karlsruhe has still many problems in scoring). Against CMUnited99, results are also rather worse. Against this team, losing the positional advantage makes the game much more tied and FC Portugal loses the pressing capability over CMUnited. The result is that the team is unable to score many goals and CMUnited99 has some scoring chances.

---

[2] Unfortunately it is not possible to present results against YowAI2000 and Magma Freiburg that were fifth in RoboCup 2000, because their binaries are still not available.

Table 4. Scores of FC Portugal with and without SBSP and DPRE against several RoboCup 2000 teams

Teams	Without SBSP				Without DPRE				Without SBSP and DPRE			
	W	D	L	Score	W	D	L	Score	W	D	L	Score
Brainstormers2K (Germany)	5	5	0	8-2	8	2	0	12-1	3	6	1	6-2
ATTCMU2000 (U.S.A)	9	1	0	34-0	10	0	0	56-0	10	0	0	28-0
CMUnited99 (U.S.A)	10	0	0	49-0	10	0	0	85-0	10	0	0	38-0
Essex Wizards2000 (England)	10	0	0	39-0	10	0	0	62-0	9	1	0	44-0
Cyberoos2000 (Australia)	10	0	0	108-0	10	0	0	184-0	10	0	0	96-0
Robolog2000 (Germany)	10	0	0	111-0	10	0	0	142-0	10	0	0	98-0
Total	54	6	0	349-2	58	2	0	541-1	52	7	1	310-2

Turning off the DPRE mechanism does not affect much the results against Essex Wizards. Analyzing the games, the explanation seems to be that Essex Wizards have a very slow type of game and so dynamic role and positioning exchange is not essential.

Tests were also performed using FC Portugal without both mechanisms against the best RoboCup2000 teams. The team is still superior to its opponents but has now lots of difficulties to overcome Brainstormers (conceding two goals and losing a game 1-0). Brainstormers are able to dominate the game and FC Portugal has lots of difficulties to enter Brainstormers middle field. However, FC Portugal communication strategy, intelligent perception, very good decision mechanisms (based on real soccer knowledge) and excellent goalkeeper, are still sufficient to win most of the games.

6   Conclusions and Future Work

In this paper we have presented a new approach to build cooperative teams of agents performing in dynamic real-time adversarial environments, based on a formalization of what should be a team strategy, a situation based strategic positioning mechanism, a dynamic positioning and role exchange mechanism and a new agent architecture. Following these guidelines we have selected the RoboSoccer simulated domain as our test bed and implemented a new RoboSoccer team – FC Portugal – that uses this team strategy. FC Portugal has shown the usefulness of the proposed approach through the results achieved in RoboCup2000, becoming the undefeated European and World champion, scoring 180 goals without conceding a single goal.

One of our main contributions in this paper is the formalization of the team strategy concept. As shown in section 2, a large part of this formalization can be applied to any domain with spatially distributed agents and any kind of team composed of homogeneous agents. In our formalization a team strategy is composed of a set of tactics and a set of possible agent types (defining agent behaviours at several levels). Each tactic is composed of several formations that are applied in different situations. Each formation is a flexible distribution of the agents in the field and has an assignment of agent types to each agent. The strategic position of the agents in the field is also dependent on the situation and of the positioning assigned in that formation to each agent. This nested strategic and tactic knowledge representation enables the development of very flexible teams, capable of assuming social behaviour (in strategic situations) and a more reactive behaviour (in active situations). Moreover the distinction between strategic and active situations gives the agents more sophisticated means of achieving global coordination of the team. When the agent is not on a critical situation (one in which he will be engaged in active behaviour soon), it assumes that it is in a strategic situation. In this situation it tries to position itself in the best possible strategic position.

It is also significant that, in our teamwork coordination approach, there is no conflict between simple agent reaction and deliberation about team coordination. In fact, situation-based analysis other than just trigger individual agent's actions, also induces appropriate tactical changes, leading all the team to adopt a new formation and therefore maintaining some sort of team coherence and coordination adjusted to the new situation. This reactively oriented change of global coordination framework (formations used for specific situations) prevents agents from performing isolated from the rest of the team while paying attention and reacting to the situation dynamics.

Our Dynamic Positioning and Role Exchange mechanism is another contribution of this work. This policy enables a better use of the team resources by exchanging their positioning and role. If, in a given situation, it is better for the team global utility that two agents switch places, the exchange is then performed. However, since the agents are homogeneous (except for the goal keeper), a role (agent type) exchange can also be performed (each agent is equally good in each one of the possible roles). This is useful to keep the formation characteristics. For heterogeneous agents a similar mechanism can be adopted extending this framework with an agent vs role capability matrix and changing the DPRE utility functions in accordance.

The results achieved by FC Portugal show the usefulness of the proposed team strategy, agent architecture and the adequacy of SBSP and DRPE in the context of the simulated RoboSoccer domain. Future work will be concerned with the application of this framework to other domains and its extension to heterogeneous agents.

Acknowledgments. The authors would like to thank to Peter Stone, Patrick Riley and Manuela Veloso for making available the low-level source code of their CMUnited99 simulation league RoboCup team. This saved us a huge amount in testing our approach in the framework of the FC Portugal project. We would also like to thank the financial support for this work of the FCT - Portuguese Foundation for Science and Technology, Compaq Portugal, PT Innovation, University of Aveiro, LIACC – Artificial Intelligence and Computer Science Laboratory and APPIA – Portuguese Association for Artificial Intelligence. Our thanks goes also to the anonymous reviewers that through their very detailed reviews contributed to increase the quality of this paper.

References

1. M. Asada and H. Kitano, editors. *RoboCup-98: Robot Soccer World Cup II*. Springer, Lecture Notes in Artificial Intelligence, 1999
2. Mike Bowling, Peter Stone, and Manuela Veloso. Predictive memory for an inaccessible environment. *In Proceedings of the IROS96 Workshop on RoboCup*, pages 28--34, Osaka, Japan, November 1996. (p. 68)
3. Emiel Corten et al. Soccerserver Manual, Version 5 rev 00 beta, at URL http://www.dsv.su.se/~johank/ Robocup/ manual, July, 1999
4. Keith Decker. Task Environment Centered Simulation. In M. Prietula, K. Carley, and L. Gasser, editors, *Simulating Organizations: Computational Models of Institutions and Groups*. AAAI Press/MIT Press, 1996
5. Klaus Dorer, The Magma Freiburg Soccer Team, in Manuela Veloso, Enrico Pagello and Hiroaki Kitano, editors. *RoboCup-99: Robot Soccer World Cup III*. Springer, Lecture Notes in Artificial Intelligence, 2000
6. B. Grosz,. Collaborating systems. *AI magazine*, 17 (2), 1996
7. B. Grosz, and S. Kraus. Collaborative plans for complex group actions. *Artificial Intelligence*, 86, 269—358, 1996
8. Hiroaki Kitano, M. Asada, Y. Kuniyoshi, I. Noda and E. Osawa. Robocup: The Robot World Cup Initiative. In *Proceedings of IJCAI95 Workshop on Entertainment and AI/Alife*, 1995
9. H. Kitano. RoboCup: The Robot World Cup Initiative, *Proceedings of the 1st International Conference on Autonomous Agent (Agents97)*, Marina del Ray, The ACM Press, 1997.
10. Hiroaki Kitano, M. Tambe, P. Stone, M. Veloso, I. Noda, E. Osawa and M. Asada. The Robocup Synthetic Agents' Challenge. *In Proceedings of the International Joint Conference on Artificial Intelligence (IJCAI)*, 1997
11. H. Kitano, et al., RoboCup-Rescue: Search and Rescue for Large Scale Disasters as a Domain for Multi-Agent Research, *Proceedings of IEEE Conference on Man, Systems, and Cybernetics (SMC-99)*, 1999
12. Kostas Kostiadis and H. Hu. A Multi Threaded Approach to Simulated Soccer Agents for the RoboCup Competition, *IJCAI'99 workshop on RoboCup*, 1999.
13. N. Jennings. Controlling cooperative problem solving in industrial multiagent systems using joint intentions. *Artificial Intelligence*, 75, 1995
14. H. J. Levesque, P. R. Cohen and J. Nunes. On acting together. *In Proceedings of the National Conference on Artificial Intelligence*. Menlo Park, California, AAAI press, 1990
15. Itsuki Noda. Soccer Server: A Simulator of Robocup. In *Proceedings of AI symposium '95 Japanese Society for Artificial Intelligence*, pp. 2934, 1995
16. Itsuki Noda, Hitoshi Matsubara, Kazuo Hiraki, and Ian Frank. Soccer server: A Tool for Research on Multiagent Systems. *Applied Artificial Intelligence*, Vol. 12, pp.233-250, 1998
17. Luís Paulo Reis and Nuno Lau, FC Portugal Team Description: RoboCup 2000 Simulation League Champion, *In Peter Stone, Tucker Balch and Gerhard Kraetzschmar, editors, RoboCup-2000: Robot Soccer World Cup IV*, Springer, Berlin, 2001, to appear
18. Luís Paulo Reis and Nuno Lau, FC Portugal Approach Overview, Accessible from http:/www.ieeta.pt/robocup/overview.htm, November of 2000
19. Martin Riedmiller et al. Karlsruhe Brainstormers 2000 - A Reinforcement Learning approach to robotic soccer. *Proceedings of the Fourth International Workshop on RoboCup*. Melbourne, August 2000
20. Peter Stone. *Layered Learning in Multi-Agent Systems*. PhD Thesis, School of Computer Science, Carnegie Mellon University, 1998

21. Peter Stone and Manuela Veloso. Task Decomposition, Dynamic Role Assignment, and LowBandwidth Communication for RealTime Strategic Teamwork. *Artificial Intelligence*, 110 (2), pp.241-273, June, 1999.
22. Peter Stone, Patrick Riley and Manuela Veloso. CMUnited-99 source code, 1999. Accessible from http://www.cs.cmu.edu/ ~pstone/RoboCup/CMUnited99-sim.html.
23. Peter Stone, Patrick Riley and Manuela Veloso. The CMUnited-99 Champion Simulator Team, in Manuela Veloso, Enrico Pagello and Hiroaki Kitano, editors. *RoboCup-99: Robot Soccer World Cup III*. Springer, Lecture Notes in Artificial Intelligence, 2000
24. Peter Stone, Tucker Balch and Gerhard Kraetzschmar, editors, RoboCup-2000: Robot Soccer World Cup IV, Springer, Berlin, 2001, to appear
25. Milind Tambe, Towards Flexible Teamwork, *Journal of Artificial Intelligence Research 7*, pp. 83-124, 1997
26. Milind Tambe. Implementing Agent Teams in Dynamic Multi-Agent Environments. *Applied Artificial Intelligence*, vol. 12, 1998
27. Manuela Veloso, Michael Bowling, Sorin Achim, Kwun Han, and Peter Stone. The CMUnited98 Champion Small Robot Team. In Minoru Asada and Hiroaki Kitano, editors, *RoboCup98: Robot Soccer World Cup II*. Springer Verlag, Berlin, 1999
28. Manuela Veloso, Enrico Pagello and Hiroaki Kitano, editors. *RoboCup-99: Robot Soccer World Cup III*. Springer, Lecture Notes in Artificial Intelligence, 2000
29. T. Wittig. ARCHON – An Architecture for Multi-Agent Systems, *Ellis Horwood Limited*, 1992

Deliberation Levels in Theoretic-Decision Approaches for Task Allocation in Resource-Bounded Agents

Maroua Bouzid, Hossam Hanna, and Abdel-Illah Mouaddib

CRIL/Université d'Artois
Rue de l'université, S.P. 16, 62307 Lens Cedex, France
{bouzid,hanna,mouaddib}@cril.univ-artois.fr

Abstract. In this paper we develop a new model of task allocation in distributed and cooperative resource-bounded agents using a theoretic-decision approach and their effect on the responsiveness of the system. Two architectures for task allocation and their level of deliberation are discussed. In both architectures the following holds: (1) Agents have limited resources and estimated distributions over resource execution tasks and (2) Agents create new tasks that they send to a central controller to distribute among them. The main difference between the two architectures resides in the place where the allocation decision-making process is performed. In the first architecture, we assume that the central controller builds an optimal and global decision on task allocation using a dynamic programming model and an estimated distribution over resources. In the second architecture, we assume that each agent builds a locally optimal decision and the central controller coordinates these distributed locally optimal decisions. In both architectures, we formulate the standard problem of task allocation as a Markov Decision Process (MDP). The states of the MDP represent the current state of the allocation in terms of tasks allocated to each agent and available resources. It is well-known that such approaches have a high-level of deliberation that can affect their efficiency in dynamic situations. We then discuss the effect of the two architectures on the balance between the deliberative and reactive behavior of the system.

1 Introduction

The development of new coordination protocols in distributed and multi-agent systems has recently been under intensive study. The importance of automated negotiation systems is increasing because of new applications requiring intelligent, autonomous and cooperative agents such as electronic commerce [5], transportation exchanges [10] or multi-rover systems [4]. Most of these applications imply agents of limited resources and share the set of tasks that the system has to achieve. The system has to be able to distribute tasks among agents such that the overall value of the system is maximized.

Strategies developed for coordination should take the overhead of computation into account. This overhead allows to evaluate the *level of deliberation*

M. Hannebauer et al. (Eds.): Reactivity and Deliberation in MAS, LNAI 2103, pp. 198–216, 2001.

that can lead to a purely *deliberative behavior* when this level is high while the behavior is assumed to be *reactive* when this level is low. Although reactive behaviors are suitable for dynamic environments, they are not able, in general, to construct a high solution quality. In the opposite, deliberative behaviors allow a high solution quality but they are less suitable for dynamic situations. The balance between the level of deliberation and the solution quality has been measured by the *utility* function that can lead to a good tradeoff between the deliberation time and the solution quality. However, the coordination strategies have to deal with this aspect in order to design an adaptive system able to define the appropriate level of deliberation to the current load of the system.

The system we are studying consists of cooperative resource-bounded agents, where each agent has an initial amount of resources and shares a set of tasks to be achieved together with the other agents. Agents have an estimated distribution over the computation resource needed to achieve a task and a reward value when the latter is achieved. The problem we study is how to distribute tasks among agents such that the overall reward value is maximized and the cost (resources used) is minimized. In other words, we use a resource-bounded agent system based on an input set of tasks and each agent's resources conditions that distributes tasks among agents. Agents are assumed to be identical. An agent can achieve any task in the input set and can accept a subset of tasks to achieve when its internal resources permit. This assumption can be relaxed by introducing to the allocation problem not only the available resources but also the operation rules (specific agents expertise). Furthermore, the computation resources of agents to achieve the tasks are uncertain. Most of the approaches dedicated to this problem [10,1,11] ignore the uncertainty on computation resources. Previous approaches for task allocation try to minimize the cost functions of agents [1] while the value rewarded when achieving the task is not taken into consideration. In these approaches, the value is uniquely measured by the cost functions when the task is allocated. However, the reward value when achieving a task combined with the cost function have to be considered as a measure of the task value.

The method we suggest is a theoretic-decision technique using the cost of achieving the task, the reward value when the task is achieved and the uncertainty on resource consumption. This mechanism is an interesting mean to coordinate agents and minimize the communication between them. All tasks are joined together in a same set. Two architectures are considered:

- *A high-level deliberative system:* This architecture uses a central controller which is in charge to distribute the set of tasks among agents. Since agents have the same competence, they are able to achieve any task. The allocation is based on series of steps. At each step a task is allocated to an agent. This process is repeated for every task until all tasks are allocated or all agent resource have been fully utilized. A dynamic programming algorithm is proposed to develop a policy to allocate tasks to agents. It uses the estimated distribution over resources. The central controller builds the whole decision based on an optimal policy of the global Markov Decision Process. Agents have a *reactive* behavior since they only execute the orders received from the central controller.

The "*Responsiveness*" of the system is highly related to the deliberation time of the central controller. The system is responsive or reactive when the deliberation time of the central controller is low. Agents have no effect on the responsiveness of the system since their behavior is reduced to execute orders coming from the central controller.

- *A low-level deliberative system:* This architecture tries to avoid the drawbacks of the previous architecture where the "responsiveness" depends only on the central controller. In this architecture, we assume that agents are able to build a local allocation decision and the central controller plays only the role of coordinating the distributed local decisions. Indeed, the decision-making process based on a local MDP reduces the deliberation level but an overhead of coordination has to be considered. In addition to that, the global optimality is lost. The decisions made by agents are locally optimal but coordinated local decisions are usually not globally optimal. However, the utility of the solution can be higher than the previous approach. The "responsiveness" of this system depends on the slower agent. Indeed, the coordination can start only when all agents finish building their decisions, the central controller acts only when the slower agent has finished its processing and returns its local decision.

Section 2 presents an example concerned with such approaches. Section 3 introduces a formal definition of the problem. In Sect. 4, we develop a theoretic-decision approach for the stated problem using the high level deliberative architecture. A discussion on the complexity of the approach is presented in Sect. 5. We propose in Sect. 6 another approach using the low-level deliberative architecture and showing the effect of the coordination startegies on reducing this complexity and on the responsiveness. Section 7 gives new directions on distributed MDPs and their coordination. Section 8 describes related work and the relationship with deliberation and reactivity and Sect. 9 concludes the paper.

2   Example: Cooperative Rovers for Science

The recent success in the areas of space exploration and planetary rovers resulted in the feasibility of sending rovers to other planets and increased the significance of such missions to scientific community. Future missions are being planned to send additional rovers to Mars. In order to optimize and maximize the science return and enable certain types of activities, a set of rovers to be in charge of gathering the desired data are required [4]. These rovers have to behave in a coordinated fashion. In fact, each rover accomplishes a subset of the overall mission goals and shares the acquired information. These rovers have also to be highly autonomous and require little communication to perform their tasks. Each rover has to be in charge of making decisions on its own as to what scientific tasks should be accomplished, which science data should be gathered, stored and communicated. The system is based on a set of goals and the rovers' initial conditions. It generates a sequence of tasks to be accomplished for achieving these goals. Each rover is responsible for planning its own tasks. The central system is responsible for distributing the tasks among individual rovers in a fashion that maximizes the reward value.

Coordinating these multiple rovers by respecting their autonomy and reducing their communication introduces some new challenges for the supporting technology. Issues of concern will be the communication, control and autonomy. Although the decentralized control increases the level of autonomy of different components of space systems to gain survivability, the coordination problem among the sub-systems to maximize their ability to achieve shared tasks is the major issue. This coordination protocol has to allow a group of rovers to explore a larger area and increase the amount of collected data. Also, it has to share tasks and resources for high performance and to make rovers cooperate to achieve complex tasks that require more than one rover. In addition to that, the coordination has to include *adaptive levels of deliberation* since in some situations, the decisions have to be available to the rovers at a given time (at given sun positions for example) and a long deliberation time can make the decisions useless. Consequently, new approaches have to be designed in such a way that they :

- reduce the communication among rovers,
- reduce tasks uncertainty on their resource availability,
- and, to develop a strategy for the allocation task problem with adaptive level of deliberation.

The approach we have adopted for this example consists of two control levels. The first level consists of the rover activity and its planification for its own tasks. This paper does not address this issue, but the interested reader can find different solutions to this problem in [9,14,15]. However, we propose that the result of the execution of each rover that can contain gathered science data or new goals to be accomplished are communicated to the system (central controller). The central controller that represents the second control level, gathers all goals together and develops the tasks to be accomplished and then distributes them among rovers. To do that two architectures could be considered as mentioned in the introduction. The main difference between them is that the decision making on the task allocation could be done by a centralized control module or by all rovers and a central module coordinates distributed decisions.

The decision making (by a central module or different rovers) is based on a sequential allocation model and a dynamic programming algorithm for constructing an optimal policy. We assume that tasks are allocated in a given order. We model the allocation problem as an MDP and describe how the system could construct an optimal (globally or locally) allocation policy for the sequence of tasks based on their evaluations.

3   Problem Statement

Let $A = \{a_1, a_2, \ldots, a_p\}$ be a set of agents that have to optimally share a set $G = \{g_1, g_2, \ldots, g_n\}$ of tasks. Each agent a_i has initially an available resource t_i allowing it to allocate a subset G_i of tasks to achieve. Each agent a_i has (1) a positive reward function r_i which reflects the expected reward value when achieving a task (2) a positive function *cost* that measures the cost of remaining resources (3) a probabilistic distribution over the amount of resources required to achieve a task. The problem of task allocation consists in deciding how to distribute tasks among agents such that the overall utilization is maximized by maximizing the reward value and minimizing the cost.

The scenario used for agents consists in initial tasks (i.e. analyzing rocks in different areas) that a central controller distributes among agents. Agents send in return collected data (pictures, chemical structure of rocks) and other goals (analyzing other rocks *one* mile in the west of the current location of the rover). The central controller collects data, sends to earth a synthetic result of the current scientific exploration and finally, determines new tasks to achieve that he will distribute among agents and so on. The task allocation policy that the central controller adopts is based on a theoretic decision mechanism.

The tasks will be allocated sequentially in a known order. This common order is $g_1, g_2, \ldots, g_n$. We use k to denote the allocation round for the task g_k. A round k of allocation denotes the allocation for task g_k. There are n rounds. Each agent a is given an initial resource t_a which it uses to allocate tasks. At the end of each round, if the agent a allocates the tasks, its set of allocated tasks increases while its resources decrease. Utility $u(g_k, t_a)$ of being in such a state at the end of the round is measured to define the reward value. We will define the utility in the next section.

4   A High-Level Deliberative Theoretic-Decision Approach

The process through which an agent allocates tasks is not one of assigning values to individual resources , but rather one of constructing an allocation policy by which the agent allocates a task considering the outcome of earlier events in the allocation. The sequential nature of the allocation process means that it can be viewed as a standard sequential decision problem under uncertainty. In other words, this problem of task allocation can be formulated as a control problem of a Markov Decision Process (MDP). The states of the MDP represent the current state of the computation of allocation tasks in terms of the subset of tasks allocated/remaining resources per agent. The rewards associated with each state are simply the rewards when allocated tasks have been accomplished and the benefit gained (abusively, we name it cost of the remaining resources). The possible actions are those concerning the allocation of a task to an agent. The transition model is defined by the resource uncertainty associated with the agent selected to accomplish the task. To compute an optimal allocation policy, we can use a standard dynamic programming algorithm such as value iteration.

We define in this section the formal definition of the resulting MDP. Then, we describe an algorithm to construct an optimal policy for task allocation. Finally, we present an analysis of this algorithm.

4.1   Preliminaries

In our context, we consider the limited computation time. In the previous example, this time consists in what is necessary to communicate data. We don't take the other resources into account such as memory or energy, but the extension to the other resources is not difficult. We can use a vector of resources and a vector of computation resources.

Definition 1 *Each agent a has a probability distribution P_a that allows it to determine the probability of the computation resources required to accomplish a task g: $P_a(\tau_a(g))$ where τ_a represents the estimated function of computation resources used to achieve a goal. τ is the amount of resource.*

This distribution is constructed off-line by analyzing the behavior of each agent in achieving the tasks. With this learning step, the distribution P_a is represented as a set of couples $\{(\tau, p)\}$ where p is the probability the computation resource takes τ units. The number of couples representing P_a affects its precision and the size of the MDP.

Definition 2 *Each agent a has a reward function $r_a(g_i)$ that measures the reward value when achieving a task g_i.*

Definition 3 *Each agent a has a Cost function $Cost(t)$. The latter measures the value of available resources t. In our context, this cost is saved by the agent since the resources are not consumed. So, for an agent a high cost is favorable and $Cost(0) = 0$*

Definition 4 *The utility function $u(g_k, t_a)$ of being in a state that the task g_k is allocated and t_a is the remaining resource represents the utility of being in such a state. One way to define this utility is to take into account the reward value, i.e. when the task has been achieved, and the cost of remaining resource, such as:*

$$u(g_k, t_a) = r(g_k) + Cost(t_a)$$

4.2   State Representation

We model the allocation task processing as a stochastic automaton with a finite set of world states $\mathcal{S} = \{\boldsymbol{S}^k | k \in \{1, 2, \ldots, n\}\}$. When the system of allocation is in state $\boldsymbol{S}^k$, task k has been allocated, $k = 0$ is used to indicate that no task has been allocated and the system is ready to start. k is used as an index of the task. The allocation of tasks is organized in rounds. At each round i we allocate task g_i. At each round i, state $\boldsymbol{S}^i$ defines the allocation of tasks $1, 2, \ldots, i$ and the state of agent resources. State $\boldsymbol{S}^i$ is represented by a vector containing at each dimension j the subset of tasks allocated by the agent j and its remaining resources. More formally:

$$\boldsymbol{S}^k = ((G_1, t_1), (G_2, t_2), \ldots, (G_p, t_p))$$

such that:

$$\bigcup_i G_i = \{g_1, g_2, \ldots, g_k\} \subset G$$

G_i denote subsets of tasks.

Initial state

$$\boldsymbol{S}^0 = ((\emptyset, t_1), (\emptyset, t_2), \ldots, (\emptyset, t_p))$$

Terminal states

Two situations represent the terminal state:

- *All resources have been fully utilized, so:*

$$\boldsymbol{S}^i_{f,0} = ((G_1, 0), (G_2, 0), \ldots, (G_p, 0))$$

- *All tasks have been allocated, so:*

$$\boldsymbol{S}^n = ((G_1, t_1), (G_2, t_2), \ldots, (G_p, t_p))$$

such as:

$$G = \bigcup_i G_i$$

4.3   Actions

An action $\mathbf{a(g)}$ consists in allocating a task g to an agent a. This action is probabilistic due to the resource uncertainty that defines the new state. At each state we have many possible actions corresponding to the number of possible allocations of a task to agents since agents are considered identical. Actions fail when their computation resources are greater than the available resources. A set $\mathcal{A}$ of actions is:

$$\mathcal{A} = \{a_i(g) | a_i \in A, g \in G\}$$

We present in the following the transition model.

4.4   Transition Model

The initial state of the MDP is S^0. This state indicates that the system is ready to start the allocation of the first task. The terminal states are all the states mentioned below, i.e. those where all tasks have been allocated S^n or where all resources have been fully utilized $S^i_{f,0}$. In every nonterminal state, there are different possible actions representing different possible agents to allocate the task. A Transition occurs when an agent allocates a task. In other words, the agent includes this task in its subset of allocated tasks and then, its resource is reduced by the amount of the expected resource to achieve the allocated task. This transition is probabilistic since the amount of expected resources to achieve a task is probabilistic.

The transition model is a function that maps each element of

$$\mathcal{S} \times \mathcal{A} = \{a_k(g_i) | 1 \leq i \leq n \; and \; 1 \leq k \leq p\}$$

into a discrete probability distribution over $\mathcal{S}$.

The rest of the paper describes the equations that define the transition probabilities for a given nonterminal state S^i and the value of terminal states.

Probability of a Successful Transition

$$Pr(S^i|S^{i-1}, a_j(g_i)) = P_{a_j}(\tau_{a_j}(g_i)), \; when \; t_{a_j} \geq \tau_{a_j}(g_i) \tag{1}$$

This equation determines the transition following successful execution when the computation resource is less than the available resource. The new state after the allocation of the task i is:

$$S^i = ((G_1, t_1), \ldots, (G_j \bigcup \{g_i\}, t_{a_j} - \tau_{a_j}(g_i)), \ldots, (G_n, t_n))$$

State S^i corresponds to the new state after the successful execution of the action $a_j(g_i)$. This execution leads to an increase of the set of allocated tasks by allocating to the agent a_j the task g_i and a decrease of the remaining resource by the expected computation resource $\tau(a_j(g_i))$.

Probability of a Failed Transition

$$Pr(S'^i|S^{i-1}, a_j(g_i)) = \sum_{\tau_j < g_i} P_{a_j}(\tau_{a_j}(g_i)) \tag{2}$$

This equation determines the transition following failure execution when the computation resource is greater than the available resource.

The new state for this transition is:

$$S'^i = ((G_1, t_1), \ldots, (G_j, 0), \ldots, (G_n, t_n))$$

State S'^i corresponds to the new state after the execution of the action $a_j(g_i)$ fails. This failure does not change the set of allocated tasks and sets the remaining resource to 0 since the expected computation resource $\tau(a_j(g_i))$ will use all the available resource. To simplify, we assume that a mechanism is added to abort an execution that requires more resources than what is available.

4.5   Rewards and Values of States

Rewards are associated with terminal states based on the agent utilities of allocated tasks and remaining resources. Therefore,

$$R(S^k) = \sum_{(G_a,t_a)\in S^k} (Cost(t_a) + \sum_{g_i\in G_a} r(g_i)) \tag{3}$$

Now, we can define the expected value function for the states of the MDP as follows:

$$V(S^i) = \max_{a\in\mathcal{A}}\{Pr(S'^{i+1}|S^i, a(g_{i+1}))V(S'^{i+1}) + \tag{4}$$
$$\sum_{\tau_{a(g_{i+1})}} Pr(S^{i+1}|S, a(g_{i+1}))V(S^{i+1})\}$$

Finally, the value function for terminal states:

$$V(S^n) = R(S^n) \tag{5}$$

and

$$V(S_{f,0}) = R(S_{f,0}) = \sum_{(G_a,0)\in S_{f,0}} \sum_{g_i\in G_a} r(g_i) \tag{6}$$

The allocation policy π makes it possible to know, for each legal state S^i, the action (to which agent the task is allocated) to perform to allocate the task $i+1$. The value $V^\pi(S^i)$ of the policy π is the expected reward obtained by executing the policy π. The expected value of π given the initial state S^0 is simply $V^\pi(S^0)$. An optimal allocation policy is any π that maximizes the expected reward for every state. This is allowed by Eq. (4).

4.6   Optimal Allocation

The resulting MDP is a case of a finite-horizon MDP with no loops, since each transition moves forward in the state space by continuously allocating a resource. This class of MDP can be easily solved for relatively large state spaces because the value function can be calculated in one sweep of the state space (backwards, starting with terminal states). This approach can be implemented by a recursive algorithm which computes the value function starting with the values of terminal states given by Eq. (5) (i.e., 3) and (6) and using Eq. (4) to compute the values of intermediate and initial states. The optimal policy is computed by using a standard dynamic programming algorithm.

Theorem 1 *Given a set of agents and a set of tasks, the optimal policy to distribute tasks among agents is the optimal policy for its corresponding MDP*

Proof: Given the one-to-one correspondence between the MDP states and the states of the task allocation processing, the optimal policy for the MDP is the optimal policy for the task allocation problem.

In his general version, the distributed allocation task problem is NP-complete. However, under the following assumption:

- tasks are ordered
- Markovian assumption

the complexity of the problem is reduced and an optimal solution is tractable.

4.7   Towards an Adaptive Deliberation Approach

Although the problem is tractable for a reasonable size as we will show in Sect. 5, the deliberation level is still high. Indeed, this is the effect of the centralized approach where agents are purely reactive while the controller is purely deliberative. This architecture is based on the principle of Master/Slave architecture. The deliberation level is completely related to the controller. However, in this architecture, the balance between the level of deliberation and the solution quality should be considered at the control level. This issue is overcome with the advantage of this approach because it allows an allocation available at any time. At least, there is *one* agent which has a task to achieve. This incremental processing avoids the combinatorial allocation problems and allows to characterize the processing by a *performance profile* that can be a function that maps rounds of allocation (level of deliberation) to the number of allocated tasks (solution quality). With *performance profile*, the system can have an adaptive deliberation by adapting the deliberation level to the load of the system.

This approach is flexible. It allows a system to deal with a transient failed agent that can occur during the allocation process. This incremental processing is more suitable than the classical ones in situations where transient overload of the system occurs. In such situations, the system is able to handle the overhead of the coordination by limiting the allocation rounds to the subset of the most preferred tasks instead of the whole set of tasks.

5   Analysis

The number of MDP states is defined by the number p of agents, the number n of tasks and the maximum number q of alternatives in estimated distribution P_a. The number of states is limited by $p^n q^p$. In our example, p and n are not potentially large since it is not economically desirable to have the number p of rovers (to be sent to Mars) large. At most $p = 5$. In the same way, the number of tasks to be allocated are in general one task created by the agent, then $n = 5$ while q is defined in a way that the distribution is accurate enough, for example $q = 5$. In this situation, the number of states is less that 10^7 and that is still a tractable size. However, in general, the number of tasks is potentially quite large. In the same way, the allocated number of alternatives is relatively small in comparison to the number of tasks. However, it can be quite large for more precision in the estimated distribution. An example for $p = 5$, $n = 20$ and $q = 5$ is approximately about 10^{17} states. For such situations, this number of states requires a substantial computation effort. Fortunately, we can make it simpler if we use some heuristics to reduce the number of tasks to be allocated. Indeed, the agent can locally select a subset of tasks and negotiates the remaining tasks with the other agents.

6   A Low-Level Deliberative Distributed Policies Approach

Obviously, the example presented above shows an explosion in the size of the MDP. Therefore, it is not feasible to compute a truly optimal policy.

The approaches we have developed to reduce the size of the policy consists in distributing the tasks among agents each of which allocates a subset of tasks using a local MDP. The problem is that different agents can allocate the same tasks or some tasks could not be allocated by any agent. To deal with this issue we develop a global coordinator and we discuss two strategies of coordination. In the following we describe, first, the local MDP and then we present the two coordination strategies and their performance.

6.1   Local Markov Decision Process

Each agent transforms the allocation task on an MDP which is a simplified version of the one described in Sect. 4. The main difference is the set of actions of the MDP that is reduced only to an action to allocate the task and an action to skip the task that means that the agent does not allocate the task. This reduces the size of the MDP to q^p where p is the number of tasks and q is the number of different alternatives of resources to achieve each task. With this simplification the local MDP at each agent is described by : the intermediate state is $S^i = (G_a^i, t_a)$ where G_a^i is the subset of G containing locally allocated tasks to a and t_a are the remaining resources. The terminal states are (G^n, t_a) (decisions on all tasks has been made (allocated or skipped)) or $(G_a^i, 0)$ (all resources has been fully utilized). The reward R associated with the state is its utility. However Eq. (3) becomes,

$$R(S^i) = u'(G_a^i, t_a) = Cost(t_a) + \sum_{g \in G_a^i} r(g) \tag{7}$$

Equations 5, 6 use this new definition of R. The transitions follow Eqs. (1) and (2) by using the state S^i instead of $\boldsymbol{S}^i$. The resulting states for successful and failed transitions, respectively, are:

$$S^{i+1} = (G_a^i \bigcup \{g_{i+1}\}, t_a - \tau_a(g_{i+1}))$$

$$S'^i = (G_a^i, 0)$$

The resulting MDP is a case of a finite horizon MDP with no loops.

Theorem 2 *Given an agent and its local set of tasks, the optimal policy to allocate a task is the optimal policy of the corresponding MDP.*

Proof: similar to Theorem 1.

The agent from this MDP, computes the subset of tasks that maximizes its local utility. We call in the following T_{max}^a the optimal allocated subset of the agent a, given by its optimal policy,

6.2   Coordination of Distributed Policies

Each agent sends to the global coordinator its optimal allocated subset T_{max}^a. The global coordinator have to detect conflicts between agents and to solve them. We recall that two agents a and a' are in conflicts when the following condition holds :

$$T_{max}^a \bigcap T_{max}^{a'} \neq \emptyset$$

The coordinator collects all conflicts and solve them agent by agent. Two strategies has been developped that we name *all_or_nothing* or *task_by_task*. We describe in the following the main idea of those strategies.

All_or_Nothing Coordination. The coordinator sends the whole set G to all agents and receives from them their local optimal allocations T_{max}^a with the expected utility $EU(a)$. The resolution of a conflict consists in validating the whole subset T_{max}^a of the agent with the maximum EU, and refusing the subsets of the other with which the agent is in conflict. The coordinator makes agents informed on the validation or cancellation of their subsets. When all the tasks has been allocated the coordination is terminated. Elsewhere, the coordinator sends the remaining tasks to the agents that have no tasks and a new cycle of allocation and coordination is fired. The agents don't need to compute again their local MDPs because the ones computed previously remain valid but only they should skip the tasks that has been already allocated in the previous cycle. The agents send new optimal subsets to the coordinator. This processing is repeated until all tasks are allocated or the set of the remaining tasks is the same in two successive cycles.

Task_by_Task Coordination. This strategy differs fundamentally from the first one, since the coordination is done step by step. Indeed, the coordinator instead of validating all the subset of the agent, it validates only the task under negotiation. The coordinator takes tasks one by one in a given order and allocates them to the agents.

The agents send, as previously, their optimal subsets to the coordinator. The coordinator allocates the task under negotiation to the agent with the highest EU (of its whole policy). The coordinator makes agents informed on his decision. The agent, for which the task is allocated, pursues his policy while the other should skip this task and then move to a new state in the MDP that allows them to suggest another new optimal subset computed from the new policy of their local MDPs. Recall that agents don't recompute the MDPs but only a new policy. This process is repeated task by task until all tasks has been allocated.

6.3   The Deliberation Level in the Distributed Deliberative Approach

The *deliberation level* of this approach depends on the coordination overhead and on the slowest deliberative agents that build local allocation decisions. In contrary to the centralized approach, we assess the level of deliberation at the coordinator module by measuring the cost of the coordination and at the deliberative distributed agents by measuring the cost of constructing the local decisions. This deliberation level can be formalized as follows :

$$Deliberation\_Level =$$

$$Cost(coordination\_time) \; + \; \max_{a \in \mathcal{A}} \; Cost(processing\_time(a))$$

The deliberation time of coordination could be assessed by exchanged messages between the coordinator and agents while the deliberation time of agents is the *cpu* time consumed when they construct their local allocation decisions. To have an adaptive deliberation level we can adapt : (1) the processing time of agents to reduce the set of tasks to allocate, and (2) to design a good coordination technique. For the latter, we compare the coordination approaches we presented and their effect on the deliberation time.

The Cost of Coordination Strategies. The costs of All_Or_Nothing (AOR) and Task_By_Task (TBT) approaches have been evaluated according to the number of tasks and agents. We have measured the load of communication in both approaches. The TBT coordination approach exchanges more messages than the AON approach. Indeed, for example, for 10 agents and 100 tasks, the TBT approach needs 2010 messages to allocate all tasks while AON needs only 108 messages. Table 1 summarizes obtained results on the communication overhead of both approaches. From this table we can see that AON is more suitable than TBT in dynamic situations. However, with the TBT coordination approach, the system can adopt an adaptive deliberation behavior by reducing the number of tasks as we mentioned in the previous approach. Indeed, we can see that TBT has the number of exchanged messages as a quick increasing function of the number of tasks. In the opposite, AON has a slow increasing function of the number of exchanged messages.

We can use these functions as "performance profile" of those approaches that allow to adapt the deliberation level to the appropriate load of the system.

The Deliberation Time of Agents. The other factor that affects the deliberation time of the entire system is the deliberation time of the allocation decision

Table 1. Number of exchanged messages for AON and TBT strategies according to the number of tasks and agents

Agents	Tasks	All_Or_Nothing	Task_By_Task
10	20	48	410
	50	78	1010
	80	100	1610
	100	108	2010
15	20	73	615
	50	123	1515
	80	145	2415
	100	183	3015
20	20	98	820
	50	168	2020
	80	230	3220
	100	258	4020
25	20	123	1025
	50	213	2525
	80	295	4025
	100	333	5025

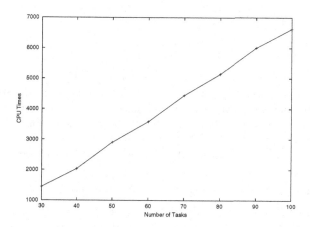

Fig. 1. Computation time of local decison according to the number of tasks

process of agents. To evaluate the deliberation time of agents, we record an average (over 10 agents) of consumed *cpu* according to the number of tasks. We derive from these gathered results a "performance profile" that it is also necessary to deal with an adaptive deliberation. Figure 1 shows this performance profile.

7   New Directions for Distributed Local MDPs Strategies

In the previous section, we discussed an approach to reduce the size of the global MDP by constructing local MDPs and then coordinating the distributed policies using two techniques of coordination. This approach is based on distributing the same set of tasks to all agents and then coordinate their local decisions. In this section, we present new directions where the whole set of tasks is not distributed among agents but each agent allocates tasks from the set of tasks it creates. In those strategies, we seek to reduce the size of the policy by defining approximation policies considering only a subset of tasks. In order to select the subset of tasks to be allocated systematically to the agents, we use a local allocation before starting the global allocation mechanism. This method will reduce the number of states to $p^{n-k}q^p$, if k tasks are locally allocated. The selection of the locally allocated tasks can be based on different heuristic approaches. These are:

7.1   Reactive Approach

In this approach, we assume that when each agent a allocates a task locally from the set G_a, it creates and starts immediately the execution. The task that has been selected is the one that maximizes the *utility* from the set of locally created ones. Each agent, then, allocates only *one* task and sends the others to the central controller that defines the allocation policy. The local allocation is then based on the following equation:

$$g_{allocated} = arg \max_{g \in G_a} u(g, t_a) \tag{8}$$

Since each agent allocates a task locally, the central controller MDP size becomes $p^{n-p}q^p$. This approach does not substantially reduce the size but allows the agents to continue their execution while the central controller constructs the allocation policy. The computation time of the allocation policy is comparable to the execution time of agents. In our example this assumption is valid, but in other applications an experimental evaluation could be necessary.

7.2   Distributed Local Markov Decision Process

Another approach consists in allowing each agent to construct a local MDP of the local set allocation. The central coordinator will be invoked only if some tasks have not been locally allocated. This means that each agent constructs a local policy for allocating a subset of its created task set G_a and sends the remaining tasks if any to the central coordinator. In the local MDPs that is similar to the one of Sect. 6, the intermediate state is $S^i = (G_a^i, t_a)$ where G_a^i is the subset of G_a containing locally allocated tasks to a and t_a are the remaining resources. The terminal states are (G_a, t_a) (all tasks has been allocated) or $(G_a^i, 0)$ (all resources has been fully utilized). The reward R associated with the state is its utility. However Eq. (3) becomes,

$$R(S^i) = u'(G_a^i, t_a) = Cost(t_a) + \sum_{g \in G_a^i} r(g) \tag{9}$$

Equations 5, 6 use this new definition of R. The transitions follow Eqs. (1) and (2) by using the state S^i instead of $\boldsymbol{S}^i$. The resulting states for successful and failed transitions, respectively, are:

$$S^{i+1} = (G_a^i \bigcup \{g_{i+1}\}, t_a - \tau_a(g_{i+1}))$$

$$S'^i = (G_a^i, 0)$$

The resulting MDP is a case of a finite horizon MDP with no loops.

Theorem 3 *Given an agent and its local set of tasks, the optimal policy to allocate a task is the optimal policy of the corresponding MDP.*

Proof: similar to Theorem 1.

Agents construct local MDPs that allow them to have an optimal local allocation policy. However the global optimality is not guaranteed. Indeed, it is obvious to prove that the local optimal MDPs do not guarantee a global optimal policy since it is not guaranteed that the utility u_a' of a locally allocated task is greater than the utility $u_{a'}'$ of another agent a'. In order to deal with a global optimality, agents need to have a stochastic information on the utilities of the other agents for a given allocated task and remaining resources. Further study is needed to analyze how a stochastic distribution on utilities can be used in local allocations. Our future work will concern the effect of introducing such information on a global optimality when we have local optimal policies. This distribution Pr_a^u will allow agent a to predict the effect of its allocation such that:

$$u_{max} = \max_{a' \in \mathcal{A} - \{a\}} u_{a'}(g, t_{a'}) \tag{10}$$

The probability that the utility of agent a is greater than the others: $Pr_a^u(u_a(g, t_a) > u_{max})$ is the probability that it has the highest utility to allocate the task g. This information will be introduced in the transition model expressed by Eqs. (1) and (2) and then recomputes the values of states as it is shown in Sect. 4.5. Our future work treats this issue.

8 Related Work

8.1 Task Allocation

The problem of distributing tasks among agents has been studied using many different coordination techniques. The *contract net* protocol [3] is one mean to do that. This protocol assumes that agents have not resource limitations. In our context, we relax this assumption and our assumption are similar to what Sandholm developed in his approach TRACONET [10]. However, in this approach Sandholm ignores the uncertainty of resource task realization. Sandholm examines a generalization of CONTRACT NET to Task Oriented Domains (TODs), where the allocation starts with an initial allocation and then agents negotiate to exchange tasks. In our case, we avoid this feedbacks from the initial allocation and reducing then the communication load.

Anderson and Sandholm [1] find that decommitment protocols increase the quality of resulting allocations in variants of TODs. This approach does not make clearly the frontier between allocation and execution where the decommitment is important when execution is progressing differently than expected. In our approach, we limit our study just to allocation and we don't deal with the execution phase. Future work will concern this point.

Walsh and Wellman [13] discussed economic effeciency to solve task allocation problems involving hierarchical dependencies and resource contention. This approach introduces also a decommitment phase to augment allocation effeciency. In contract to our approach, this approach does not deal with uncertainty of resource consumption while our approach is not suitable to situation where tasks are hierarchically dependent.

Finally, Shehory and Kraus [12] propose methods for task allocation via coalition formation. In contrast to our approach, agents are designed in such a way that they are not able to solve a task solely. In our approach agents are designed in such a way that they can solve more than one task solely.

8.2   Combinatorial Auction

This work has the same motivation as combinatorial auction. Combinatorial auction where agents can bid on combination of items, e.g. tasks, have recently received a lot of interest because they often result in better allocations than traditional auction where the item values are not additive. A special case of combinatorial auction has been studied in [1] where one agent, which initially has all tasks, later allocates them to the other agents. Combinatorial auctions are one-to-many, i.e. there is one seller and many buyers. Unlike the combinatorial auction, our agents are sellers and buyers and we use a special case of combinatorial auction which is many-to-many. Furthermore, unlike the approach described in [1], initially, the agents have no tasks. They construct their subset of allocated tasks through a series of allocations. The advantage of this is to avoid a re-allocative combinatorial allocation. Besides, with initial allocation, some agents may receive the tasks they don't want. Our agents have a preference on tasks which is measured by the reward value.

Unlike classical approaches studied for resource allocations [8,7,6] where agents share resources, this approach reduces the communication between agents and takes uncertainty on items, e.g. tasks and resources. Other approaches have been developed to use auction mechanisms for resource allocation [2] and present a new approach for allocation of resources in multi-agent systems. Our work is similar to this approach by allocating tasks.

8.3   Reactivity and Deliberation

Most of task allocation approaches assume agents to be purely reactive. By reactive we mean that an agent has no ability to construct a decision but it only acts depending on the order it receives. In our approach, we deal with *reactive agents* using a *deliberative central controller* using an MDP method. We show that with such agents, the complexity is relatively high and we have to give agents a relative ability to construct decisions and then to submit it to the community, which commits or not to the decision of the agent with coordination strategies. In addition to that, agents have no ability nor knowledge about the other agents in order to find a good tradeoff between their ability to construct a decision and the ability to execute the agreed decision. This tradeoff gives a balance between the reactive and deliberative behavior of our agents. In contrast to that, the central controller is purely deliberative and we are developing new strategies that can decide the level of deliberation appropriate to the situation given by the load of the overall system.

9   Concluding Remarks

It is well-known that task allocation mechanisms in multi-agents systems have a high level of deliberation that can affect their efficiency in dynamic situations. We have presented two architectures based on a task allocation MDP technique and discussed the effect of these architecture on their deliberation level. This deliberation level allows to assess the "responsiveness" (degree of reaction) of the system.

This study starts by describing a new model for allocation tasks in a resource-bounded agent system whose resource availability is uncertain. We present an approach of allocation model that reformulates the allocation problem as a Markov Decision Process (MDP) and uses a dynamic programming algorithm. This approach uses a theoretic-decision mechanism that allows the central coordinator to construct a global allocation policy. This approach avoids a reallocation stage that can lead to a substantial communication overhead. However, its deliberation level, although it remains feasible, is still high. Indeed, the resulting MDP of this approach, although it suggests an optimal solution, can have a large size that requires a substantial computation effort. To reduce this size we suggest different approaches and studying their integration and their effect on the size and on the global optimality.

A new work has been focused on using distributed local MDPs and coordination of these local MDPs. We have developed two approaches of coordination and their performances. In this approach, we show the effect of the coordination overhead and the local computation of agents on the deliberation level of the whole system and how to derive an adaptive deliberation level.

A future direction that we can follow is to extend this approach to multiple resources. Indeed, in our multi-rovers system, rovers handle their resources on communication time, energy and memory to store data. This issue can be addressed as an optimizing multi-criteria decision quality problem where each resource can be assumed as a criterion of the multi-resources problem.

Acknowledgements. The authors would like to thank the reviewers for their constructive comments.

References

1. M. Andersson and T. Sandholm. Time-quality tradeoffs in reallocative negotiation with combinatorial contract types. In *AAAI*, pages 3–10, 1999.
2. G. Boutilier, Moisés, and B. Sabata. Sequential auctions for the allocation of resources with complementaries. In *IJCAI*, 1999.
3. Davis and Smith. Negotiation as a metaphor for distributed problem solving. *Artificial Intelligence*, 20:63–109, 1983.
4. T. Estlin, A. Tobias, G. Rabideau, R. Castana, S. Chien, and E. Mjolsness. An integrated system for multi-rover scientific exploration. In *AAAI*, pages 613–613, 1999.
5. R. Kalakota and A. Whinston. *Frontiers of Electronic Commerce.* Addison-Wesley, 1996.
6. A.-I. Mouaddib. Progressive negotiation for time-constrained autonomous agents. In *First International Conference on Autonomous Agents*, pages 8–16, 1997.
7. A.-I. Mouaddib. Multistage negotiation for distributed scheduling of resource-bounded agents. In *AAAI Spring Symposium on Satisficing Models*, pages 54–59, 1998.
8. A.-I. Mouaddib. Anytime coordination for progressive planning agents. In *AAAI-99*, pages 564–569, 1999.
9. A.-I. Mouaddib and S. Zilberstein. Optimal scheduling for dynamic progressive processing. In *ECAI-98*, pages 499–503, 1998.
10. T. Sandholm. An implementation of the contract net protocol based on marginal cost calculations. In *AAAI*, pages 256–262, 1993.
11. S. Sen. An automated distributed meeting scheduler. *IEEE Transactions Expert*, accepted, 1996.
12. O. Sheory and S. Kraus. Methods for task allocations via agent coalition formation. *Artificial Intelligence*, 101:165–200, 1998.
13. W. Walsh and M. P. Wellman. Effeciency and equilibrium in task allocation economies with hierarchical dependencies. In *IJCAI-99*, pages 520–526, 1999.
14. S. Zilberstein and A.-I. Mouaddib. Reactive control for dynamic progressive processing. In *IJCAI-99*, pages 1268–1273, 1999.
15. S. Zilberstein and A.-I. Mouaddib. Optimizing resource utilization in planetary rovers. In *2nd NASA Workshop on Planning and Scheduling for Space*, 2000.

Cognition, Sociability, and Constraints

Gerhard Weiß

Institut für Informatik, Technische Universität München
80290 München, Germany.
weissg@in.tum.de

Abstract. This paper focuses on the challenge of building technical agents that act flexibly in modern computing and information environments. It is argued that existing agent architectures tend to inherently limit an agent's flexibility because they imply a discrete cognitive and social behavior space. A novel, generic constraint-centered architectural framework (CCAF) is proposed that aims at enabling agents to act in a continuous behavior space. Though some aspects of this framework are still tentative in flavor, it offers two remarkable characteristics. First, it approaches flexibility in terms of cognition (ranging from reactive to proactive) *and* sociability (ranging from isolated to interactive). Second, it treats flexibility as an *emergent* property (more specifically, as a property that emerges as a result of an agent's continuous attempt to handle local and global constraints). A key implication of the considerations in this article is the need for integrating various existing constraint-handling approaches into a coherent whole in order to obtain really flexible agents.

1 Introduction

Modern computing platforms and information environments are becoming more and more distributed, large, open, dynamic, and heterogeneous. Computers are no longer stand-alone systems, but have become tightly connected both with each other and their users. The increasing technological complexity of such platforms and environments goes together with an increasing complexity of their potential applications. This development has led to a rapidly growing research and application interest in agents as a powerful concept and guideline for designing, implementing, and analyzing complex information processing systems in which decentralized data are processed in an asynchronous but concerted way by several computers that act more as "individuals" rather than just "parts." There is no universally accepted definition of the term agent (see e.g. [18,64] for more detailed considerations on this term), but generally it is used to refer to a *computational autonomous entity*, that is, an entity that runs on a computing device and decides upon the activities he takes in order to meet his design objectives independent of humans and other agents. Building agents that deserve to be called flexible is one of the major driving forces in the field of agent-based computing, where flexibility is usually assumed to be composed of the following three basic ingredients [32]:[1]

---

[1] Flexibility, understood in that way, is often equated with intelligence.

M. Hannebauer et al. (Eds.): Reactivity and Deliberation in MAS, LNAI 2103, pp. 217–235, 2001.

- *reactivity*: the ability to respond in a timely fashion to environmental changes;
- *pro-activeness*: the ability to generate and rationally pursue goals; and
- *sociability*: the ability to interact with other agents and possibly humans by exchanging information, coordinating activities, and so forth.

In view of the requirements and challenges that arise in the context of modern computing systems and their applications, it is obvious that flexibility is a key property that agents need to possess in order to operate successfully. The realization of computational flexibility thus constitutes a grand challenge in the field of agents and multiagent systems. This article takes a closer look on how to build flexible agents. It starts from the observation that existing, standard agent architectures result in inherently restricted flexibility because they induce discrete behavior spaces. A generic constraint-centered architectural framework (CCAF) is proposed that aims at avoiding this serious restriction. This framework is significantly different from conventional architectures in two key respects:

- it relates flexibility to cognition *and* sociability, rather than to just cognition or just sociability; and
- it treats flexibility as an *emergent* property, and not as a property that can be directly implemented.

With that, this framework captures and reflects an alternative way of thinking about computational flexibility and flexible agent construction. It is obvious that an experimental and/or theoretical validation of the correctness and completeness of such a generic framework is a long-term scientific endavor. What is therefore necessarily required in a first basic and feasible step is to provide a broad range of qualitative arguments and considerations that together make this framework plausible and conclusive. This is what this article seeks to do. To avoid expectations that can not be fulfilled at this stage of research it is explicitly pointed out that some of the arguments and considerations presented here are clearly tentative in flavor.

The article is structured as follows. Section 2 characterizes existing standard architectures from the point of view of computational flexibility. Section 3 introduces an alternative, constraint-centered view of achieving flexibility. Section 4 presents the CCAF which integrates the main thoughts and ideas of this alternative view. Finally, Sect. 5 discusses this alternative view and overviews its implications on future research.

2   Existing Agent Architectures

A wide variety of architectures – particular methodologies (including arrangements of data, algorithms, and control and data flows) for building agents – have been described in the literature; see, e.g., [25,40,63] for overviews. Reviewing all of them is beyond the scope of this article. Instead, some standard representatives are described in the following that indicate the broad structural and functional

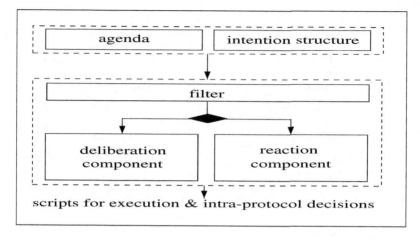

Fig. 1. The "reasoning, deciding, and reacting component" of COSY

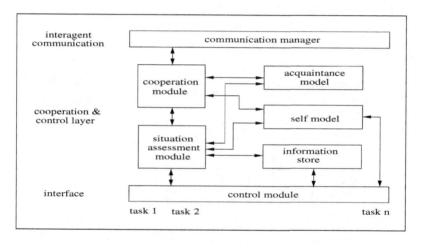

Fig. 2. GRATE*

range of existing architectures: COSY [8], GRATE* [31], INTERRAP [17], and TouringMachines [15]. Figures 1, 2, 3, and 4 illustrate these architectures. Existing architectures are typically built of logically separate parts (usually called modules, components, or layers), each responsible for generating one of the three abilities – reactivity, pro-activeness, and inter-activeness – that are considered as essential to flexibility. While COSY (via the reaction and deliberation components) and TouringMachines (via the reactive and planning layers) are examples of architectures that primarily aim at capturing the notion of agents that are able to behave reactively *as well as* pro-actively, GRATE* focuses on agents that are able to act in an isolated *as well as* an interactive manner (where several of the components shown in Fig. 2 are involved in both types of actions).

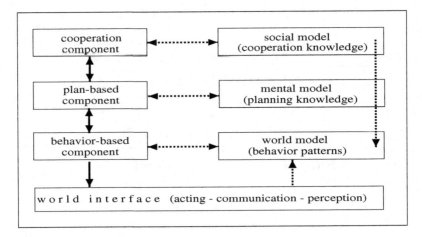

Fig. 3. INTERRAP

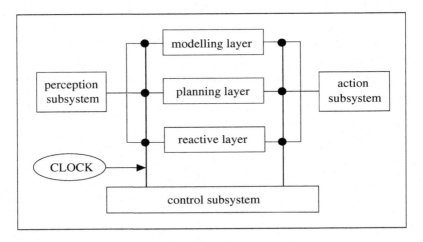

Fig. 4. TouringMachines

INTERRAP is intended to capture all three "flexibility patterns" via its three components and their associated information bases. The modules either run in a parallel (e.g., TouringMachines) or a mutually exclusive way (e.g., COSY, IN-TERRAP). The decision on which module "dominates" the others in a given context (i.e., determines the external actions to be carried out) is realized either in a centralized or a decentralized way. For instance, in COSY a specific "filter" decides between behaving reactively and behaving pro-actively; in GRATE* the situation assessment module decides which action should be performed locally and which action should be delegated; and in INTERRAP the different components sequentially (from bottom to top) analyze a situation until one of them decides to be competent to deal with it.

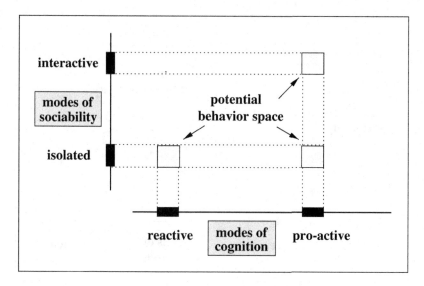

Fig. 5. The discrete behavior space metaphor

As these considerations indicate, a major characteristic of many existing architectures is that they are implicitly based on the assumption that reactivity, pro-activeness and inter-activeness are "pure," disjoint behavioral modes: there is nothing in between them, and every goal or task (or every context in which a goal or task is pursued) allows to uniquely and correctly determine at every time which of the "pure modes" is appropriate. This assumption is very critical and inherently restricts an agent's flexibility, because the "pure modes" define a discrete behavior space composed of just a few, disconnected behavioral "isles" or repertoires. (Throughout this article the term repertoire is used to refer to some part of a behavioral space.) Figure 5, which is based on the standard view of reactivity and pro-activeness as cognitive characterizations and of interactivity (as opposed to isolatedness) as a social characterization of an agent's behavior, illustrates this drawback.[2] (This figure, as well Fig. 6 below, is not intended to show all aspects that may be of relevance w.r.t. an agent's behavior; instead, these figures are just intended to highlight the key aspects – sociability and cognition – considered in this article.) Obviously, the repertoires allow only a very limited form of "graceful degradation" in an agent's behavior. Most importantly, "discrete behavior space architectures" require a mapping of *all* potential environmental situations and activity contexts to a few discrete repertoires at design time. This simply is not possible in most real-world applications. Moreover, they require the identification of the criteria for switching between the pure modes,

---

[2] This figure takes care of the fact that many existing architectures do not capture what could be called "reactive interactivity" or "interactive reactivity"; instead, reactivity is usually associated with isolated behavior.

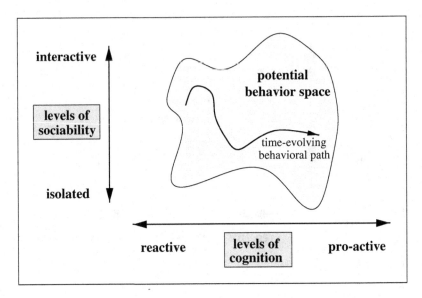

Fig. 6. The continuous behavior space metaphor

which is to say that they require to foresee all conditions and circumstances under which an agent will have to act reactively, pro-actively, and interactively in order to fulfill his mission. Again this is not possible in more complex applications.

3   Flexibility Reconsidered

In order to avoid the flexibility restrictions implied by existing architectures, an extended and more natural view of an agent's behavior space is required. An obvious alternative would be to not assume the existence of just two social and two cognitive discrete modes, but to have continuous levels of sociability and cognition. According to this view, an agent is not flexible in that he switches between a few behavioral repertoires, but is flexible at various levels: sociability now varies from isolated to interactive, and cognition now varies from reactive to pro-active as a continuum. Figure 6 illustrates this view. From an external observer's point of view, the different levels may be distinguished in terms of the number of exchanged messages, the number of agents involved in the solution process or its subprocesses, the number of negotiation iterations, the number of steps taken for plan generation, and so forth. In the following it is argued that this alternative can be realized under certain conditions through constraint handling.

From what has been said above it follows that some sort of behavior-influencing mechanism is needed that enables an agent to act in a continuous behavior space on multiple levels of sociability and cognition. An intuitively obvious and appealing candidate for such a mechanism is constraint handling. It is an *obvious* candidate because agents can be considered, in a very natural way, as entities that are surrounded by and must cope with various constraints that do have, or should have, a significant impact on both their social and cognitive behavior. The most common examples of constraints are time bounds, cost bounds, and requirements on the desired solution quality. These three constraints are present in one or another form in most, if not all, application domains. Other examples of constraints that are available at the agent and group levels are an agent's individual preferences, collective preferences of groups, psychological or social commitments, limitations on resources an agent or a group wants to use, roles an agent is expected to play in joint processes, norms an agent has to take into consideration, conventions that apply in an agent's application domain, and so forth. It is an *appealing* candidate because if offers a new perspective of isolated activity, interactivity, reactivity, and pro-activeness as observable properties that *emerge* as a result of an agent's continuous attempt to handle local and global constraints while he tries to meet his design perspective. Constraint handling inherently offers the possibility, or even requires, to act at different levels of sociability and cognition, and an agent can be said to be cognitively and socially flexible to the degree he can handle – identify and (fully or partially) satisfy – the constraints he is confronted with. This is in clear contrast to the standard, discrete behavior space perspective that aims at achieving flexibility through directly implementing pure behavioral modes and appropriately switching between them. Of course, just saying that constraint handling is an obvious and appealing mechanism for achieving continuous behavior is not sufficient. What has to be done is to identify *specific conditions* under which continuous flexibility can be achieved through constraint handling.

3.1 Condition 1 – Intertwining of Constraints and Activities

Most obviously, constraints on the one hand and an agent's internal activities (ranging from environmental analysis over planning and learning to communication) on the other must be tightly intertwined:

– an agent should be able to dynamically modify and refine the set of constraints as he runs any of his internal activities such that ideally each internal activity can result in a modified constraint set (*constraint identification and acquisition*); and
– an agent should be able to execute each of his internal activities under the given constraints such that ideally none of his activities violates constraints (*constraint satisfaction*).

Here are some basic illustrations of the kind of flexible behavior that becomes possible through the fulfillment of this intertwining condition:

- An agent carrying out a time-critical mission takes care of the time spent for each of his activities. Whenever he identifies several possible solution paths (and no other constraints are available), then he chooses the one requiring minimal overall time. This identification and choice is also done under the available time constraints.
- An agent analyzing his current sensor input finds out that the resources he would need for successfully pursuing some of his goals are limited and that access to these resources needs to be coordinated with other agents. The limitation constraint has a significant impact on his goal ranking, and the coordination constraint requires him to initiate negotiation and contracting activities.
- As a side effect of negotiation and contracting activities, an agent is being confronted with new constraints in form of commitments, roles, and responsibilities. In response to this, the agent checks whether his planned future activities are compatible with these new constraints; a consequence of this compatibility check may be the initiation of local or joint plan revision activities.

These illustrations also show that an agent has to be able to cope with the fact that constraints can dynamically raise or disappear as a result of his own activities. Obviously, realizing this intertwining is particularly difficult in domains in which constraints change dynamically due to the activities of other agents or humans. Related work dealing with dynamic constraint satisfaction is, e.g., [4, 11,56].

3.2   Condition 2 – Constraint-Induced Cooperation

An agent must be able to carry out each activity he considers as relevant for a solution process in cooperation with other agents, whenever the constraints he faces require this. (Here coordination means that an agent carries out an activity together with others or that an activity is completely delegated to one or several other agents. Note that available architectures typically restrict coordination to script generation/planning, whereas e.g. situation analysis and failure analysis are often treated as a local activities that are not distributed.[3]) The following examples illustrate what it means to have this condition fulfilled:

- If an agent is unable to provide a detailed, qualitatively sufficient analysis of the current environmental situation, then he asks other agents for support.
- An agent considers the possibility to share some time-critical control task with one or several other agents, if control appear to be too time-consuming for him. After having communicated with other agents (where this communication itself is subject to the time constraint), the agent comes to the conclusion that distribution of control would result in a faster solution and thus tries to establish "control contracts." The set of agents he considers as

---

[3] Of course, there are exceptions; e.g., see [9].

potential cooperators may be constrained by commitments in which he is already involved, and time pressure also guides him in his choice of the method he uses for selecting cooperators (e.g., iterated negotiation or voting).

- If an agent is required to provide a low-cost solution but communication with other agents is expensive due to limited available bandwidth, then he will avoid negotiation activities even if this results in a solution of low(er) quality.

As these examples show, taking the constraint-centered view serious means that communicative and coordinative acts among agents have to be designed, to a large extent, in a strictly constraint-triggered way. This also means that the contents of communicative acts are determined by constraints to a remarkable degree. Taking an extreme position, it can be even argued that constraints (and nothing else) constitute the "necessary and sufficient conditions" for communicative and coordinative acts – the agents communicate and coordinate *if and only if* this is required by the constraints they have to fulfill.

It is important to see that this condition does also concern an agent's constraint handling process itself: constraints can require an agent to identify and satisfy constraints in cooperation with others. This can be the case, for instance, if constraint identification requires to search through databases which the agent simply is not allowed to access or if constraint satisfaction is too complex to be solvable by the agent without violating available time/cost constraints. Available work that is relevant w.r.t. the distribution of the constraint handling process is, e.g., [27,54,55,65,66].

3.3   Condition 3 – Meta-Reasoning

Agents must be able to reason about their constraints, and to involve other agents into this reasoning process whenever necessary. Following the argumentation in [35] (see also [12] for earlier considerations on this subject), this kind of reasoning must be quantitative in nature, because qualitative, purely symbolic reasoning about constraints like time and costs can be extremely complex especially in large-scale agent and multiagent contexts. More specifically, this means that achieving continuous flexibility through constraint handling requires an agent to be able

- to assign quantitative values to the constraints that express their relative importance they have for him;
- to assign quantitative values to the constraints that express the degrees to which he is willing to violate them;
- to assign quantitative values to the constraints that express the estimated risk of violating them (given the current environmental circumstances and the activity sequence he intends to execute); and
- to communicate (exchange, negotiate, refine, etc.) these quantities with other agents and humans.

This ability constitutes a profound basis for applying efficient mechanisms for (joint) constraint relaxation and propagation. In particular, based on these quantities an agent or a group of agents can efficiently evaluate the worth of alternative activities or activity sequences under the given constraints, supervise (joint) solution processes, and gracefully redirect solution processes in the case of constraint violation. Here are some simple illustrations of flexible behavior induced by this meta-reasoning constraint:

- An agent quantitatively expresses the degree to which he prefers a qualitatively high to a cheap solution in the case of his goal A, and how he weights the costs compared to the processing time in the case of his goal B.
- An agent quantitatively describes to what extent he is willing to relax role and normative constraints under the condition that this relaxation helps to cope with resource constraints.
- An agent decides to follow a cheaper "computation-sensitive" solution path rather than a more expensive "communication-sensitive" path. If it turns out during the solution process that the quality of the solution tends to be lower than he expected, then he reconsiders his choice and decide in a quantifiable way how to proceed from that point of the solution process such that the violation of the quality constraint is kept as minimal as possible.
- An agent asks other agents for analyzing the current situation and informs them about his "constraint preferences." The other agents make offers and quantitatively specify to what degree they could fulfill the constraints.

Related work dealing with the quantification of constraints in the context of scheduling is presented in [22,21] (design-to-time scheduling) and [57,59,58,61] (design-to-criteria scheduling). Related research on the quantification of motivations, which can be also viewed as constraints an agent has to satisfy, is reported in [60].

3.4   Condition 4 – Centralized Realization

An agent must be able to efficiently handle constraints as he carries out his activities. This requires that an agent's reasoning about constraints (including key activities like constraint identification, relaxation, and quantification) is realized in a centralized way. In principle, it would be possible to treat a single agent's constraint reasoning as a distributed, internal process. In this case, different internal activities (e.g., negotiation and exception handling) would independently of each other take care of available constraints. However, because in general *(i)* constraints are highly dynamic (they appear and disappear continuously as a result of an agent's own and other agents' activities), *(ii)* different internal activities are concerned by the same constraints, and *(iii)* constraint handling itself should not violate available constraints, it is most likely that a distributed internal constraint handling process is inefficient and results in a poor performance both at the agent and the group level. (Note that several agents may work together to handle constraints; the point made here is that the constraint handling activities occuring *within* an individual agent are likely to be most efficiently realized in a centralized manner.)

It is noted that the above mentioned conditions are not disjoint, but related to each other. It is also stressed that this list of conditions is not claimed to be complete; instead, it is argued that these conditions are most elementary for achieving sophisticated flexibility through constraint handling.

4   An Architectural Framework Based on Constraints

Figure 7 shows a generic architectural agent framework, called Constraint-Centered Architectural Framework (CCAF), that aims at capturing the constraint-centered view of flexibility and its conditions. According to this generic framework, an agent is composed of several kernel management modules (coordination, adaptation, script, execution, and constraints), where each module consists of several elementary activities or processes that are carried out by an agent in order to meet his design objectives. The activities within the management modules use and modify different data or information sets, as indicated by the data flow arrows. The figure also shows the basic flow of control between the internal activities, where a control link from a box A to a box B means that B (or its components) can be invoked or activated by A (or its components). The CCAF includes several standard data links. For instance, as indicated by the corresponding data flow arrows, the communication and interaction protocols mainly concern the coordination management, and the performance data are of particular relevance to the adaptation and execution management modules. Similarly, the CCAF includes several standard control links. For instance, the control link from the script management module to the execution management module indicates that script activities are usually followed by execution activities, and the control link from the execution management module to the adaptation module indicates that an agent usually tries – on the basis of the monitored performance data – to improve his overall performance through failure analysis and learning. In addition to that, the CCAF integrates the "constraint-specific conditions" mentioned in the previous section. Condition 4 ("centralized realization of an agent's constraint handling activities") requires the separate constraint management module in which all basic constraint handling activities run in a centralized manner. Condition 3 ("quantitative reasoning about constraints") requires the reasoning and quantification processes located within the constraint management module. Condition 1 ("tight intertwining between internal activities and constraints") results in the bidirectional data flow links between the set of constraints and each of the management modules. Condition 2 ("constraint-induced cooperation") implies the control links from all other modules to the coordination management module. Finally, Conditions 1 and 2 additionally require that there are control links from the constraint management module to all other management modules.

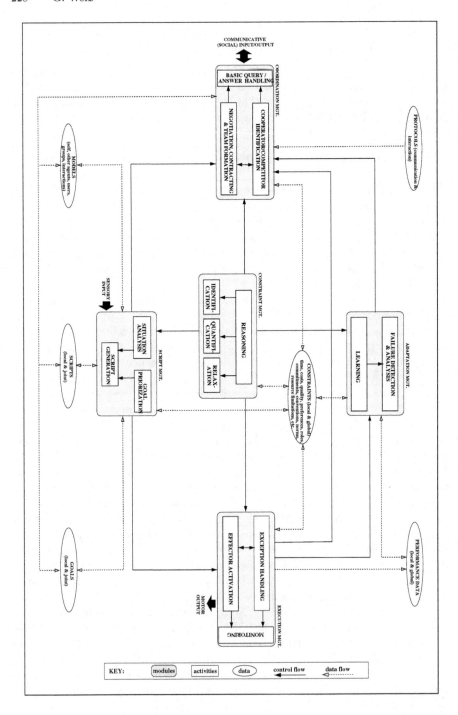

Fig. 7. The Constraint-Centered Architectural Framework (CCAF)

5 Discussion

5.1 Summary

The concept of agents has the capacity to play an important role in understanding, managing and using distributed, large-scale, dynamic, open, and heterogeneous computing and information environments. Flexibility, that is, the ability to act reactively, pro-actively, and socially, is a desirable key property of agents. This article attempts to contribute to our understanding of what it means to build "really flexible agents" and to lay the foundation for an alternative approach to build agents that behave flexibly in complex domains. It was argued here that flexibility achieved through many existing agent architectures is inherently limited, because they tend to generate a discrete behavior space that consists of just a few behavioral repertoires. A generic architectural framework called CCAF was introduced that aims at avoiding this limitation. The basic idea underlying the CCAF is that *flexible behavior emerges along two continuous axis – cognition and sociability – as a result of an agent's attempt to handle constraints*. "Emergence rather than direct implementation" and "integration of cognition and sociability" are the two characteristics that make the CCAF unique. In particular, it is argued that these two characteristics make continuous behavior spaces possible. Four key conditions were identified that are considered to be essential for achieving continuous flexibility through constraint handling. Under these conditions the constraints inherently determine an agent's behavioral path by both preventing and enforcing activities that an agent carries out in order to achieve his goals. The CCAF thus brings two contrary perspectives of constraints together: constraints as "a bad thing" an agent has to cope with, and constraints as "a good thing" that supports an agent in navigating through the space of possible cognitive and social behaviors. It is pointed out again that some of the aspects of the proposed framework are tentative in flavor and leave room for further improvement and refinement.

5.2 Related Work

Constraint handling is a well known topic in artificial intelligence in general (e.g., see [37] and the constraints archive at http://www.cs.unh.edu/ccc/archive/) and in the field of agent-based systems in particular (e.g., [19]). Various pointers to related work have been already provided above and several others follow below. Two agent architectures that should be mentioned here because of their interesting relationships to CCAF are EXCALIBUR (e.g., [42]) and WAFFLER (e.g., [1]). Both EXCALIBUR and WAFFLER focus on agents acting in real-time scenarios and both aim at exploiting constraint-oriented reasoning as a method for balancing reactivity and pro-activeness. For that reason both architectures can be viewed as instantiations of the CCAF. Compared to EXCALIBUR and WAFFLER the CCAF is much broader in its scope and vision of the potential role of constraints and constraint handling for agents. In particular, CCAF does not only deal with the cognitive dimension ("reactivity versus pro-activeness") but also with the social dimension ("isolatedness versus interactivity") of flexibility from a unified constraint-centered perspective.

5.3 Open Issues

The constraint-oriented view of building flexible agents brings up several research issues, where the following appear to be particularly challenging:

- An agent's or a group's quantitative reasoning about constraints must be bounded, that is, like all other activities this reasoning has to be conducted under the available constraints. In principle, this would require something like a "meta-reasoning process" whose purpose is to make sure that the process of reasoning about constraints itself does not violate any constraints. Thus, the need for "reasoning about constraints" would imply the need for "reasoning about reasoning about constraints." This in turn would imply, for the very same reason, the need for "reasoning about reasoning about reasoning about constraints," and so forth – resulting in an infinite and computationally intractable loop of meta-reasoning processes. Even a restriction of this loop to some predefined depth does not work in general, because for any depth it is possible to specify time and cost constraints that can not be fulfilled. Currently it is unknown how the problem of "constraint violation through constraint handling" can be solved efficiently. More generally, this requires to clarify how the CCAF and its "quantitative meta-reasoning about constraints" conception is related to the concepts of metalevel rationality (e.g., [45,46,47]) and social rationality [28] and to utilitarian – decision-theoretic – meta-reasoning (e.g., [7,29]).
- There is a need for a "global constraint metrics" that allows agents to unambiguously reason and communicate about their constraints and how to handle them. Such a metrics must be unique and known to all cooperating agents within a task domain, but may vary for different domains.
- As coordination and communication themselves are subject to the constraints, it has to be clarified whether this raises specific requirements on the coordination/communication languages and protocols used by the agents.
- It is broadly accepted that autonomy is a key feature of agents, but it is unclear how this feature on the one hand and constraints on the other are related to each other. Intuitively, it appears that constraints require, or inherently imply, variability and adjustability in an agent's autonomy ("constraints constrain autonomy"). Details of this requirement – its formalization and practical realization – still need to be clarified. Work that may be of help in this respect can be found in [41].
- The algorithms that realize an agent's internal activities need to be highly constraint-sensitive, that is, they should be designed such that an agent can act in accordance with available constraints and in response to changes in his constraint set at each point of the overall problem solving process in which he is engaged. In view of the three most common constraints – time, costs, and quality –, this means that there is a strong need for "any-time, any-cost,

and any-quality algorithms." Related works that are of particular interest in this respect are the following: reactive and anytime planning (e.g., [5,6,13,14, 16,23,24,43] and also [33,38]), real-time search (e.g.,[26,30,34]); constraint-based negotiation (e.g., [44,50,53]); negotiation/interaction-based constraint satisfaction (e.g., [10,36]); anytime constraint satisfaction (e.g., [39,62,67]); "soft contracting" that allows agents to break contracts and thus to act more flexibly e.g. in response to unexpected changes in their constraints (e.g., [2, 51,52,49]); coalition/team formation under time and cost constraints (e.g, [48]); deadline-based multiagent scheduling [20]; and real-time learning (e.g., [3]).

Each of these items constitutes a specific line of future research. The CCAF should be viewed as a starting point for further discussion and research on computational flexibility, and as a plea for combining and integrating the various related approaches mentioned throughout this article into a unified, monolithic and coherent whole. It is a long-term challenge to fully identify the benefits and limitations of the CCAF through practical and theoretical analysis.

Acknowledgments. Many of the ideas described above were stimulated by the various research efforts referred to in this article. Victor Lesser draws my attention to the important role of an agent's ability to meta-reasoning about constraints. Thanks also to the reviewers for their valuable comments on an earlier draft.

References

1. J. Anderson. Waffler: A constraint-directed approach to intelligent agent design. In E.C. Freuder, editor, *Constraints & Agents. Papers from the AAAI Workshop (Technical Report WS-97-05)*, pages 70–75. AAAI Press, Menlo Park, CA, 1997.
2. M.R. Andersson and T.W. Sandholm. Leveled commitment contracts with myopic and strategic agents. In *Proceedings of the 15th National Conference on Artificial Intelligence (AAAI-98)*, pages 38–45, 1998.
3. A.G. Barto, S.J. Bradtke, and S.P. Singh. Learning to act using real-time dynamic programming. *Artificial Intelligence*, 72:81–138, 1995.
4. C. Bessier. Arc-consistency in a dynamic constraint satisfaction problem. In *Proceedings of the Ninth National Conference on Artificial Intelligence (AAAI-91)*, pages 221–226, 1991.
5. M. Boddy and T.L. Dean. An analysis of time-dependent planning. In *Proceedings of the 7th National Conference on Artificial Intelligence (AAAI-88)*, pages 49–54, 1988.
6. M. Boddy and T.L. Dean. Deliberation scheduling for problem solving in time-constrained environments. *Artificial Intelligence*, 67:245–285, 1994.
7. J.S. Breese and M.R. Fehling. Control of problem-solving: Principles and architecture. In R.D. Shachter, T. Levitt, L. Kanal, and J. Lemmer, editors, *Uncertainty in Artificial Intelligence 4*. Elsevier/North-Holland, Amsterdam, London, New York, 1990.

232   G. Weiß

8. B. Burmeister and K. Sundermeyer. Cooperative problem-solving guided by intentions and perception. In E. Werner and Y. Demazeau, editors, *Decentralized A.I. 3*, pages 77–92. North-Holland/Elsevier, Amsterdam et al., 1992.
9. N. Carver and V.R. Lesser. The DRESUN testbed for research in FA/C distributed situation assessment: Extensions to the model of external evidence. In *Proceedings of the First International Conference on Multi-Agent Systems (ICMAS-95)*, pages 33–40, 1995.
10. S.E. Conry, K. Kuwabara, V.R. Lesser, and R.A. Meyer. Multistage negotiation for distributed constraint satisfaction. *IEEE Transactions on Systems, Man, and Cybernetics*, 21(6):1462–1477, 1991.
11. R. Dechter and A. Dechter. Belief maintenance in dynamic constraint networks. In *Proceedings of the Seventh National Conference on Artificial Intelligence (AAAI-88)*, pages 37–42, 1988.
12. K.S. Decker and V.R. Lesser. Quantitative modeling of complex environments. *International Journal of Intelligent Systems in Accounting, Finance, and Management*, 2(4):215–234, 1993.
13. V. Decugis and J. Ferber. Action selection in an autonomous agent with a hierarchical distributed reactive planning architecture. In *Proceedings of the Second International Conference on Autonomous Agents (Agents'98)*, pages 354–361, 1998.
14. M. Drummond and J. Bresina. Anytime synthetic projection: Maximizing the probability of goal satisfaction. In *Proceedings of the Eight National Conference on Artificial Intelligence (AAAI-90)*, pages 138–144, 1990.
15. I.A. Ferguson. Integrated control and coordinated behavior: a case for agent models. In M.J. Wooldridge and N.R. Jennings, editors, *Intelligent Agents*, Lecture Notes in Artificial Intelligence, Vol. 890, pages 203–218. Springer-Verlag, Berlin et al., 1995.
16. R.J. Firby. Modularity issues in reactive planning. In *Proceedings of the Third International Conference on AI Planning Systems*, pages 78–85, 1996.
17. K. Fischer, J.P. Müller, and M. Pischel. A pragmatic BDI architecture. In M.J. Wooldridge, J.P. Müller, and M. Tambe, editors, *Intelligent Agents II*, Lecture Notes in Artificial Intelligence, Vol. 1037, pages 203–218. Springer-Verlag, Berlin et al., 1996.
18. S. Franklin and A. Graesser. Is it an agent, or just a program?: A taxonomy for autonomous agents. In J.P. Müller, M.J. Wooldridge, and N.R. Jennings, editors, *Intelligent Agents III*, Lecture Notes in Artificial in Artificial Intelligence, Vol. 1193, pages 21–36. Springer-Verlag, Berlin et al., 1997.
19. E.C. Freuder (Chair). Constraints & agents. Papers from the AAAI workshop. Technical Report WS-97-05, AAAI Press, Menlo Park, CA, 1997.
20. S. Fujita and V.R. Lesser. Centralized task distribution in the presence of uncertainty and time deadlines. In *Proceedings of the Second International Conference on Multi-Agent Systems (ICMAS-96)*, pages 87–94, 1996.
21. A. Garvey, K. Decker, and V.R. Lesser. A negotiation-based interface between a real-time scheduler and a decision-maker. In M. Klein and S. Lander, editors, *Models of Conflict Management in Cooperative Problem Solving. Papers of the AAAI Workshop (Technical Report WS-94-04)*. AAAI Press, Menlo Park, CA, 1994.
22. A. Garvey and V.R. Lesser. Design-to-time real-time scheduling. *IEEE Transactions on Systems, Man, and Cybernetics*, 23(6):1491–1502, 1993.
23. E. Gat. Integrating planning and reacting in a heterogeneous asynchronous architecture for controlling real-world mobile robots. In *Proceedings of the Tenth National Conference on Artificial Intelligence (AAAI-92)*, pages 802–815, 1992.

24. M.P. Georgeff and A.L. Lansky. Reactive reasoning and planning. In *Proceedings of the 6th National Conference on Artificial Intelligence (AAAI-87)*, pages 677–682, 1987.
25. A. Haddadi and K. Sundermeyer. Belief-Desire-Intention architectures. In G.M.P. O'Hare and N.R. Jennings, editors, *Foundations of Distributed Artificial Intelligence*, pages 169–186. Wiley, New York et al., 1996.
26. B. Hamidzadeh and S. Shekhar. Deadline compliance, predictability, and on-line optimization in real-time problem solving. In *Proceedings of the 14th International Joint Conference on Artificial Intelligence (IJCAI-95)*, pages 220–226, 1995.
27. S. Haridi, P. Van Roy, and G. Smolka. An overview of the design of Distributed Oz. In *Proceedings of the Second International Symposium on Parallel Symbolic Computation (PASCO'97)*, pages 176–187, 1997.
28. L.M. Hogg and N.R. Jennings. Socially rational agents. In *Proceedings of the AAAI Fall Symposium on Socially Intelligent Agents*, pages 61–63, 1997.
29. E.J. Horvitz. Problem-solving design: reasoning about computational value, trade-offs, and resources. In *Proceedings of the Second Annual NASA Research Forum*, pages 26–43, 1987.
30. T. Ishida. Real-time search for autonomous agents and multiagent systems. *Autonomous Agents and Multi-Agent Systems*, 1:139–167, 1998.
31. N.R. Jennings. Specification and implementation of a belief-desire-joint-intention architecture for collaborative problem solving. *Journal of Intelligent and Cooperative Information Systems*, 2(3):289–318, 1993.
32. N.R. Jennings, K. Sycara, and M.J. Wooldridge. A roadmap of agent research and development. *Autonomous Agents and Multi-Agent Systems*, 1:7–38, 1998.
33. K. Kanazawa and T. Dean. A model for projection and action. In *Proceedings of the 11th International Joint Conference on Artificial Intelligence*, pages 985–990, 1989.
34. R.E. Korf. Real-time heuristic search. *Artificial Intelligence*, 42(2-3):189–211, 1990.
35. V.R. Lesser. Reflections on the nature of multi-agent coordination and its implications for an agent architecture. *Autonomous Agents and Multi-Agent Systems*, 1:89–111, 1998.
36. J. Liu and K.P. Sycara. Exploiting problem structure for distributed constraint optimization. In *Proceedings of the First International Conference on Multi-Agent Systems (ICMAS-95)*, pages 246–253, 1995.
37. A.K. Mackworth. Constraint satisfaction. In S.C. Shapiro, editor, *Encyclopedia of Artificial Intelligence*, pages 285–293. Wiley, New York, 1992.
38. P. Maes. Situated agents can have goals. *Robotics and Autonomous Systems*, 6:49–70, 1990.
39. P. Morris. The breakout method for escaping from local minima. In *Proceedings of the Eleventh National Conference on Artificial Intelligence (AAAI-93)*, pages 40–45, 1993.
40. J.P. Müller. The right agent (architecture) to do the right thing. In J.P. Müller, M.P. Singh, and A.S. Rao, editors, *Intelligent Agents V*, Lecture Notes in Artificial in Artificial Intelligence, Vol. 1555, pages 211–226. Springer-Verlag, Berlin et al., 1999.
41. D. Musliner and B. Pell (Cochairs). Agents with adjustable autonomy. Papers from the AAAI spring symposium. Technical Report SS-99-06, AAAI Press, Menlo Park, CA, 1999.
42. A. Narayek. Constraint-based agents. In E.C. Freuder, editor, *Constraints & Agents. Papers from the AAAI Workshop (Technical Report WS-97-05)*, pages 45–50. AAAI Press, Menlo Park, CA, 1997.

43. A. Narayek. A planning model for agents in dynamic and uncertain real-time environments. In *Proceedings of the AIPS Workshop on Integrating Planning, Scheduling and Execution in Dynamic and Uncertain Environments*, pages 7–14, 1998.

44. A. Roth, J. Murnighan, and F. Schoumaker. The deadline effect in bargaining: Some experimental evidence. *American Economic Review*, 78:806–823, 1988.

45. S.J. Russell. Rationality and intelligence. In *Proceedings of the 14th International Joint Conference on Artificial Intelligence (IJCAI-95)*, 1995.

46. S.J. Russell and E.H. Wefald. *Do the right thing: Studies in limited rationality.* The MIT Press, Cambridge, Mass., 1991.

47. S.J. Russell and E.H. Wefald. Principles of rationality. *Artificial Intelligence*, 49(1-3):361–395, 1991.

48. T. Sandholm, K. Larson, M. Andersson, O. Shehory, and F. Tohmé. Anytime coalition structure generation with worst case guarantees. In *Proceedings of the 15th National Conference on Artificial Intelligence (AAAI-98)*, pages 46–53, 1998.

49. T. Sandholm, S. Sikka, and S. Norden. Algorithms for optimizing leveled commitment contracts. In *Proceedings of 16th International Joint Conference on Artificial Intelligence (IJCAI-99)*, 1999.

50. T. Sandholm and N. Vulkan. Bargaining with deadlines. In *Proceedings of 16th National Conference on Artificial Intelligence (AAAI-99)*, 1999.

51. T.W. Sandholm and V.R. Lesser. Issues in automated negotiation and electronic commerce: Extending the contract net framework. In *Proceedings of the First International Conference on Multi-Agent Systems (ICMAS-95)*, pages 328–335, 1995.

52. T.W. Sandholm and V.R. Lesser. Advantages of a leveled commitment contracting protocol. In *Proceedings of the 13th National Conference on Artificial Intelligence (AAAI-96)*, pages 126–133, 1996.

53. A. Sathi and M.S. Fox. Constraint-directed negotiation of resource reallocations. In M.N. Huhns and L. Gasser, editors, *Distributed Artificial Intelligence, Volume 2*, pages 163–193. Pitman/Morgan Kaufmann, Cambridge, MA, 1989.

54. G. Solotorevsky, E. Gudes, and A. Meisels. Modeling and solving distributed constraint satisfaction problems. In *Proceedings of the 2nd International Conference on Principles and Practice of Constraint Programming (CP-96)*, pages 561–562, 1996.

55. K. Sycara, S. Roth, N. Sadeh, and M. Fox. Distributed constrained heuristic search. *IEEE Transactions on Systems, Man, and Cybernetics*, 26(1):1446–1461, 1991.

56. G. Verfaillie and T. Schiex. Solution reuse in dynamic constraint satisfaction problems. In *Proceedings of the Twelfth National Conference on Artificial Intelligence (AAAI-94)*, pages 307–312, 1994.

57. T. Wagner, A. Garvey, and V.R. Lesser. Satisficing evaluation functions: The heart of the new design-to-criteria paradigm. Technical Report 1996-82, Computer Science Department, University of Massachussetts at Amherst, 1996.

58. T. Wagner, A. Garvey, and V.R. Lesser. Complex goal criteria and its application in design-to-criteria scheduling. In *Proceedings of the 1997 National Conference on Artificial Intelligence (AAAI-97)*, pages 294–301, 1997.

59. T. Wagner, A. Garvey, and V.R. Lesser. Criteria-directed task scheduling. Technical Report 1997-59, Computer Science Department, University of Massachussetts at Amherst, 1997.

60. T. Wagner and V.R. Lesser. Relating quantified motivations for organizationally situated agents. In *Proceedings of the 6th International Workshop on Agent Theories, Architectures, and Languages (ATAL-99)*, 1999.

61. T. Wagner, A. Raja, and V.R. Lesser. Modeling uncertainty and its implication on design-to-criteria scheduling. Technical Report 1999-51, Computer Science Department, University of Massachussetts at Amherst, 1999.
62. R.J. Wallace and E.C. Freuder. Anytime algorithms for constraint satisfaction and SAT problems. *SIGART Bulletin*, 7(2), 1996.
63. M.J. Wooldridge. Intelligent agents. In G. Weiss, editor, *Multiagent Systems*, pages 27–77. The MIT Press, Cambridge et al., 1999.
64. M.J. Wooldridge and N.R. Jennings. Agent theories, architectures, and languages: A survey. In M.J. Wooldridge and N.R. Jennings, editors, *Intelligent Agents*, Lecture Notes in Artificial in Artificial Intelligence, Vol. 890, pages 1–39. Springer-Verlag, Berlin et al., 1995.
65. M. Yokoo. Asynchronous weak-commitment search for solving distributed constraint satisfaction problems. In *Proceedings of the First International Conference on Principles and Practice of Constraint Programming (CP-95)*, pages 88–102, 1995.
66. M. Yokoo, E. Durfee, T. Ishida, and K. Kuwabara. Distributed constraint satisfaction for formalizing distributed problem solving. In *Proceedings of the Twelfth IEEE International Conference on Distributed Computing Systems*, pages 614–621, 1992.
67. M. Yokoo and K. Hirayama. Distributed breakout algorithm for solving distributed constraint satisfaction problems. In *Proceedings of the 2nd International Conference on Multi-Agent Systems (ICMAS-96)*, pages 401–408, 1996.

Author Index

Atkin, M. S.   92

Behnke, S.   125
Bouzid, M.   198
Bredenfeld, A.   111

Carpin, S.   35
Cohen, P. R.   92

Ferrari, C.   35

Gérard, P.   150

Hanna, H.   198
Hannebauer, M.   3

Iocchi, L.   9

Kobialka, H.-U.   111

Lau, N.   175

Malec, J.   76
Mavromichalis, V. K.   53

Moore, A.   137
Mouaddib, A.-I.   198

Nardi, D.   9

Oliveira, E. C.   175

Pagello, E.   3,   35
Patuelli, P.   35

Reis, L. P.   175
Riedmiller, M.   137
Rojas, R.   125

Salerno, M.   9
Schneider, J.   137
Sigaud, O.   150

Vouros, G.   53

Weiß, G.   217
Wendler, J.   3
Westbrook, D. L.   92

Lecture Notes in Artificial Intelligence (LNAI)

Vol. 1891: A.L. Oliveira (Ed.), Grammatical Inference: Algorithms and Applications. Proceedings, 2000. VIII, 313 pages. 2000.

Vol. 1902: P. Sojka, I. Kopeček, K. Pala (Eds.), Text, Speech and Dialogue. Proceedings, 2000. XIII, 463 pages. 2000.

Vol. 1904: S.A. Cerri, D. Dochev (Eds.), Artificial Intelligence: Methodology, Systems, and Applications. Proceedings, 2000. XII, 366 pages. 2000.

Vol. 1910: D.A. Zighed, J. Komorowski, J. Żytkow (Eds.), Principles of Data Mining and Knowledge Discovery. Proceedings, 2000. XV, 701 pages. 2000.

Vol. 1916: F. Dignum, M. Greaves (Eds.), Issues in Agent Communication. X, 351 pages. 2000.

Vol. 1919: M. Ojeda-Aciego, I.P. de Guzman, G. Brewka, L. Moniz Pereira (Eds.), Logics in Artificial Intelligence. Proceedings, 2000. XI, 407 pages. 2000.

Vol. 1925: J. Cussens, S. Džeroski (Eds.), Learning Language in Logic. X, 301 pages 2000.

Vol. 1930: J.A. Campbell, E. Roanes-Lozano (Eds.), Artificial Intelligence and Symbolic Computation. Proceedings, 2000. X, 253 pages. 2001.

Vol. 1932: Z.W. Raś, S. Ohsuga (Eds.), Foundations of Intelligent Systems. Proceedings, 2000. XII, 646 pages.

Vol. 1934: J.S. White (Ed.), Envisioning Machuine Translation in the Information Future. Proceedings, 2000. XV, 254 pages. 2000.

Vol. 1937: R. Dieng, O. Corby (Eds.), Knowledge Engineering and Knowledge Management. Proceedings, 2000. XIII, 457 pages. 2000.

Vol. 1952: M.C. Monard, J. Simão Sichman (Eds.), Advances in Artificial Intelligence. Proceedings, 2000. XV, 498 pages. 2000.

Vol. 1955: M. Parigot, A. Voronkov (Eds.), Logic for Programming and Automated Reasoning. Proceedings, 2000. XIII, 487 pages. 2000.

Vol. 1967: S. Arikawa, S. Morishita (Eds.), Discovery Science. Proceedings, 2000. XII, 332 pages. 2000.

Vol. 1968: H. Arimura, S. Jain, A. Sharma (Eds.), Algorithmic Learning Theory. Proceedings, 2000. XI, 335 pages. 2000.

Vol. 1972: A. Omicini, R. Tolksdorf, F. Zambonelli (Eds.), Engineering Societies in the Agents World. Proceedings, 2000. IX, 143 pages. 2000.

Vol. 1979: S. Moss, P. Davidsson (Eds.), Multi-Agent-Based Simulation. Proceedings, 2000. VIII, 267 pages. 2001.

Vol. 1991: F. Dignum, C. Sierra (Eds.), Agent Mediated Electronic Commerce. VIII, 241 pages. 2001.

Vol. 1994: J. Lind, Iterative Software Engineering for Multiagent Systems. XVII, 286 pages. 2001.

Vol. 2003: F. Dignum, U. Cortés (Eds.), Agent-Mediated Electronic Commerce III. XII, 193 pages. 2001.

Vol. 2007: J.F. Roddick, K. Hornsby (Eds.), Temporal, Spatial, and Spatio-Temporal Data Mining. Proceedings, 2000. VII, 165 pages. 2001.

Vol. 2014: M. Moortgat (Ed.), Logical Aspects of Computational Linguistics. Proceedings, 1998. X, 287 pages. 2001.

Vol. 2019: P. Stone, T. Balch, G. Kraetzschmar (Eds.), RoboCup 2000: Robot Soccer World Cup IV. XVII, 658 pages. 2001.

Vol. 2033: J. Liu, Y. Ye (Eds.), E-Commerce Agents. VI, 347 pages. 2001.

Vol. 2035: D. Cheung, G.J. Williams, Q. Li (Eds.), Advances in Knowledge Discovery and Data Mining – PAKDD 2001. Proceedings, 2001. XVIII, 596 pages. 2001.

Vol. 2039: M. Schumacher, Objective Coordination in Multi-Agent System Engineering. XIV, 149 pages. 2001.

Vol. 2056: E. Stroulia, S. Matwin (Eds.), Advances in Artificial Intelligence. Proceedings, 2001. XII, 366 pages. 2001.

Vol. 2062: A. Nareyek, Constraint-Based Agents. XIV, 178 pages. 2001.

Vol. 2070: L. Monostori, J. Váncza, M. Ali (Eds.), Engineering of Intelligent Systems. Proceedings, 2001. XVIII, 951 pages. 2001.

Vol. 2083: R. Goré, A. Leitsch, T. Nipkow (Eds.), Automated Reasoning. Proceedings, 2001. XV, 708 pages. 2001.

Vol. 2086: M. Luck, V. Mařík, O. Stěpánková, R. Trappl (Eds.), Multi-Agent Systems and Applications. Proceedings, 2001. X, 437 pages. 2001.

Vol. 2099: P. de Groote, G. Morrill, C. Retoré (Eds.), Logical Aspects of Computational Linguistics. Proceedings, 2001. VIII, 311 pages. 2001.

Vol. 2101: S. Quaglini, P. Barahona, S. Andreassen (Eds.), Artificial Intelligence in Medicine. Proceedings, 2001. XIV, 469 pages. 2001.

Vol. 2103: M. Hannebauer, J. Wendler, E. Pagello (Eds.), Balancing Reactivity and Social Deliberation in Multi-Agent Systems. VIII, 237 pages. 2001.

Vol. 2109: M. Bauer, P.J. Gmytrasiewicz, J. Vassileva (Eds.), User Modeling 2001. Proceedings, 2001. XIII, 318 pages. 2001.

Vol. 2111: D. Helmbold, B. Williamson (Eds.), Computational Learning Theory. Proceedings, 2001. IX, 631 pages. 2001.

Lecture Notes in Computer Science

Vol. 2071: R. Harper (Ed.), Types in Compilation. Proceedings, 2000. IX, 207 pages. 2001.

Vol. 2072: J. Lindskov Knudsen (Ed.), ECOOP 2001 – Object-Oriented Programming. Proceedings, 2001. XIII, 429 pages. 2001.

Vol. 2073: V.N. Alexandrov, J.J. Dongarra, B.A. Juliano, R.S. Renner, C.J.K. Tan (Eds.), Computational Science – ICCS 2001. Part I. Proceedings, 2001. XXVIII, 1306 pages. 2001.

Vol. 2074: V.N. Alexandrov, J.J. Dongarra, B.A. Juliano, R.S. Renner, C.J.K. Tan (Eds.), Computational Science – ICCS 2001. Part II. Proceedings, 2001. XXVIII, 1076 pages. 2001.

Vol. 2075: J.-M. Colom, M. Koutny (Eds.), Applications and Theory of Petri Nets 2001. Proceedings, 2001. XII, 403 pages. 2001.

Vol. 2076: F. Orejas, P.G. Spirakis, J. van Leeuwen (Eds.), Automata, Languages and Programming. Proceedings, 2001. XIV, 1083 pages. 2001.

Vol. 2077: V. Ambriola (Ed.), Software Process Technology. Proceedings, 2001. VIII, 247 pages. 2001.

Vol. 2078: R. Reed, J. Reed (Eds.), SDL 2001: Meeting UML. Proceedings, 2001. XI, 439 pages. 2001.

Vol. 2081: K. Aardal, B. Gerards (Eds.), Integer Programming and Combinatorial Optimization. Proceedings, 2001. XI, 423 pages. 2001.

Vol. 2082: M.F. Insana, R.M. Leahy (Eds.), Information Processing in Medical Imaging. Proceedings, 2001. XVI, 537 pages. 2001.

Vol. 2083: R. Goré, A. Leitsch, T. Nipkow (Eds.), Automated Reasoning. Proceedings, 2001. XV, 708 pages. 2001. (Subseries LNAI).

Vol. 2084: J. Mira, A. Prieto (Eds.), Connectionist Models of Neurons, Learning Processes, and Artificial Intelligence. Proceedings, 2001. Part I. XXVII, 836 pages. 2001.

Vol. 2086: M. Luck, V. Mařík, O. Štěpánková, R. Trappl (Eds.), Multi-Agent Systems and Applications. Proceedings, 2001. X, 437 pages. 2001. (Subseries LNAI).

Vol. 2089: A. Amir, G.M. Landau (Eds.), Combinatorial Pattern Matching. Proceedings, 2001. VIII, 273 pages. 2001.

Vol. 2091: J. Bigun, F. Smeraldi (Eds.), Audio- and Video-Based Biometric Person Authentication. Proceedings, 2001. XIII, 374 pages. 2001.

Vol. 2092: L. Wolf, D. Hutchison, R. Steinmetz (Eds.), Quality of Service – IWQoS 2001. Proceedings, 2001. XII, 435 pages. 2001.

Vol. 2093: P. Lorenz (Ed.), Networking – ICN 2001. Proceedings, 2001. Part I. XXV, 843 pages. 2001.

Vol. 2094: P. Lorenz (Ed.), Networking – ICN 2001. Proceedings, 2001. Part II. XXV, 899 pages. 2001.

Vol. 2095: B. Schiele, G. Sagerer (Eds.), Computer Vision Systems. Proceedings, 2001. X, 313 pages. 2001.

Vol. 2096: J. Kittler, F. Roli (Eds.), Multiple Classifier Systems. Proceedings, 2001. XII, 456 pages. 2001.

Vol. 2097: B. Read (Ed.), Advances in Databases. Proceedings, 2001. X, 219 pages. 2001.

Vol. 2098: J. Akiyama, M. Kano, M. Urabe (Eds.), Discrete and Computational Geometry. Proceedings, 2000. XI, 381 pages. 2001.

Vol. 2099: P. de Groote, G. Morrill, C. Retoré (Eds.), Logical Aspects of Computational Linguistics. Proceedings, 2001. VIII, 311 pages. 2001. (Subseries LNAI).

Vol. 2101: S. Quaglini, P. Barahona, S. Andreassen (Eds.), Artificial Intelligence in Medicine. Proceedings, 2001. XIV, 469 pages. 2001. (Subseries LNAI).

Vol. 2102: G. Berry, H. Comon, A. Finkel (Eds.), Computer-Aided Verification. Proceedings, 2001. XIII, 520 pages. 2001.

Vol. 2103: M. Hannebauer, J. Wendler, E. Pagello (Eds.), Balancing Reactivity and Social Deliberation in Multi-Agent Systems. VIII, 237 pages. 2001. (Subseries LNAI).

Vol. 2105: W. Kim, T.-W. Ling, Y-J. Lee, S.-S. Park (Eds.), The Human Society and the Internet. Proceedings, 2001. XVI, 470 pages. 2001.

Vol. 2106: M. Kerckhove (Ed.), Scale-Space and Morphology in Computer Vision. Proceedings, 2001. XI, 435 pages. 2001.

Vol. 2109: M. Bauer, P.J. Gymtrasiewicz, J. Vassileva (Eds.), User Modelind 2001. Proceedings, 2001. XIII, 318 pages. 2001. (Subseries LNAI).

Vol. 2110: B. Hertzberger, A. Hoekstra, R. Williams (Eds.), High-Performance Computing and Networking. Proceedings, 2001. XVII, 733 pages. 2001.

Vol. 2111: D. Helmbold, B. Williamson (Eds.), Computational Learning Theory. Proceedings, 2001. IX, 631 pages. 2001. (Subseries LNAI).

Vol. 2118: X.S. Wang, G. Yu, H. Lu (Eds.), Advances in Web-Age Information Management. Proceedings, 2001. XV, 418 pages. 2001.

Vol. 2119: V. Varadharajan, Y. Mu (Eds.), Information Security and Privacy. Proceedings, 2001. XI, 522 pages. 2001.

Vol. 2121: C.S. Jensen, M. Schneider, B. Seeger, V.J. Tsotras (Eds.), Advances in Spatial and Temporal Databases. Proceedings, 2001. XI, 543 pages. 2001.

Vol. 2126: P. Cousot (Ed.), Static Analysis. Proceedings, 2001. XI, 439 pages. 2001.